Astrology Made Easy
A Handy Reference Guide

Barbara Goldsmith

Barbara Goldsmith
Your Astrology Signs
www.yourastrologysigns.com

Copyright Barbara Goldsmith 2008

This book is copyright. Except for the purpose of fair reviewing, no part of this publication may be reproduced or transmitted in any form or by any means, electronic or mechanical, including photocopying, recording, or any information storage or retrieval system, without prior permission in writing from the publisher.

Table of Contents

Introduction 1
Chapter 1 6
   Composition of the 12 signs 6
   Positive/Receptive or Masculine/Feminine Signs 6
   The Triplicities 7
   The Fire Signs: Aries, Leo, Sagittarius 8
   The Earth Signs: Taurus, Virgo, Capricorn 10
   The Air Signs: Gemini, Libra, Aquarius 11
   The Water Signs: Cancer, Scorpio, Pisces 13
   The Modes – Cardinal, Fixed, Mutable - Quadruplicities
   18
Chapter 2 26
   Where to start – tips for getting into the chart 26
   Quadrants 29
   Colour Balance 32
Chapter 3 34
   The Sun Signs 34
Chapter 4 101
   The Ascendant or Rising Sign 101
Chapter 5 120
   The Planets 120
Chapter 6 147
   The Houses 147
Chapter 7 187
   Interpretive Guidelines 187
   Sun in Signs and Houses 187
   Moon in Signs and Houses 198
   Mercury in Signs and Houses 212

- Venus in Signs and Houses 221
- Mars in Signs and Houses 229
- Jupiter in Signs and Houses 237
- Saturn in Signs and Houses 246
- Uranus in Signs and Houses 258
- Neptune in Signs and Houses 271
- Pluto in Signs and Houses 281

Chapter 8 298
- Aspects 298
- Conjunction 301
- Opposition 302
- Sextile 302
- Trine 303
- Semi-sextile 303
- Square 303
- Inconjunct (Quincunx) 303

Chapter 9 306
Astrological humour 303
APPENDICES 313
- Appendix I: Zodiac signs and body parts in more detail
  314
- Appendix II: Natal Charts of Famous People 316
- Appendix III: Glossary 328

Acknowledgements

To Connie H Deutsch who has been badgering me for over a decade to write a book. Thank you for all your encouragement, love, endless support and patience. Here it is at last!

and

I would like to express my deepest thanks to Elizabeth van Til who laboured for endless hours and supported me with humour and kindness in getting the job done.

"Astrology is a science in itself and contains an illuminating body of knowledge. It taught me many things and I am greatly indebted to it."

Albert Einstein, physicist.

Introduction

Welcome to the wonderful, amazing and intriguing world of astrology. My book attempts to create an easily understood handbook that incorporates the widely applicable meanings that come from the basics of astrology.

Let me share with you my first experiences with astrology. When I was 19 years of age, a friend of mine recommended I go for a reading from a local astrologer. I was a bit nervous at first as I'd never done anything like this before, but gave her my date, time and place of birth and arranged to go and see her the next week. Her reading was phenomenal – I couldn't get over her accurate knowledge of my behaviour patterns, my emotional needs, my romantic attachments, my health, my finances, my family dynamics and my soul purpose. This ignited my interest and a lifelong passion for the subject of astrology.

Astrology is a language. Learning astrology is like learning any foreign language. You already have the ideas, concepts, and experiences of your life within you; you are just learning a new language for what you are already experiencing. To learn a language, you need to know its alphabet, and in astrology, this is made up of the Planets, Signs, Houses and Aspects.

Think of yourself as being the Director of the play of your life. As the Director, you have free will to script your play as you choose, but you need to know the nature of the cast you are working with. The actors and actresses are the planets; the signs are the roles the characters came to play; the houses are the settings for this all to take place in; and the aspects reveal how all of the characters get along with one another.

Planets: The characters; the actors and actresses in the play of your life.
Signs: The scripts and roles the characters are to perform.
Houses: The settings where the characters play out their roles.
Aspects: How the characters either support, or are in conflict with, each other.

Your birth chart itself is a map to all of these players in your life and how they are best staged to work out the individual roles in a way that doesn't interfere with the needs of the other players in the chart. Otherwise, problems erupt. Every chart has its inconsistencies. You can explore one part of your chart that describes part of you that is equally true, yet is in conflict with the first part. This goes on until you script a lifestyle that allows for all of these differences in your own life. Then the outer problems seem to disappear, or at least the impact they make on you diminishes.

Consider your horoscope to be a roadmap. It shows the conditions you are going to meet in your life. Some of the roads on which you will travel will be smooth and easy whilst others will be in poor condition and in need of repair. If you restore them to good condition, your car will not break down and cause you difficulties and delays.

The point of using astrology is to help you accept what you have been given to work with, and then to help you find healthy ways to incorporate this into your life. Your birth chart is the map to living in harmony with yourself and the world around you.

I wish to help the beginner/intermediate student/teacher of astrology with simple ways to begin the process of understanding the basic information in an astrology chart. The book focuses on the major factors in any birth chart and does not include the minor factors that often confuse the beginning student and often unnecessarily divert the attention of more experienced practitioners. I have concentrated on understanding the natal chart only and will present the transits and progressions in a later book.

This book is aimed at assisting you in learning how to interpret birth charts. It supplies the practitioner, teacher, or student with a starting point for carrying out an astrology reading. However, please be aware, that this is "cookbook astrology": i.e. the delineation of planets by sign and house with a paragraph or two for each. For example, Saturn in the 1st House, Saturn in the 2nd House etc. Whilst being very helpful in the process of learning astrology, rarely can delineation operate effectively in a vacuum – each element being isolated and separately interpreted. The planets in a chart are tied to each other by aspects, by rulership of Signs and Houses, and by reinforcement of certain indications.

There comes a point in interpretation where a cookbook just cannot go. This is where the "art" of astrology comes into play. A living human brain is required to tie all the elements together to weigh and balance influences and use judgment about how much and in what way to pass the conclusions on to the client. The process of learning how to synthesise all the elements within a birth chart is similar to the process of learning how to speak a language fluently. It takes years of experience and practice to get to the stage where you are thinking and totally immersed in that language. This book is a stepping stone towards that final aim.

New students of astrology often ask: "what shall I focus on in a chart?" My response is that even if you feel that you understand only a small part of a chart, follow what you do understand and it will lead you to the structure and the main themes of the rest of the chart. Don't worry about doing a "complete chart interpretation" as it is not possible. Instead of getting lost in the endless details of a chart, it is better to focus on what is important in the person's nature and on what kind of person he or she is.

This book is intended to make your life easier – I only wish I had had something similar to this when I was learning astrology. This is in fact what prompted me to write this book. There are of course no definitive answers and it is important that you use this book as a starting point and develop your own style and way of doing a reading.

This book is divided into nine chapters.

Chapter 1 examines the various qualities of the Astrological Signs:
* ✭ Positive and Receptive Signs
* ✭ The Elements – Fire, Earth, Air, Water
* ✭ Modes of expression: Cardinal, Fixed and Mutable

Chapter 2 gives you tips for easy ways into the chart
Chapter 3 covers the Sun Signs and their major characteristics
Chapter 4 discusses the Planets and their meanings
Chapter 5 includes a description of the Houses of life experience
Chapter 6 relates to the Ascendant and its meaning
Chapter 7 is a handy, easy-to-use reference guide giving you simple interpretative explanations of the various planets in each Sign and then in each House
Chapter 8 gives you an outline of the meaning of the major aspects in a chart
Chapter 9 is some astrological humour to show you the funny side of the signs and their characteristics.

I trust you will find this an invaluable guide to enable you to quickly determine the major characteristics and basic motivations in a birth chart.

Chapter 1

"I have studied the matter. You sir, have not."
Sir Isaac Newton – Physicist
(Said in defence of astrology, to sceptic Edmund Halley)

Composition of the 12 signs

The signs can be remembered by three basic signatures:
- ★ Positive/Negative or Masculine/Feminine
- ★ The Triplicities – Fire, Earth, Air, Water
- ★ The Quadruplicities – Cardinal, Fixed, Mutable

Positive/Receptive or Masculine/Feminine Signs

There is a division of the signs into Positive (Masculine), and Receptive (Feminine) signs. The Masculine signs are all the Fire and Air signs: Aries, Gemini, Leo, Libra, Sagittarius and Aquarius correspond to the 1st, 3rd, 5th, 7th, 9th, and 11th Houses. The Receptive or Feminine signs include all the Earth and Water signs: Taurus, Cancer, Virgo, Scorpio, Capricorn, and Pisces and correspond to the 2nd, 4th, 6th, 8th, 10th, and 12th Houses.

Count the planets in Masculine and Feminine signs in order to understand the polarity of the individual.

Those with a majority of Masculine/Positive signs tend to be self-initiating and they take action in order to achieve results rather than waiting for things to come to them.

Wherever these signs are placed in your chart, you are likely to take the initiative and go for what you want.

A strong preponderance of planets in Masculine signs indicates a self-starter with positive outgoing tendencies.

The Receptive/Feminine signs indicate passivity. At times, however, people born under them are capable of acting in a forcible manner, although they usually wait for things to come to them before taking direct action. In this respect, they are passive and interact with what happens to come their way. They work on the principle of attracting what they want rather than attempting to go out and conquer it.

If there is a strong balance of planets in Receptive passive signs in your chart, then you probably will not be aggressive in your actions, but rather possess great strength in terms of passive endurance.

The Triplicities

The Elements – Fire, Earth, Air and Water – each represent a basic kind of energy and consciousness that operates within everyone. Each person is consciously more attuned to some types of energy than others.

Fire signs express the warming, radiating, energising life principle which can manifest as enthusiasm, faith, encouragement, passion and the drive to express the self.

Earth signs have practical abilities and are more attuned to the physical nature of the world, with the ability to utilise and improve the material world. They tend to seek security and stability.

Air signs are correlated with the mind, perception and expression, especially related to personal interaction and communication and to geometrical thought forms and abstract ideas.

Water signs are associated with emotions, feelings, sensations and encompass healing, intuition and the feeling response and empathy with others.

The Elements have traditionally been divided into two groups: Fire and Air being considered active and self-expressive and Water and Earth considered passive, receptive and self-containing.

Water and Earth signs are more self-contained than Fire and Air signs in that they live more within themselves and don't allow themselves to project this essential energy outwardly without a good deal of caution and forethought. This enables them to build a solid foundation for action. The Fire and Air signs are more self-expressive and want to "get it out." They tend to pour forth their energies and life substance unreservedly: the Fire signs by direct action and the Air signs by social interaction and verbal expression.

The Fire Signs: Aries, Leo, Sagittarius

The Fire signs express radiance, enthusiasm, initiative, confidence and colour. They exemplify high spirits, great faith in themselves, unending strength and a direct honesty. The Fire signs want to get on with life, they are easily bored, crave variety and are great starters and notoriously poor finishers. They love the thrill of the chase and need excitement and constant stimulation in their lives. Fire signs need action, passion and aliveness in every moment.

With Aries, the Fire manifests as decisiveness in spearheading new efforts and ideas. Aries could be described as "the ignition key of the zodiac."

Leos possess the managerial capability for acting as the central dramatic figure around which an organisation or group gather.

Sagittarians have the ability to act as spiritual and philosophic leaders. They are often concerned with law and higher education and with the ways in which society is built.

All three have something in common with the nature of Fire, which actively burns, crackles, consumes, warms, delights or annoys. People with many Fire signs in their charts can delight others with their exuberance and warmth. Their faults can be rashness, over-excitability, extravagance and thoughtlessness, leading to harmful and destructive ways.

Fire judges that Water will extinguish it, Earth will smother it, but Air will fan the flames.

Keywords:
Fearless, impulsive, enthusiastic, strong, honest, blunt, outgoing, extrovert, demonstrative, impatient, ardent, creative, aggressive, positive, self-motivated, spontaneous, energetic, intense, stimulating, inspirational, self-confident, independent, idealistic, optimistic.

The Earth Signs: Taurus, Virgo, Capricorn

The Earth signs rely heavily on their senses and practical reasoning. Their innate understanding of how the material world functions gives the Earth signs more patience and self-discipline than other signs. The Earth Element tends to be cautious, conventional and generally dependable. Knowing their niche in the world is especially important to the Earth signs, for security remains a constant goal for them throughout their lives. The Earth signs respond to the Fire signs by saying: "what's the rush?" "can we afford it?" They like to take their time before coming to a decision and they crave security. Never try to push an Earth sign – the more pushed they feel, the more they will dig their heels in.

Taurus' practical quality appears as the ability to accumulate money and material resources.

Virgo manifests practicality as intelligence and diligence in labour and detailed hard work and service. Virgo is also associated with health.

With Capricorn, there is the practical ability to organise and manage vast business and governmental enterprises, and, on a more mundane level, the ability to structure and organise ordinary business affairs.

Earth is solid, dependable, motionless, dry and often thought of as uninteresting. People with Earth signs strongly influencing their charts are capable and hard working in sensible ways, either in actual building or in the building of careers and organisations. They are careful and trustworthy with possessions or finance and will look after the small matters which go towards making the complete whole. They tend to be suspicious or dubious about more lively agile-minded people, thinking them disturbing or trivial.

They can be overly materialistic, lacking interest in more abstract and inspirational things in life. They can have too narrow an outlook on life and be devoted to order and routine.

Earth senses that Air will dry it, Fire will parch it, but Water will refresh it.

Keywords:
Practical, patient, self-disciplined, persistent, cautious, dependable, conventional, attuned to physical world, materialistic, down-to-earth, security-minded, realistic, productive, methodical, exacting, thorough, orderly, patient, enduring, stable.

The Air Signs: Gemini, Libra, Aquarius

The Air signs express thought, words and ideas. The Air signs have the inner need to detach themselves from their immediate experiences of daily life in order to gain objectivity, perspective and a rational, reflective approach to everything they do. The Air signs need to talk about their experiences and to share them with others. Telephone bills are frequently higher for the Air signs than for other signs. The Air signs constant questions are: "why?" "how?" There is the need to understand, work it all out and then share and discuss the information. Air signs manifest strong mental abilities and intellectual attributes.

In Gemini, this intellectualism shows itself as the ability to acquire, utilise and communicate factual information. Gemini goes around like a Hoover, sucking up every piece of information it can find.

In Libra, these qualities are shown in the ability to weigh and balance, making just and fair comparisons. Librans can often be indecisive as they see all sides in a situation.

In Aquarius, this is expressed as an intuitive grasp of universal principles along with a desire for the well being of humanity as a whole.

Air is the medium for carrying sound waves and Air signs tend to stress communication in some way. People with lots of Air signs in their chart have a leaning towards reasoning, intelligent pursuits and working in the area of ideas.

They can lack depth and there is sometimes a tendency to immerse themselves in schemes and theories.

Air thinks that Water will saturate it, Earth will confine it, but Fire will answer with a leaping response.

Keywords:
Intellectual, questioning, conceptualising, synthesising, observant, objective, detached, perceptive, expressive, curious, indecisive, talkative, interacting, cooperating, sharing, unrealistic, communicative, expressive, mentally stimulating, rationalising.

The Water Signs: Cancer, Scorpio, Pisces

The Water signs are in touch with their feelings, in tune with nuances and subtleties that many others do not even notice. Water represents deep emotion and feeling responses, ranging from compulsive passions to overwhelming fears to an all-encompassing acceptance and love of creation. Water signs need space and privacy to recharge their batteries. Water signs feel everything more intensely than the other signs, so once hurt, they retreat for a while to recover. Whilst the Fire signs easily forget, the Water signs remember and hold onto unpleasant experiences for longer.

Cancer shows strong feelings about home, family and often about food and nourishment.

Scorpio shows strong emotions about death, joint resources and the deeper mysteries of life. Scorpios will often use the word "intense."

In Pisces, it is shown as an unconscious telepathic communication with other people.

Water reflects, dissolves, washes away and helps growth. Like the sea it can be stormy or have a calm exterior with a deceptive, hidden undercurrent which can drag down. As it has no shape of its own, water takes on the shape of its container. Once contained, it can be calm and useful though often dampening. Those with a strong Water influence in their charts are naturally sensitive, intuitive and inspirational which they can express in caring for others or in music, art, poetry and dance, or in using psychic faculties.

Water people are deep, emotional, secretive and protective. Their faults may be that they are unstable like Water, too easily being a reflection of the last person they were with, too sensitive to other influences, too inclined to emotional storms and to be a drag on others.

Water feels that Fire will make it boil, Air will make it vapourise, but Earth will contain it.

Keywords:
Emotional, moody, empathic, sensitive, intuitive, compassionate, psychic, secretive, private, reflective, vulnerable, sentimental, responsive, dependent, nurturing, protective, personal, flowing, imaginative, passive, changeable, malleable, caring.

The above Keywords for each of the Elements should help you to interpret the emphasised Elements in a chart. A well-balanced chart would have three to four counts each of Fire, Earth, Air and Water signs. Five counts of any Element is an emphasis; six or more counts is an extreme emphasis.

To determine the predominant Element in a chart, add up the number of Fire, Earth, Air and Water signs which contain planets, as well as the signs on the Ascendant and the Midheaven. Using a 14 point scale, count the Sun and Moon signs as 2, the signs of the other planets, the Ascendant and Midheaven as 1.

Here is an example:

	Fire	Earth	Air	Water
Sun 2 Scorpio 20				2
Moon 27 Taurus 13		2		
Mercury 9 Libra 48			1	
Venus 24 Libra 15			1	
Mars 15 Scorpio 11				1
Jupiter 17 Capricorn 08		1		
Saturn 23 Capricorn 19		1		
Uranus 18 Leo 42	1			
Neptune 19 Scorpio 45				1
Pluto 9 Virgo 31		1		
Ascendant 13 Gemini 33			1	
M.C. 19 Aquarius 27			1	
Totals	1	5	4	4

People with 6 or more Fire signs may be fast-paced and dominating and inclined to invest all of themselves in their activities. They may become self-absorbed and find it hard to perceive other people as separate individuals with their own valid needs and desires.

People with 6 or more Earth signs are likely to be concerned with concrete details and tangible results. They will operate most frequently in the world of their senses, attuned to their immediate environment and their physical bodies.

People with 6 or more Air signs usually live in their minds, restlessly seeking knowledge and sharing their thoughts with other people. They can be impersonal, but they will thrive on communication and social interaction.

People with 6 or more Water signs often lose themselves in their feelings and emotions. Their extreme sensitivity may cause them to withdraw into themselves. Often quite psychic, they respond with great compassion to the needs of other people.

Weakest Element

As most people who are weak in an Element have not developed most of that Element's characteristics, they usually are aware of their lack and strive to overcome it. Initially, their attempts to compensate for an inherent lack may make them appear as if the Element in question is strong in their charts. However, as they usually hunger so deeply to function on this energy level, they may try too hard and create problems for themselves.

However, in my experience, I have often found that someone with no planets in a certain Element often exerts so much effort to learn the characteristics of that Element and incorporate them into their life, that they become even more adept than someone who has an abundance of planets in that Element. For example, a person with no Air planets in their chart can be an absolute genius especially in the field of communications. They develop the Air Element to such a degree that they become masters in it.

What also happens is that if you are lacking an Element in your chart, you will draw other people into your life who have planets in that Element that you are deficient in. It's amazing how many charts I have seen of very successful relationships where one partner has an abundance of planets in Earth signs, while their partner has one or none.

Lack of Fire:
Pessimistic, uninvolved, unmotivated, apathetic, depressed, unexcitable.

Lack of Earth:
Impractical, disorganised, compulsive, unproductive, unstable, ungrounded, security-conscious.

Lack of Air:
Subjective, searching, disconnected, isolated, lonely, simple, misunderstood.

Lack of Water:
Controlled, closed, unresponsive, impersonal, insecure, out of touch, insensitive.

Whilst the above are negative characteristics, they can be overcome.

Fire Signs
Aries: the innovator
Leo: the organiser
Sagittarius: the executive

Earth Signs
Taurus: the concentrator
Virgo: the discriminator
Capricorn: the practical idealist

Air Signs
Gemini: the friendly one
Libra: the diplomat
Aquarius: the individualist

Water Signs
Cancer: the insistent
Scorpio: the passionate
Pisces: the compassionate

The Modes – Cardinal, Fixed, Mutable - Quadruplicities

The signs can be further defined by the way they use energy. These are called Quadruplicities. They are also referred to as qualities or modalities. There are three modes and they relate to how the signs use their energy in the environment. These modes or qualities, consist of Cardinal, Fixed and Mutable signs and they reveal significant personality characteristics. Using the same 14 point scale as in the Elements, count up the number of Cardinal, Fixed and Mutable signs in the chart.

The Cardinal signs are Aries, Cancer, Libra and Capricorn. In whatever houses or areas of life the Cardinal signs are found, there will be activity and the ability to initiate new enterprises. Positively expressed, these signs manifest constructive initiative, but on the negative side, there can be busybody tendencies and thoughtless actions.

Aries show their Cardinal side by using their Fire energy to start new things, to inspire others and to innovate. For example an Aries might demonstrate its Cardinal nature by creating a new gadget or inspiring other people to get in touch with their creative side. Aries is about the desire for its immediate expression and expansion.

Cancer is about security, foundation and depth. Cancerians often show their Cardinal side by leading in the health field, nursing or the food industry. For example, I know a Cancerian who used his Cardinal energy to start up his own Homoeopathic College.

Libra is concerned with relationships and breadth. A Libran might show their Cardinal side by leading a political party or being instrumental in changing the law for the better. For example, Margaret Thatcher demonstrated her Libran Cardinal energies by serving as Prime Minister of the UK and making huge changes to the balance of power between the Unions and the Government.

Capricorn is about the attainment of goals and success. Capricorns use their Cardinal drive to create new structures – anything from a new business to a large construction project. The Cardinal energy of Capricorn is to organise and to strategise. Conrad Hilton showed the Cardinal energy of Capricorn in the vast hotel empire he created.

Aries and Libra have to do with individuality and its striving to broaden its horizons and find a complementary partner, of the self coming to meet the other, of individual expansion, projection, exploration, and discovery. Cancer and Capricorn are the maternal and paternal, respectively. Cancer is the home and the mother – insular, nurturing, and protective. Capricorn is the father, his means of provision, and the rules of society that ensure his position in it and its order and success.

People with 7 or more Cardinal signs would rather be overly active than bored. Although very concerned with their activities and projects, they also focus their attention on the crucial areas of life – home and family, love and profession and are usually intent on meeting challenges and resolving crises.

Keywords:
Active, involved, restless, energetic, busy, driving, ambitious, opportunistic.

The Fixed signs are Taurus, Leo, Scorpio and Aquarius. Fixity implies stability, steadfastness but lack of variation. People who have lots of Fixed signs in their charts are stable in their ways. They will not be so good at getting things going, but will guard and conserve that which is started and may be depended upon to see that what they think is to be done, truly is done. Their faults may be inertia, lack of imagination and an inability to quickly adapt to changing circumstances.

Taurus acquires and utilises the energies and materials at its direct disposal. It expresses its Fixed nature by being very cautious before making any investments. Taurus does not rush into any new business venture without checking everything out thoroughly in advance.

Leo expresses itself intuitively and dramatically in the name of some cause or enterprise. Leo shows its Fixed nature by stealing the limelight and staying there! For example, many actors and actresses display this Leo trait.

Scorpio is adept at using the resources of others, particularly those of a mate or partner for their mutual benefit. It demonstrates its fixity by seeing things in black or white – there is no in-between. It also creates intensity in all life areas and this too shows its Fixed nature.

Aquarius provides the form and currency of communication and ideas that benefit friends and associations bound by common interests. Aquarians tend to be more fixed in their opinions and views. Once they have made up their minds and feel strongly about something, they will fight endlessly for their beliefs. For example, Paul Newman, an Aquarian Sun, helped children with cancer in the Third World – a humanitarian cause.

Taurus and Scorpio, complementary signs, deal with the accumulation and disposal of resources. Each reminds the other of their mutual but opposite purpose. Leo and Aquarius face the problems of self-expression, as a singular individual in Leo and in relationships and partnerships in Aquarius.

People with 7 or more Fixed signs focus their attention on their values and goals, and the satisfaction of their desires. Slow to start, they are powerhouses once they determine their course of action. They resist changing direction and refuse to be pushed, pulled or pressurised.

Keywords:
Determined, purposeful, stubborn, inflexible, powerful, persistent, strong-willed, slow and deliberate.

The Mutable signs are Gemini, Sagittarius, Virgo and Pisces. Mutability makes them changeable and sometimes inconstant. They are versatile and adaptable. People with a predominance of Mutable signs have a desire to serve others. They tend to act for others in either self-seeking or selfless ways. They are much more varied than the Cardinal and Fixed signs. Their faults can be over-diffuseness and lack of stability.

Gemini shows its Mutable side with its constant changeability. It needs variety, movement, and flexibility which are all Mutable qualities. This is especially true in Gemini's voracious quest for learning and communicating.

Sagittarius expresses its Mutable nature in its optimistic outlook and its ability to see the good side of everything –

even the most serious situations don't seem to get them down for too long.

Virgo demonstrates its Mutable side through needing variety in the workplace, paying attention to lots of different details and having a good memory.

Finally, Pisces shows its Mutable nature through the constant dreaming, imagining and escapist nature of the sign. The fish are going in opposite directions which denote changeability and instability.

The Mutable mindset is interested in pursuing and refining the ideas set in motion by the Cardinal and Fixed signs. It develops rather than creates and in so doing plants the seed from which the Cardinal and Fixed signs can begin once again to create anew. The power of the Mutable signs is based on the accumulated achievements and knowledge of the Cardinal and Fixed signs.

Gemini and Sagittarius are concerned with the intellect, the accumulation and relationship of ideas, and journeying into new and foreign realms both physically and mentally. They are the travellers, concerned with mobility and learning. Gemini acquires information, and Sagittarius takes it and expands upon it, infusing it with new ideas and insights gleaned along the way. Gemini is the wandering minstrel, the vagabond poet collecting stories to tell, while Sagittarius is the serious explorer, travelling with a lot more luggage and equipment and sedulously making notes.

Virgo is the travelling merchant, filled with practical and commercial goals, and Pisces is the pilgrim on the solitary, holy journey. Each has a remarkable story to tell. The role of the Mutable signs is to serve, aid, heal and support, to give rather than take.

People with 7 or more Mutable signs are concerned with personal relationships and thrive on variety and change. More inclined to flow with the current than swim against the tide, they adapt themselves readily to the people and circumstances of their lives. Frequently, however, they do not know what they want or where they want to go.

Keywords:
Adaptable, versatile, changeable, variable, personal, personable, flighty, restless, indecisive, easily influenced.

Lack of Cardinal:
These people often enjoy observing and simply "being" without necessarily "doing." But if they have 0 or 1 Cardinal sign, they may feel driven to prove themselves through activity or may substitute an emotionally intense inner life for active involvement in external challenges.

Lack of Fixed:
These people may have difficulty completing what they have begun and developing structure and stability in their lives. They may, as a result, become obsessed with organising or finishing, and may test their willpower by committing themselves to overly-demanding projects or goals.

Lack of Mutable:
These people usually know what they want. Frequently unwilling to compromise, they may insist that other people be adaptable and accommodate them. Because they have difficulty in bending with circumstances and making personal changes, they often attempt to force change in their external circumstances, sometimes in dramatic ways.

Chapter 2

"There shall be the signs in the Sun, the Moon and the Stars." *Jesus Christ, Luke 21:25*

Where to start – tips for getting into the chart

More planets on left hand side or on the right hand side of the chart?

When I look at a chart, I examine its basic structure – just from glancing at the patterns in the chart, you can see a great deal straight away. For example, are most of the planets on the left hand side of the chart, or are they on the right hand side? If someone has lots of planets on the left side of the chart, they are usually self-sufficient and like to come up with their own ideas and ways of doing things. They do not like too much interference from other people and often are quite private. This is where they learn about themselves and is mainly subjective. This is about their private space and is what motivates them physically, emotionally and mentally.

On the other hand, people with more planets on the right hand side of the chart look to others for validation and ideas and tend to look outside themselves to a greater extent. They can become dependent on others and need to watch out that this does not become unbalanced and that they develop their own thinking abilities. Planets on this side of the chart tend to show how you relate to your environment. Here we experience a reflection of ourselves and a means to go out and meet others.

Look at the Ascendant and all the planets in the 10th, 11th, 12th, 1st, 2nd, 3rd houses as being on the "I" side of the chart. This is the inside of your cave and you do not venture out of here too easily. The planets in the 4th, 5th, 6th, 7th, 8th, and 9th houses could be referred to as the "You" side of the chart where you actively seek out other people and are coming right out of your cave into the outside world. For example, someone with their Sun in the 7th house, will have a strong Libran feel to them and will want to connect with people and form relationships. However, someone with the Sun in the 1st house, the "I" part of the chart, will be more focused on their own self-development and might be slower at forming relationships.

More planets above the Horizon or below the Horizon?

The horizon represents the ground you stand on. Anything below it is hidden under the Earth and is therefore hidden from your view and beyond your ability to recognise it. This is where you tend to act from impulses and instincts, usually without knowing why. You seek common roots and bonds with people. You want to belong. If more planets are below the horizon, you will tend to live close to your family and friends and will not venture out too far until later in life.

Planets above the horizon are in full view. There is conscious perception, planning, achievement and the development of self-awareness. It is not ruled by unconscious factors. From here, you can see the world clearly. You can make conscious decisions about yourself and your life. You can set goals. This is where you become an individual and formulate and express your own uniqueness. You must be careful not to lose sight of your roots and the need for humility.

A greater number of planets in the upper half of the chart indicates someone who looks to the future, may want to travel extensively or even live abroad. This also shows someone who may think ahead of their time. The lower part of the chart indicates self-development, while the upper part of the chart shows co-development and interdependence with other people.

Direction

Are the aspect lines more of a vertical or more of a horizontal nature? Vertical charts have a desire to progress upwards. They wish to break away from the restrictions of the collective. There is a desire for individuality.

Horizontal charts have the desire for more human contact than personal or business success in the world.

Shaping

Is the chart Linear, Fixed or Dynamic?

A linear chart is one that is composed mainly of lines that do not connect with each other. This is a chart of someone who is always on the go, has lots of energy and goes off in lots of different directions. They are often searching but not sure what they are looking for. It does not mean they cannot be successful, but they may not always recognise it. This type of chart has a Cardinal emphasis.

A fixed shaping is one that is made up of 4, 5, or 6 sided shapes. This indicates a need for stability and security. The more symmetrical it is, the stronger the security motivation. This type of chart has the quality of the Fixed Element. These people need an underpinning of security in their lives to function more efficiently and happily.

Dynamic shaping consists of mainly triangles within the chart. This is changeable, adaptable and goal oriented. There are creative talents and the ability to transform surroundings. In crisis this is easier to handle than the fixed structure as they are able to adapt and adjust to changing circumstances. They can go with the change quite willingly and like to be changeable and flexible. This type corresponds to the Mutable element.

There may be a mixture of different shapes – however, you will find that there is usually a predominant one that stands out more than any other.

Quadrants

The distribution of planets in the four quadrants enables you to see in which areas of life a person functions easily and naturally and where their main areas of interest lie. For example if one quadrant has most planets, this will be the life area they will relate to the most. This is where their talents will lie.

If there is a fairly equal distribution of planets in all 4 quadrants, there will be an interest and ability to express oneself in all areas of life. The difficulty may be in staying focused.

1st Quadrant
This is the Fire quadrant, comprising the first three Houses, and could be described as the impulsive part of the chart. Planets in this quadrant are about self-preservation and self-assertion. There is the need for survival and to establish a place for ourselves in the world. Natural defense mechanisms often surface. You are seeking a separate identity in order to conform to the rules of the environment you are in. You learn through your own experience and you may tend to act before thinking and may be quite impulsive.

2nd Quadrant
This is the Earth part of the chart, containing the 4th, 5th and 6th Houses, and can be defined as the instinctive part of the chart. You are no longer concerned with your self and your own space. You are seeking to connect with others. In all forms of relationships – parents, teachers, lovers, employers – you develop certain stereotyped action-reaction mechanisms. You acquire know-how to deal with the outside world and other people. You are learning about unconscious patterns of behaviour. These can come in challenging family relationships, challenges in love, sickness etc. These situations help you to learn more about unconscious behaviour patterns. Growth comes from your interaction with others. People with a strong second quadrant are often good at counselling as they can give safety and security to their clients.

3rd Quadrant

This is the Air part of the chart, consisting of the 7th, 8th and 9th Houses and here there is a conscious awareness of the needs of others. You need to develop conscious awareness of the needs of others and to your own relationship needs. There is the ability to think objectively. Give and take in relationships in which the energy exchange is modulated by conscious agreement – you share. There is an exchange of ideas.

Planets here are about conscious self-expression, action, creativity outward into the world. Here you learn through conscious adaptation and by considering the thoughts and examples of others. It's about expanding your horizons, conscious communication and learning how to gain a more objective view of yourself as others see you.

4th Quadrant

This section of the chart relates to the element of Water and comprises the 10th, 11th and 12th Houses. Here you withdraw from the world, distill your experiences and bring about conscious self-knowledge. There is a more conscious sense of self. Here you are no longer dependent on the environment for confirmation. You choose how you express yourself. It's all about the integration of the self. You no longer need experiences "out there" to learn, but can be true to yourself and give back to the world what you have gleaned from your experience. Here you can teach and help others toward their own self-realisation, free of unconscious impulses, demands, projections and expectations.

You can feel safe and self-confident in who you are and what you have achieved and turn your energy inwards to examine yourself in your essence. You can be self-assured or you may try to distance yourself from the world so it cannot encroach upon or threaten you. You must accept full responsibility for yourself and remain true to your innermost being.

Colour Balance

The colour balance is made up of the different aspects: Conjunctions, Squares and Oppositions are red, Sextiles and Trines are blue and the Quincunx (Inconjunct) and Semisextiles are green. An "ideal" mix would be 4 red, 2 green and 6 blue. However, there are very many variations and this is just a guideline. (See Chapter 8 for more information about the different Aspects.)

Take a look at the colour balance in the chart. Is there a preponderance of red, blue or green? Red aspects are Cardinal in nature and indicate activity, "doing" energy, blue aspects are Fixed and indicate the ability to rest, relax and enjoy the moment, while green which are Mutable, confer awareness, thinking and sensitivity. You will come across huge varieties and combinations in the birth charts that you examine. For example, someone may have no green lines. A lack of green aspects can indicate a lack of awareness, giving a motivation of seeing things in a black/white, either/or way. This is often found in the charts of famous athletes. They need to have a black and white attitude with no shades of grey in order to dedicate themselves to the rigorous training required to reach their goals.

On the other hand, someone with a lot of green and red and not very much blue, might find it very hard to relax, always being on edge and having to do something. This probably indicates a very stressful, restless person who will have to learn how to "chill out" and enjoy life.

The above elements give you a quick and easy way to get into the chart from the outset. You do not need to do any deep calculations at this stage and you can easily get an overall picture of the person.

Chapter 3

"Millionaires don't use astrology, billionaires do."
JP Morgan – First Billionaire

The Sun Signs

Aries ♈

March 21st – April 19th
(Note: Because of leap years, time zones, and other factors, the exact day and time when the Sun enters a particular sign of the zodiac varies slightly from year to year.)

"I thought I'd begin by reading a poem by Shakespeare, but then I thought, why should I? He never reads any of mine." *Spike Milligan (comedian) Aries Sun Sign.*

"Live all you can; it's a mistake not to. It doesn't so much matter what you do in particular, so long as you have your life. If you haven't had that what have you had?"
Henry James (writer) Aries Sun Sign.

"Iron rusts from disuse; stagnant water loses its purity and in cold weather becomes frozen; even so does inaction sap the vigour of the mind."
Leonardo da Vinci (artist / inventor) Aries Sun Sign.

Personal creed : I am
Positive / Masculine sign

Symbol: The Ram
Element: Fire
Quality: Cardinal
Body part: The head
Ruler: Mars

People with an Aries Sun Sign are generally:
Enthusiastic, individualistic, outspoken, alert, quick to act and speak, ambitious, candid, generous friends, energetic, courageous, confident, quick- witted, innovative, excitable.

On the other hand they can be:
Selfish, quick-tempered, impulsive, impatient, foolhardy, lacking in real direction, poor finishers.

Arians love:
Action, coming first, challenges, championing causes, spontaneity, leading the way, going fast, something new.

They cannot stand:
Waiting around, admitting failure, other people's advice, slow speeds.

You always know when you've met a "typical Aries" when they come marching into a room full of people, and they go straight for the buffet with the food on and help themselves. They don't wait to be asked, they presume it's there to be enjoyed as they see all the lovely colours and off they go! Aries is about the self and can be described as "me, myself and I." They like to be first on the bus and first off the bus. Aries can be notoriously self-centred or wonderfully assertive.

It's lethal for me to go shopping with my Arian friend. She'll pick out a $3000 leather and sheepskin jacket and insist that I try it on. "Go on, it's just your colour and it will look great on you," she'll say. Once I've got it on, she'll do everything in her power to persuade me to buy it. Impulsive Aries loves to be in the excitement of the moment and doesn't always stop to think about the consequences. If you're doing some brainstorming and need new and creative ideas, it's always a good idea to have an Arian on the team.

Aries is about learning the boundaries of individualism. Aries comes to every situation as though it is brand new and they need to burn their fingers to learn, and no one can tell them they're wrong. Aries can be quite childlike in their enthusiasm for an idea, especially if it's one of their own, and this enthusiasm can be infectious. Aries are rarely cynical and this refreshing approach makes them attractive to others.

Aries make courageous leaders, with a genuine and gentle concern for those they command. But they are rather ordinary followers because they are usually convinced they have a much better way of doing things. A tremendous number of people with Aries planets succeed in their own businesses, or in fields where they are pretty much left to their own devices. Aries rules the 1st House of the horoscope wheel. Being first, and doing it by yourself, is a constructive way of channelling all your excess energy.

With all this boundless energy and self-belief, Arians can easily be irritated by slowness or moderation. They sometimes march straight over the sensibilities of others to get where they are going.

This is the sign of new beginnings. Arians are full of creative energy and enthusiasm and because Aries is a Cardinal sign, they initiate new activities which keep them occupied until the novelty wears off. Arians have a tremendous drive to prove themselves through action. They are not satisfied merely to intellectualise their concerns; they are impatient to do something about them.

Don't try to direct the life of anyone born in Aries. They want to do what they want to do when they want to do it. Arians are the self-starters of the zodiac, but they do tend to lose interest if the pace slows down or things become complicated. They are very self-confident on the surface but this conceals a feeling of inadequacy on the subconscious level. The three qualities that Arians would benefit from learning are: coordination, conservation of energy and completion.

If Arians can learn to think before taking action, their energetic natures will enable them to accomplish a great deal. However, their impulsiveness and inability to listen to the advice of others tends to involve them in challenges. Arians are also likely to be impatient and do not always finish what they start, leaving follow-up actions to those with Fixed and Mutable signs.

The most highly evolved Arian types possess great willpower, spiritual self-confidence and regenerative ability due to the Sun's exaltation in this sign.

You identify with: champions, heroes, winners, sports stars, pioneers, inventors.

You're an authority on: assertiveness skills, doing it alone, winning, letting off steam.

You need: fitness pursuits, a dynamic role in your work, friends who will argue with you, friends who will forgive you, a cause, a fast set of wheels, people who operate at your speed.

Arian Symbols:
Rams, Mars, Crimson, Red, Redheads, Rouge, Athletes, Competitions, Danger, Races, Motorbikes, Sports cars, Formula One, Champions, Fighters, Heroes, Heroines, Fights, Speed, Adrenalin, Pioneers, One, Accidents, Scars, The Head, Guns, Police, Gyms, War, Masculinity, Defence, Fire, Anger, Emergencies, High Temperatures, Fevers.

Famous Arians:
Warren Beatty, Elton John, Vincent Van Gogh, Spike Milligan, Diana Ross, Marlon Brando, Johann Sebastian Bach, Charlie Chaplin, Guy Fawkes, Rene Descartes.

Taurus ♉
April 20th – May 20th

"Wealth is not a hindrance, but rather a help towards attaining a proper standing in a chosen field of activity. I confess that as far as I am concerned, it has done me some service as it has preserved my character from many a crookedness poverty might have exposed it to."
Henryk Sienkeiwicz (writer) Taurus Sun Sign

"You can have either the Resurrection or you can have Liberace. But you can't have both."
Liberace (entertainer) Taurus Sun Sign

Personal creed: I have
Receptive / Feminine sign
Symbol: The Bull
Element: Earth
Quality: Fixed
Ruler: Venus
Body part: Throat, neck

People with Taurus Sun sign are generally:
Patient, reliable, warm-hearted, loving, persistent, placid, artistic, gentle, loyal, domestic, sensual, good with money and resources, stable, secure.

On the other hand, they can also be:
Jealous, possessive, resentful, inflexible, self-indulgent, greedy, unenterprising, cautious, careful.

Taureans love:
Security, stability, practicality, consistency, sensual pleasures from food and drink to nature, routine, fine food and good linen, a good provider (either being one or having one.)

They cannot stand:
Risks, cheating, waste, change, uncertainty, cheap things, being uprooted without their initiative.

Now imagine this: Aries has got all these great ideas going, and now Taurus comes along and says: "can we afford it?" "will it work?" "there's a lot of hard work to be put into this project." Taurus, being a Fixed sign, now has to put all the energy into making the wonderful Arian idea a reality. Taurus literally has to bring it down to earth.

Taureans can and do drive the Air and Fire signs nuts because they like to do things slowly. In fact, my Gemini friend describes her Taurean husband as having two speeds: slow and stop. However, they are precise and consistent and very good at finishing projects and making ideas a reality.

Taurus rules money and personal resources. Anything connected with making money, profits, business, investments, stock markets and economics relates to the sign of Taurus. Why? It's because they have an innate understanding of how money works. They are able to save for a rainy day and always have a bit of money put aside for a "rainy day" fund. Generally they are not extravagant and will save every penny they earn. They are equally as frugal with other peoples' finances. They hate to see anything wasted and will keep and hoard the money like a squirrel. A Taurean friend of mine used to be the Treasurer for a local charity. Whenever anyone wanted even so much as $1 out of the fund for an expense, there was a whole interrogation by the Taurean treasurer as to how this money was going to be spent and was it really necessary?

Another Taurean colleague always takes his time when buying anything and makes sure that it really works. Not only is he concerned about the finances, he wants to be sure that there's nothing wrong with it. For example, we went out to buy a chest of drawers. He checked that each drawer worked properly at least three times! And of course, being a Taurean, he did it very slowly and deliberately. Enough to drive his Gemini wife hopping mad!

Taurus is the sign of purposeful determination and power. The Element Earth teaches and guides them to become efficient in practical matters. They are fond of the good things in life and often focus their attention on material acquisitions. Love of comfort, satisfaction and pleasure is also a characteristic. They want money, not for its own sake, but so they can enjoy the things it enables them to purchase.

The hub of the Taureans' universe is security, both emotional and material. They do not tend to be aware of inner motives as a rule. They are endowed with strong willpower, which enables them to make plans from a distance, perhaps even years in advance. They strive assiduously toward their goals, firm in their acquisitive instincts. Success usually follows their efforts.

Taureans have their own methods of doing things, and if one wants a smooth relationship with them, it is wise not to interfere with them or attempt to make them over.

The bed is the prized possession of most Taureans. They are luxuriant sleepers and will seek out a perfect sleeping position. Most people's first big purchase will be a car or a stereo – the Taurean is more likely to buy a good double mattress.

The Taurean nature is a kind one, and they can enjoy helping people out of sticky situations. They can sometimes be unassuming in this regard and may find themselves being taken advantage of. If this happens too often, watch out! The Bull will charge when it is very upset.

Taurus is intensely practical, understands the market, and knows how to buy and sell at the right time. Self-made businesspeople figure heavily in the Taurus story, and so do thoughtful investors. Taureans are often experts in areas like commerce and economics. Taurus is associated with the stock market through bullion, and also through bull markets. It is common in the charts of high earners, wealthy investors and small business success stories.

Taureans often put a higher price on human values – commonly human lives. "I wouldn't touch a leper for a thousand pounds," said the late Mother Teresa, a Taurus Moon, "yet I willingly cure him for the love of God."

Priceless integrity is the domain of Taurus above all other signs. Getting there seems to involve a lot of trial and error, but when a Taurean has fixed a price on the things that cash cannot purchase, it's very hard to go back.

Taureans possess a steady, relentless quality that is very hard to beat. The steadiness and slowness of Taurus results in a stubborn refusal to give in or give up. Taureans are always in it for the full distance. Think of Taurus as the marathon runner and Aries the sprinter. The quality the most necessary for the Taurean to acquire is detachment.

You identify with: the natural world, musicians, businesspeople, collectors, connoisseurs, artists, idealists.

You're an authority on: beautiful things, moral values, the market, selling out versus making money, valuables.

You need: career stability, an attractive work environment, plants, no pressure deadlines, a comfortable chair, long gourmet lunches, an expense account.

Taurean Symbols:
The Bull, Venus, Flowers, Pearls, Love, Cupid, Hair, Beauty, Jealousy, Fashion, Sales, Money, Possessions, Values, Trade, Economics, Commerce, Stock markets, Bull markets, Bullion, Antiques, Art, Collectors, Wealth, Dogs, Shopping, Earning, Selling, Equity, Budgets, Currency, Barter, Exchange, Bankers, Gold, Platinum, Silver, The Arts.

Famous Taureans:
Barbra Streisand, Queen Elizabeth II, Al Pacino, Fred Astaire, Ryan O'Neal, Andre Agassi, Jack Nicholson, Grace Jones, Golda Meir, Socrates, Karl Marx.

Gemini ♊
May 21st – June 21st

"Husbands are chiefly good as lovers when they are betraying their wives."
Marilyn Monroe (actress) Gemini Sun Sign

"We make out of the quarrel with other, rhetoric, but of the quarrel with ourselves, poetry."
W B Yeats (poet) Gemini Sun Sign

"I'm a very natural flirt, but I don't see it in a sexual way…a lot of the time I'm like an overexcited puppy. I think I'm being friendly with someone, they think I'm flirting with them."
Kylie Minogue (singer) Gemini Sun Sign

Personal creed: I think
Positive / Masculine sign
Symbol: The Twins
Element: Air
Quality: Mutable
Ruler: Mercury
Body parts: Shoulders, arms, hands, lungs

People with a Gemini Sun Sign are generally:
Adaptable, intellectual, witty, logical, busy, spontaneous, good at writing and languages, lively, inquisitive, communicative, sociable, imaginative, persuasive, agile, positive, teasing, cheerful, curious.

On the other hand, they can also be:
Tense, superficial, inconsistent, restless, two-faced, irresponsible, exaggerating, over-optimistic, cold, restless.

Geminis love:
Variety, being occupied with many things simultaneously, new people, new subjects, new ideas, flexible thinking, being knowledgeable and well-informed, fun, telling stories and jokes.

They cannot stand:
People with nothing interesting to say, people without curiosity, overly emotional and irrational behaviour, possessiveness, jealousy.

Gemini is the sign of thinking, communicating and distributing information. The Gemini lifestyle is characterised by diversity, change and collaboration with a variety of different people and venues.

Geminis are the communicators of the zodiac. Whereas Aries has come up with all the exciting new projects and ideas and Taurus is busy trying to implement and ground them, Gemini wants to communicate them to the world. Having a Gemini is like having a loudspeaker – they get across excitement, enthusiasm in an articulate and enticing way. They make wonderful reporters, interviewers, chat-show hosts – anything that involves discussion, gossip, chit-chat, information – this is what turns the Gemini on.

Individuals born under the intellectual Air sign Gemini are ruled by Mercury and think and act swiftly. Since Mercury has to do with communication, Geminis must identify and classify. Speech is especially important to them, serving as a framework for their activities. Words are anchoring or safety devices as the mind jumps from one thing to another. They are highly intelligent and need lots of stimulation in their lives. Because their minds are so quick, they often speak very quickly too. I have a Gemini friend who can hardly pause for breath between sentences. She is so excited about what she is telling you and she often tells it with such a great sense of humour that you are left spinning at the end of the conversation.

Geminis are great at breaking the ice in a new group. Often when I am starting a new astrology class, the Gemini will walk in and start a conversation with everyone in the room, chattering away, and very soon everyone is laughing and the initial reserve, especially of the more timid signs such as Virgo, has disappeared.

Make sure you are on a special all-inclusive plan with your phone company if you have a Gemini in the house. They love to talk and especially like the telephone.

The Gemini Sun sign can often appear to be interested and interesting, but somehow emotionally detached. They are constant questioners and often dominate conversation, imparting information but often not of a very personal kind. Also, don't immediately try to hug a Gemini – make sure that you give them plenty of space. They don't like you to get too friendly, especially at the start of a relationship and like all the Air signs, they don't like to feel stifled. They prefer verbal, intellectual communication to touching and feeling.

Geminis love to see both sides of the argument. They are excellent at debating and can hold a contradictory view unflinchingly until they have won the argument. This is when they will exasperate you all over again by revealing that they actually agreed with you in the first place! They see no problem with changing their minds to suit the situation. This makes them lightning quick thinkers.

They are thirsty for knowledge and eager to study. Generally they have a highly developed learning capacity. Their inventive imagination qualifies them for professions in writing, experimentation and criticism.

Geminis' reactions are prescribed by the mood of the moment; hence the dual quality to their personality. Variety is the spice of life as they see it, and this philosophy makes them highly strung. They are happiest when they have more than one dominant interest.

Geminis use sex as they use most activities – to avoid boredom. Sometimes the flirting is much more satisfying than the consummation of lust. They love talking themselves into, and then back out of bed with all sorts of people.

When they use their famous Gemini wit, they will charm or distract absolutely anybody into absolutely anything.

The Geminian side can also be expressed through a sister or brother figure, or real-life sibling issues. Many people with Gemini Sun have platonic, sisterly relationships with men. They often say that someone in their life is "just like a brother" or "just like a sister."

Gemini is the most dual of all the signs and it is vital for you to understand the function of the mind and learn how to control it. For everyone, getting the mind under control is an extremely difficult take, but for Geminis, it is a must.

You identify with: talkers, teachers, students, travellers.

You are an authority on: sibling relationships, the neighbourhood, news, words, journeys, facts.

You need: intellectual challenges, space for private phone calls, endless variety, good talkers and listeners, intelligent clients or employers, courses and seminars tied to your work.

Geminian Symbols:
Diaries, Shorthand, Stamps, Letters, Dictionaries, Messages, Couriers, Taxis, Nicknames, Names, Doubles, Multiples, Abbreviations, Twins, Fingers, Hands, Nerves, Secretaries, Tape recorders, Journalists, Editors, Novelists, Languages, Pens, Email, Photocopiers, Notes, Schools, Buying, Selling, Pagers, Wit, Messengers, Speech, Merchants, Vocabulary, Thoughts, Opinions, Telephones, Mass Media, Voicemail, Desks, Memos, Documents, Handwriting.

Famous Geminians:
Marilyn Monroe, Prince Philip, Paul McCartney, Donald Trump, Cilla Black, Kylie Minogue, John F. Kennedy, Anne Frank, Jamie Oliver, Joan Collins.

Cancer ♋
June 22nd – July 22nd

"House ordering is my prayer, and when I have finished, my prayer is answered. And bending, stooping, scrubbing, purifies my body as prayer doesn't."
Jessamyn West (writer) Cancer Sun Sign

"When indeed shall we learn that we are all related one to the other, that we are all members of one body."
Helen Keller (Diarist) Cancer Sun Sign

"After every war, someone has to tidy up."
Wislawa Szymborska (poet) Cancer Sun Sign

Personal creed: I feel
Receptive / Feminine sign
Symbol: The Crab
Element: Water
Quality: Cardinal
Ruler: The Moon
Body parts: Breasts, stomach, digestive system

People with Cancer Sun sign are generally:
Sensitive, caring, nurturing, loving, home-loving, protective, supportive, creative, charitable, productive, psychic.

On the other hand, they can also be:
Moody, worriers, insecure, clingy, jealous, manipulative, dependent, possessive, touchy, indirect, fussy.

Cancers love:
Nurturing, planning for the future, security for their money, parenthood, home-making, business, food, security, routine, the predictable.

They cannot stand: spontaneity, people intruding on their family's harmony, tactless criticism, practical jokes, being away from home for too long.

With Cancer, we arrive at the first of the Water signs. This is the sign of the emotions and if you can imagine the wide ocean, limitless, boundless and vast, then you have a good idea about the vastness of the emotional nature of a Cancer. I have a Cancerian friend and all her family are Water signs. She said, "We are all very emotional – we cry at sad things and we cry at the happy events in our lives." That is the characteristic of the Cancerian. They are so very sensitive and finely tune into everything around them.

As a contrast to the somewhat detached nature of the Gemini, the Cancer does like to be hugged and touched. They don't mind being loved in a physical way. They need to "feel" you rather than "talk" to you. Often they are quite happy to be with you in utter silence. For this reason, the Water signs often feel more comfortable in each other's company because they can tune into one another without the need for words.

Cancers were born under the sign of emotional sensitivity. This is the strongest of the Water signs and is most strongly linked to domesticity and homemaking. Cancers possess highly developed protective and defensive instincts. Cancers protect themselves from the possibility of emotional hurt by withdrawing and finding their security in solitude. In a marriage this acute sensitivity can be a challenge. For example, I know a married couple: she is an Aries Sun and he is a Cancer Sun. Every time they have any kind of argument he says: "You've chipped away at a part of my heart and my love." For the Aries, this makes her furious as she then cannot reach him as he goes into his shell. He punishes her for having an argument with him in the first place.

Because of their strong need for security, they will do whatever is needed to establish and serve that security. They seldom gamble unless they have safely put away their "rainy day money." Even then, gambling is rarely a means of a livelihood, since they are reluctant to jeopardise their security.

They seek to avoid any mental or physical discomfort. Since neatness and cleanliness are conspicuous with this sign, it follows they dislike activities which prevent absolute cleanliness. They prefer a refined atmosphere. They love to mother and take care of people, especially in their home. Even if someone just drops by, they can muster up a whole dinner in less than half an hour if needed. They don't like to hear that anyone could go hungry before leaving their home.

Cancers are masters of the art of passive resistance. This is a powerful weapon which, when wielded, makes the individual unapproachable. With kindness, Cancers can be directed easily, since they are basically understanding. If they are forced, they become immovable. You can't reason with them when they are emotionally disturbed. Wait until they quiet down and then talk to them.

They are averse to being told how to do things; they must complete tasks on their own, since the ideas of others confuse them. At times, they shun responsibility. However, if they work on an enterprise that promotes or requires it, they are punctual, exact and efficient, willing to guide things through to a successful conclusion.

The Cancer ability to make a home can superficially appear to be similar to the Taurean desire to nest, but they have completely different motivations. For a Taurus, making a home is about making a beautiful house to enjoy, whereas for Cancer a beautiful home is a by-product of their desire to make a harmonious nest for their loved ones.

Cancers find a Zen-like serenity in the routine of everyday life. When this routine is thrown out, it can cause a great deal of stress for the Cancer, but like water, they will find their level. They have a knack for creating a home virtually anywhere. They have to, in order to feel safe.

Cancers have a deep yearning to be part of a big flourishing family. If this is not possible, they will try and create a family out of the people around them.

Cancers avoid confrontation and will not say anything that they think will cause an argument, but that does not mean they hide their feelings well. Cancers wear their hearts on their sleeve, so you don't have to be the most perceptive person to know when they are upset with you. Cancers do not take criticism well, no matter how well-intentioned, and they can be terribly hurt by the slightest of insults.

Planets in Cancer describe how you feel about being a mother, how you feel about your own mother and the role of women as mothers in general. If you decide to go ahead and have a child, it will be a bigger deal for you than for most other women. If you skip parenthood, then similarly, it's going to be a very big deal. You will certainly be family conscious in one way or another. There will be very little that you do which can take place without reference to your family, to your place in the family and to your relationship with those people.

Today's maternal feelings encompass a variety of different roles for example: nurse, doctor, psychologist, counsellor, chef, sports coach, taxi driver, entertainer, waitress, cleaner, interior decorator, vet, home renovator, teacher, nanny, nutritionist, caterer, masseur.

All of these roles, in Cancerian terms, are done for love and they are accomplished protectively. As with all things associated with this sign, the accent is on caring and caretaking.

Cancer rules the public: mass consciousness. Mass consciousness is ruled by feeling, never by reason. Advertising agencies know this fact and make full use of it in dealing with the public.

You identify with: homemaking, nurturing, independence, spirited and active people.

You're an authority on: the home, family relationships, putting down roots, making and enjoying good food.

You need: a caring role, emotional satisfaction, people who need you on the most basic level, a decent selection of cafes and restaurants nearby, somewhere to run wild occasionally, space to make private phone calls.

Cancerian Symbols:
The Moon, Crabs, Houses, Flats, Homes, Property, Cooks, Chefs, Mothers, Doctors, Nurses, Children, Babies, Teenagers, Patriotism, Family, Trees, Shelters, Caves, Domesticity, Food, Health, Diet, Nutrition, Breasts, Pregnancy, Roots, Birth, Baths, Female Friends, Cleaners, Nannies, Care, Adoption, Healing, Feeding, Nurturing, Architecture, Building.

Famous Cancerians:
Princess Diana, Meryl Streep, Duke of Windsor, Nelson Mandela, Robin Williams, George Orwell, Muhammed Yunus, Dalai Lama, Mary Baker Eddy, Ringo Starr.

Leo ♌
July 23rd – August 22nd

"What really flatters a man is that you think him worth flattering." *George Bernard Shaw (writer) Leo Sun Sign*

"I believe it is better to be looked over than it is to be overlooked." *Mae West (actress) Leo Sun Sign*

"Take care of the luxuries and the necessities will take care of themselves." *Dorothy Parker (writer) Leo Sun Sign*

Personal creed: I will
Positive / Masculine Sign
Symbol: The Lion
Element: Fire
Quality: Fixed
Ruler: Sun
Body part: Heart, upper back

People with a Leo Sun are generally:
Generous, self-assured, warm-hearted, creative, enthusiastic, broad-minded, flamboyant, verbose, vivacious, faithful, loving, ambitious, dominant, gracious, courageous, strong-willed, independent, popular, natural leaders, dramatic, daring, intelligent.

On the other hand, they can also be:
Pompous, spendthrifts, proud, self-centred, patronising, bossy, dogmatic, opinionated, ruthless, jealous, liars, egotistical.

Leos love:
Luxury, power, sex, money, the spotlight, gambling, pleasure, overindulgence, acclaim, making a wonderful impression, being desirable and attractive, feeling pampered, being the boss, being appreciated.

They cannot stand:
Apathy, being ignored, criticism, nagging, competition, lying, deceit, laziness, introspection.

If you have planets in this sign, there may literally be some royal or aristocratic link in your life. Leo's have this amazing knack to get you to do the grunt work and to persuade you that you are enjoying it. I have a Leo friend, she's very sunny and warm, and she can get a whole score of people carrying boxes, bags, equipment for several hours if required on a film shoot and have them smiling and singing whilst they are doing it! That is the skill of the "typical" Leo.

Leo stands for rank and privilege. Leo leads to gold medals and the company of winners. Very commonly, people with Leo planets have a connection to people in the world of film, television, music, sporting success, politics, radio or media – which is where the new Kings and Queens come from.

Leo points towards the special, the starry, the important, and the well-known. Very often, especially in women, they have a gorgeous mane of red hair.

Leos were born under the sign of generosity and nobility of feeling. Leo is a Fire sign ruled by the Sun. Since it is the

Sun's function to bestow upon the world heat, light and life, it is the benefactor of every living creature. In our planetary system it is the centre around which the planets rotate. Leos, then, are generous. They must have the spotlight, and once in it, they must shine. They enjoy being the centre of attention.

They dislike repetition. Once they see the point, they become quite impatient, and often obstinate, in discussions. Those who disagree with a Leo's opinions should be tactful, for he will surrender so long as his dignity is recognised. He wants people to think well of him.

The symbol of this sign is the lion, denoting majesty, power, and dignity. Leo is a kingly sign, and Leos express pride in every movement. As long as Leos feel they are in a position of authority and responsibility, they will leave no stone unturned in order to justify the confidence that has been placed in them. Leos whose desire for authority is unfulfilled may develop traits of indolence, laziness, impetuousness and inconstancy.

Leos make great friends who are always up for a bit of fun. They are embarrassingly generous, but you should never turn down a gift, no matter how extravagant, because their pride will be hurt. Leos don't take a blow to their pride very lightly.

Leos need constant appreciation and adoration and they will reflect it back to you. When a Leo has found the perfect partner, they give themselves over completely.

They are completely loyal as partners and never take flirting any further.

Leos are charismatic leaders who know how to get things done. They are courageous decision-makers and masterful at delegating, as they know how to charm people into doing the work for them. This isn't to say that they won't do their share, it's just that they will make sure all the drudge work will fall to someone else.

Leos' faith and loyalty to those they love is very strong. Being a Fixed sign, once they give their affections they do not change easily. Where their opposite sign, Aquarius, is too impersonal and indifferent in relationships, Leo people are too attached where those they love are concerned. They have to learn true detachment.

You identify with: leaders, performers, stars, VIPs.

You're an authority on: leadership, children, youth, the creative process, the entertainment world and above all else, yourself!

You need: space for your soaring ambition, a leading role, special privileges and perks, an important title, centre stage, recognition for your achievements, your own office, and impressive business card, someone else to do the menial tasks, glory – reflected or personal.

Leonine Symbols:
The Sun, The Lion, Gold, Fire, Orange, Queens, Kings, Cats, Crowns, Thrones, Tigers, Babies, Children, Teenagers, The Heart, Ego, Creativity, Presidents, Prime

Ministers, Politicians, The Spine, Fur, Manes, Stars, VIPs, First class, Rings, Jewels, The Stage, Limelight, Velvet, Drama, Empires, Ceremony, Princes, Princesses, Glory, Suntans, Red Carpets, Nobles, Aristocrats, Cinemas, Theatres, Music venues, Palaces.

Famous Leos:

Princess Margaret, Princess Anne, Robert Redford, Kevin Spacey, Barack Obama, Mick Jagger, Coco Chanel, Louis Vuitton, Napoleon Bonaparte, Jackie Onassis.

Virgo ♍
August 23rd – September 22nd

"The learner always begins by finding fault, but the scholar sees the positive merit in everything."
Georg Hegel (philosopher) Virgo Sun Sign

"Life is paint and the enjoyment of love is an anaesthetic."
Cesare Pavese (writer), Virgo Sun Sign

"We cannot all do great things, but we can do small things with great love."
Mother Teresa (humanitarian) Virgo Sun Sign

Personal creed: I analyse
Receptive / Feminine Sign
Symbol: The Virgin
Element: Earth
Quality: Mutable
Ruler: Mercury
Body parts – Intestines, nervous system

People with a Virgo Sun are generally:
Detailed, precise, skilled communicators, devoted, hardworking, observant, shrewd, loving, nurturing, articulate, well-spoken, ordered, neat, meticulous.

On the other hand, they can also be:
Cold, critical, reserved, self-serving, jealous, fearful, distrustful, critical, phobic about hygiene and sanitation.

Virgos love:
Feeling secure, personal cleanliness, routines, loyalty, being pampered, equality, dedication, being active, perfection, attention to detail, conventions and rules.

They cannot stand:
Tardiness, vulgarity, loud displays of affection, personal untidiness, hypocrisy, weakness, complaining, idleness, forming new relationships, being wrested away from the grindstone.

Mercury, the planet associated with Virgo, lends you a gift for communication, analysis and understanding that only Gemini can equal. Virgos enjoy naming things. Since Mercury rules Virgo, they are forever seeking knowledge. Virgos are meticulous in their work, paying a great deal of attention to detail and doing things carefully and efficiently. They like to bring order out of chaos.

In its best form, this sign is efficient and reliable. At times, however there can be a narrowness of outlook and they may be unable to talk about anything other than work. Virgos subject their world to microscopic analysis.

As Virgo rules health, they must learn not to exhaust their body energies by worrying or overworking. This sign has a marvellous physical resistance to disease, once the mind develops discipline. If Virgos can keep out of the clutches of sickness, they become effective healers, exercising a very positive influence on the sick.

Because Virgo is an Earth sign, they admire material progress. They like good food and are fond of comfort and good clothes. Virgos also need cleanliness as well as order in their environment. In fact, you may often go into a Virgo's house or office and it looks as though there is no order at all. But you ask them to find something and they know exactly where to look.

Virgo is all about synthesising knowledge for the greater good rather than personal gain, and about the altruistic goal of serving others. Virgos can see the big picture, but they love to revel in the minutiae. If they are feeling off-balance or unconfident, they will often retreat into the detail and let someone else deal with the consequences. The Virgo mind is enormously patient and will pick over at a pace that ensures no mistakes are made. They make great subeditors and software writers because they can keep their mind on track for great lengths of time.

It is the critic in Virgo that is their inner tormentor. They have a keen eye for earthly flaws. They almost automatically notice the imperfection in everything, including themselves.

Caring and serving others is what they do best. They will attend to your needs, but try to be aware of their intense desire for sacred space. They are the loners of the zodiac, so give your Virgo a space that you don't enter, so they can pick every speck of lint off the floor if they want.

When a Virgo falls in love, it is a love not given lightly. As a Mutable Earth sign, the movement of the Virgo's mind is controlled, filtered through the senses and ultimately grounded. They may allow their mind to wander a little into romance but they are too practical to embark on anything that is not a relatively safe bet. But when their heart is captured, all the feelings and passion that Virgo has been keeping under lock and key are lavished upon the loved one. They are devoted, loyal and nurturing.

Virgo's memory is amazing and they like to file away the most trivial facts. They make great writers and teachers, as they always seem to have the answer for the most challenging of questions. They combine mental ingenuity with the ability to produce a clear analysis of the most complicated problems. They also see the shades of grey in any given issue.

The Virgo individual's greatest weakness is being too critical. Their analytical mind can cause them to degenerate into fault-finding, criticism and irritability. Virgos' real satisfaction lies in the realm of work and service. They are one of the best workers in the zodiac.

Because of their own inner feelings of inadequacy, they can be very demanding where their loved ones are concerned. Their need is to learn to be less critical and more loving.

Virgo thrives on information, communication and the world of words. Only planets in Gemini and Sagittarius are as deeply concerned with knowledge. Getting the message across correctly is a chief concern of Virgo. Your Virgo side is there to question, record, nod, contradict, agree, check – and then transmit. There is a strong sense of dedication and responsibility surrounding your messenger role. Whatever is passed on by your Virgo side to others has to be researched, checked, double-checked and word perfect.

You identify with: writers, teachers, students, dieticians, workaholics, media people.

You are an authority on: words, vitamins, illness, muscles, communication, the education system.

You need: routine, routine, routine, colleagues with high standards, space for your writing skills, an organised workspace, the best cleaner in town.

Virgo symbols:
Virgins, Mothers, Daughters, Healing, Health, Mercury, Communication, Language, Writing, Speech, Commerce, Merchants, Travellers, Libraries, Neighbours, Illness, Speeches, Computers, Letters, Postcards, Memos, Roads, Shops, Sales, Brothers, Sisters, Nature, Climate, Medicine, Cures, Lists, Order, Cleaners, Ritual, Routine, Sorting, Method, Publication, Teaching, Learning, The Voice.

Famous Virgos:
Sophia Loren, Greta Garbo, Lauren Bacall, Raquel Welch, Howard Hughes, Warren Buffett, John McCain, Maria Montessori.

Libra ♎

September 23rd – October 22nd

"So far as we are human, what we do must be either evil or good: so far as we do evil or good, we are human: and it is better, in a paradoxical way, to do evil than to do nothing: at least we exist." *T S Eliot (poet) Libra Sun*

"It is better to be unfaithful than to be faithful without wanting to be." *Brigitte Bardot (actress) Libra Sun*

"May we never confuse honest dissent with disloyal subversion."
Dwight D Eisenhower (US President) Libra Sun

Personal creed: I balance
Positive / Masculine Sign
Element: Air
Symbol: The Scales
Energy: Cardinal
Ruler: Venus
Body parts: Kidneys and lower back

People with Libra Sun are generally:
Objective, intellectual, independent, valuing of others, principled, respectful, civilised, tasteful, charming, good-looking, artistic, perceptive, observant, compromising, romantic, committed in marriage.

On the other hand they can also be:
Opinionated, indecisive, promiscuous, gullible, inclined to give in to keep the peace.

Librans love:
Beauty, harmony, love, communicating, making people happy, elegance, morality, designer clothes, expensive things, beauty, balance.

They cannot stand:
Conflict, distasteful things, unprincipled behaviour.

The one thing that any Libran will tell you straight away is that they have trouble making decisions. This is because they can always see both sides of the argument. When I go out with my two Libran friends, they can never make their minds up about which film they'd like to see, which café we should eat at today, and even down to: "do you need to go to the bathroom?" "Well, I'm not sure… do you?" and so it goes, back and forth. It's interesting that they only do this with each other. When an Aries friend comes along, she leads the way, telling them which film they are going to see, where they will eat and so on…

Libra is the turning point in the evolutionary process. The nadir of selfness has been reached and in this sign, relationships involving cooperation are born. The development of relationships is the most important attainment for Libra. One of Libra's weaknesses is their wanting to be all things to all men. So great is their desire to be liked by everyone, they will not take a stand on an issue, even when they know it to be right inwardly. "Peace at any price" is their motto, but sometimes the price is too high. When integrity is involved, it is well to be willing to pay the price.

Librans are ruled by the planet Venus, which gives them charm and grace in expression, combined with a desire for popularity and the approval of others. Because Libra is a Cardinal sign, they are concerned with the present and will initiate activities. However, they usually seek the cooperation of others rather than continuing alone.

Libra has a strong sense of justice and fair play arising from Saturn's exaltation in this sign. Thus they demand that their partners work as hard as they do. Librans are anything but lazy because of this Saturn influence. The more highly evolved the individual, the more likely they are to be hard-working, especially after their 29th year (on account of the 29 year cycle of Saturn and Saturn's exaltation in Libra).

These Venus-ruled natives rarely express anger, but when they do it is as though a tornado has gone through a room – they leave nothing unsaid. They will tell you exactly what you said fifty years before and under what circumstances you said it. Yet, like the tornado their anger soon spends itself, leaving them shaken and unwell.

You can never be truly sure what a Libra really thinks. Until they have made up their mind they can be quite gullible. Once they have weighed up the evidence and come to a conclusion, their mind is set in concrete.

Libras love people and they love to be near people. They tend to gather a large circle of friends, and unlike Cancer, Libras consider friends and family of equal importance.

Libra energy tends to seek good relations with the energy of all the other signs. So they are inclined to bend the truth a little in the cause of harmony.

Librans make wonderful diplomats and do well in the fields of psychology and social work, where an understanding of the contradictory nature of the human mind is an advantage. They are good to have around the meeting table because they make a genuine effort to understand all points of view, and are often better at crystallising other people's arguments than the people themselves. Coupled with a strong sense of justice, they do well in the fields of law and mediation.

They are wonderful at publicity and event management. Some work philanthropically with great self-discipline and significant results. Libra has a well-developed sense of social justice. They support causes that value human dignity.

It is common for strongly Libran people to marry across their social class, across their nationality, across their background or across their status. Why? Because Libra wants the perfect formula that will make two radically different species appear to be equal. Also, perhaps, because Libra needs the challenge of differences in order to understand what equality and balance are really all about.

You identify with: lovers, wives, partners, peacemakers, artists, designers, law makers, defenders of justice.

You're an authority on: aesthetic concerns, social, political or ideological issues, relationships.

You need: a pleasant work environment, a position that gives you authority without compromising your popularity, the freedom to dress according to your taste, rewards for your diplomatic skills, enough time out for your love life.

Libran symbols:
Venus, Scales, Balance, Art, Hair, Make-up, Clothes, Love, Romance, Passion, Design, Beauty, Marriage, Weddings, War, Peace, Enemies, Equality, Partnerships, Image, Dance, Courtship, Justice, The Law, Harmony, Cupid, Counsellors, Allies, Softness, Colour, Diplomacy, Popularity, Artists, Beauticians, Designers, Models, Lawyers, Barristers, Solicitors, Judges, Mediators, Graphics, Public Relations.

Famous Librans:
Mahatma Ghandi, John Lennon, Margaret Thatcher, Cliff Richard, Olivia Newton-John, Julie Andrews, Luciano Pavarotti, Oscar Wilde, Susan Sarandon, Brigitte Bardot.

Scorpio ♏
October 23rd – November 21st

"You mustn't always believe what I say. Questions tempt you to tell lies, particularly when there is no answer."
Pablo Picasso (artist) Scorpio Sun

"Dying is an art, like everything else. I do it exceptionally well."
From Lady Lazarus by Sylvia Plath (poet) Scorpio Sun

"Do you not see how necessary a world of pains and troubles is: to school an intelligence and make it a soul?"
John Keats (poet) Scorpio Sun

Personal creed: - I create
Receptive / Feminine Sign
Symbol: The Scorpion
Element: Water
Energy: Fixed
Rulers: Pluto, Mars
Body parts: Genitals, bladder

People with a Scorpio Sun are generally:
Strong-willed, stubborn, complex, able to get things done when nobody else can, deeply emotional, lusty, perceptive, searching for inner values, intense, industrious, thoughtful, reserved, sensitive, passionate lovers, loyal, supportive, protective, able to reason with imagination.

On the other hand, they can also be:
Demanding, possessive, jealous, unforgiving of faults, grudge-holders, creators of life enemies, obsessive -

especially with sex, suspicious, secretive, self-pitying, self-justifying.

Scorpios love:
Sex, loyalty in a partner, mystery, secrets, privacy, trust, sensuality, passion, strength, knowing where they stand, acknowledgment, honesty, integrity.

They cannot stand:
Surprises, lying and deceit, apathy, being analysed or questioned, being "understood", excessive compliments, insincerity, being embarrassed, passivity.

In many ways Scorpio is the most powerful sign of the zodiac, because it is ruled by Mars and Pluto, while Uranus, the planet of sudden release of energy, is exalted in it. My Scorpio friend cannot have a telephone conversation without using the words: "I had such an intense talk," or "I felt like I could be dying..." – they do tend to take life seriously and always have clear motives for their actions.

More than any other sign, Scorpio deals with the processes of fundamental transformation at all levels. This transformation can be on a high or low plane, depending on the motivation behind the change. However, as a rule, Scorpios work to improve the status quo.

Scorpios possess power, will, and intense emotional desires. Their life is likely to be a constant struggle to conquer desire through the creative use of the will.

Since this sign is strongly related to the desire principle and the sex drive, there is tremendous emotional force behind the Scorpio's romantic involvements. When out of proper control this can lead to possessiveness, jealousy and violence. No sign is more potent for good or evil as Scorpio.

Because Scorpios act with all their power, it is of utmost importance that they set out on the proper course from the start. They never deal with life superficially, and whatever they become involved with is generally of serious consequence. Sometimes their desire to do everything perfectly makes them unable to delegate responsibility, so they overwork themselves, seeking perfection in all the details.

Although they despise weakness in themselves and do not like to see it in others, they are often generous and compassionate and will extend themselves in order to help someone else. Scorpios expect, however, that the individual, once helped, will stand independently and continue to help themselves.

They are not always diplomatic, since they believe in expressing their ideas and feelings with unfiltered truthfulness. They would rather remain silent than give a watered-down version of their true opinions and emotions.

They have an intense drive to investigate the nature of things and discover the causes behind any outward manifestation. Consequently, they excel in work involving detection, science, research and occult investigations.

Scorpio is very much concerned with death, birth and rebirth. It is a period of darkness and introspection after the social interaction of Libra. The difference between Libra and its neighbour Scorpio is quite radical. Probably the most pertinent difference is their attitudes to truth. For Libra, the truth is changeable; for Scorpio, the truth is a given, and it is their life's mission to seek it out. They would never bend the truth to placate someone, but will tell the story as they see it, good or bad, because the truth cannot be tampered with. In a relationship, it can be deeply frustrating for the Scorpio, as they see things in black and white. "What do you mean you're not sure? There's nothing to be unsure about," the Scorpio will say to the Libra. But true to form, the Libra will not be able to give impatient Scorpio a quick, clear response.

Scorpios are a deeply emotional sign with a great need and desire to partner. You may not be able to insult them, but you can easily break their heart once it has been given to you. The Scorpio is a deeply compassionate sign that can suffer from intense feelings of loneliness.

Civilised society is most comfortable handling death inside the walls of life insurance offices and quiet, enclosed hospitals. Any discussion of Scorpio has to include death, though. People with Scorpio planets or Pluto chart signatures have a deep understanding of death and dying issues. Elisabeth Kubler-Ross had Pluto next to her Sun on the day she was born. Whoopi Goldberg, Scorpio Sun, worked in a morgue.

One of the reasons Scorpio seems to carry such a depth charge around with you is this: you've been through crisis, survived and changed. Perhaps it is these qualities that attract you to others going through intense experiences and transformations, or maybe they gravitate towards you because of the signals they read that you cannot see!

You identify with: powerful people, survivors, healers, confidantes, dark horses, sexual dynamos.

You're an authority on: any taboo subject – sex, death, race, power or money, the dark side, human survival.

You need: a locked filing cabinet, a private phone line, a little black book, informants, a powerful or influential position, people you can trust, intense challenges, room to change direction, respect for your privacy, goals you are passionate about.

Scorpionic Symbols:
The Scorpion, Pluto, Sex, Death, Black, Blood, Transformation, Power, Money, Ghosts, Resurrection, The Phoenix, Night, Darkness, Taboo, Sin, Control, Invisibility, Intensity, Caves, Atomic Power, Sewers, Obsession, Mystery, Near-death Experience, Spirits, The Underworld, Survival, Healing, Secrets, Lust, Crime, Revenge, Passion, Depth, The Occult, Rebirth, Temptation, Forbidden fruit, Dark Horses.

Famous Scorpios:
Richard Burton, Prince Charles, Pablo Picasso, Hillary Clinton, Julia Roberts, Leonardo Di Caprio, Martin Scorsese, Bill Gates, John Cleese, Meg Ryan.

Sagittarius ♐

November 22nd – December 21st

"I don't respond well to mellow, you know what I mean, I-I have a tendency to…if I get too mellow, I-I ripen and then rot."
Woody Allen (comedian / film director) Sagittarius Sun

"The only rules comedy can tolerate are those of taste, and the only limitations those of libel."
James Thurber (writer) Sagittarius Sun

"A fanatic is one who can't change his mind and won't change the subject."
Winston Churchill (political leader) Sagittarius Sun

"I never know how much of what I say is true."
Bette Midler (entertainer) Sagittarius Sun

Personal creed: I see
Positive / Masculine Sign
Symbol: The Archer
Element: Fire
Energy: Mutable
Ruler: Jupiter
Part of body: Thighs

People with a Sagittarius Sun are generally:
Loyal, impulsive, independent, lucky, talkative, outgoing, broad-minded, straightforward, enthusiastic, idealistic, ambitious, optimistic, honest, passionate, charming, funny, far-sighted, adventurous, non-possessive.

On the other hand they can be:
Impatient, impetuous, aggressive, irrational, selfish, prone to exaggeration, flighty, sarcastic, unreliable, dogmatic, judgmental, careless with possessions and money.

Sagittarians love:
Freedom, intellectual compatibility, taking risks, socialising, philosophical and political debate, feeling trusted, an active partner, daydreaming, literature, theatre, family, friends, travel, music and dance.

They cannot stand:
Jealousy, possessiveness, routine, being doubted, having to explain themselves, control, apathy, laziness, duplicity, shallow people, inward-looking institutions, convention, housework.

You are committed to a strong sense of meaning or purpose in your life.
You exercise your sense of humour wherever possible.
You are continually learning and educating yourself.

Sagittarius, born under the sign of honesty and straightforwardness, is represented by the arrow that flies swiftly to its goal. Sagittarians deeply love liberty and freedom.

They are energetic and naturally outgoing, achieving their goals through the power of positive thinking. Since the beneficent Jupiter rules and preserves Sagittarians, help always appears when they need it, even if only at the eleventh hour. Think of the "typical" Sagittarian as being very jolly, maybe a bit plump (due to the rulership of Jupiter and going over the top) and having a hearty laugh.

They are honest, just, and generous, because of their concern for the approval and harmony of the society in which they live. However, they may also have a tendency to be narrow-minded and bigoted if the social standards to which they subscribe are limited ones.

In Sagittarius, we reconcile the spiritual level discovered in Scorpio with the external world. Sagittarius searches for the magic moment where universal principles are glimpsed through personal experience.

Sagittarians radiate energy and vitality and possess alert minds. They crave experience. They love to travel and once they have stepped out, their itchy feet will have them planning the next trip. When they are at home, they quench their thirst for experience by reading avidly.

Sagittarians are explorers both of the world and of the mind. Though they love to experience new people, places and cultures, they are also happy to sit at home in front of an open fire exploring ideas with good friends.

They are an engaging mix of teacher and student. Their Mutable energy is about giving and taking, but their Fire Element puts them more on the giving side. Jupiter is the planet of good luck and many Sagittarians experience lots of good fortune. They always seem to fall on their feet.

Sagittarians love to talk and argue. They have sharp and inquiring minds and enjoy examining new ideas and use friends and family as sounding boards. Sagittarians have been known to read a dictionary if there was no other reading matter available. The Sagittarian is always on the lookout for a new book to read.

They are good researchers and read widely. Being able to synthesise many different streams of thought into one coherent piece makes them shine in the areas of science, the arts, religion and philosophy. They will fight for what they believe to be right, sometimes to the point of being dogmatic or judgmental.

Sagittarius influenced people often have issues about their own or other people's bodies to deal with. If this sign is especially strong in your chart, you may always have felt as though bits of you were too tall, too short, too fat or too thin. You may also be sensitive to other people around you being giants or midgets, skeletons or beachballs. More than anything else, Sagittarians lend themselves to thinking about proportions. It may be one of the challenges of this sign to learn that there is really no such thing as average.

The Sagittarius planets which lead to a preoccupation with size also give you a talent to inflate, exaggerate and over-emphasise – and also to play things down in a deadpan way. Dramatic situations become tiny. Trivia becomes over the top. In situation comedy, the funniest characters are usually the ones who are larger than life. By over-stressing the trivial and underplaying what is serious, you create comedy. Sometimes your Sagittarian side means to be funny, sometimes you just are – effortlessly.

If you can possibly fly to it, walk towards it, swim around it, jump off it or drive ahead of it, then you probably will. When your Sagittarian side catches sight of vast, open spaces, it doesn't really matter if you're looking at the local golf course or the ski fields of Europe – the response is the same. British Airways, predictably enough, was incorporated on 13th December 1983, which gives the airline Sun in Sagittarius. Apart from a lust for global roaming, BA also displays that other Sagittarian characteristic – comedy on tap.

If your Sagittarian side is particularly strong, you may emigrate, work in a field which involves a lot of interstate or international juggling, or "adopt" somewhere suitably far-flung or exotic.

Sagittarius is associated with the mass media, education, and all aspects of the printed word. Having a Sagittarius planet is a little like having a library of the best fiction and non-fiction locked inside your head, and when you are not planning your next trip, you will probably be curled up with a book.

Australia's two most successful media proprietors are a Sagittarius Sun and Sagittarius Moon respectively – Kerry Packer and Rupert Murdoch. Alongside Gemini and Virgo, Sagittarius is the sign which repeats more than any other in the world of mass communications.

You identify with: explorers, adventurers, idealists, philosophers, gurus, academics, politicians.

You're an authority on: at least one "ology" or "ism" – and sometimes more than one, other countries, cultures and beliefs.

You need: long holidays, work-related travel, long-distance connections, people who laugh at your jokes, the big picture, space to take a few risks, continual opportunities for expansion, people who share your enormous vision, amusing colleagues or clients, permission to go over the top once in a while.

Sagittarian Symbols:
Centaurs, Jupiter, Airplanes, Size, Humour, Travel, Philosophy, The Law, Education, International Organizations, The World, The Heavens, Passports, Ships, Foreign Ports, Explorers, Politics, Religion, Horses, Gambling, Casinos, Cartoon Characters, Maps, Globes, Justice, Wisdom, Imports, Exports, Legislation, Rules, Beliefs, Broad Horizons, Courses, Seminars, Foreign Affairs, Foreign Languages, Mass Media, Libraries, Academies, Encyclopedias, Trips, Mind Expansion.

Famous Sagittarians:
Ludwig van Beethoven, Steven Spielberg, Andrew Carnegie, Mark Twain, Frank Sinatra, Woody Allen, Billy Connolly, Charles M Schulz, Tina Turner, Uri Geller, Walt Disney.

Capricorn ♑
December 22nd – January 19th

"No one is so old as to think he cannot live one more year."
Cicero (orator/ writer) Capricorn Sun

"Ambition can creep as well as soar."
Edmund Burke (political theorist) Capricorn Sun

"Darkness cannot drive out darkness; only light can do that. Hate cannot drive out hate; only love can do that."
Martin Luther King Jr (civil rights leader) Capricorn Sun

Personal Creed: I use
Receptive / Feminine Sign
Symbol: The Goat
Element: Earth
Energy: Cardinal
Ruler: Saturn
Body parts: Bones, skeletal system, knees, teeth

People with a Capricorn Sun are generally:
Loyal, ambitious, dedicated, focused, honest, disciplined, deliberate, logical, patient, kind, supportive, serious, dependable, tolerant, practical, prudent, humorous, reserved.

On the other hand they can be:
Anxious, stubborn, retaliatory, suspicious, severe, possessive, controlling, cold, calculating, pessimistic, fatalistic, miserly.

Capricorns love:
Loyalty, security, financial stability, ambitious partners, feeling committed, making long-term plans, dependability, perseverance.

The cannot stand:
Flightiness, bossiness, coarseness, dominance, game-playing, ego displays, extravagance, indecisiveness.

Underneath that dependable, dry, buttoned-down exterior beats the heart of the warmest furnace. Capricorns have the most caring nature, it's just that they don't think they should show it in company.

As they mature, Capricorns start to get that spark of playfulness, and begin to dally with irreverence, as they grow more comfortable with themselves and their place in the world.

The three most important Capricorn goals are security, respect and authority. Everything else falls in line with them.

Since they are born under an Earth sign, Capricorns will never be content merely to keep body and soul together. They have a persistent feeling that they must develop into something. They must have some accomplishment to point to, some property to look after, or some obligation to fulfill, which may be business, politics or the social or intellectual fields.

They have excellent intuitions and use them in their struggle to achieve personal independence and economic security. They love law and order and are dogmatic in their view that a rule is a rule and an order is an order. Since they are of the Earth element, everything has to be sensible.

Capricorns are never deterred by things that stand in the way of their climb to the top. Their extreme capacity for hard work is linked with their notion that success means material security, and they will work and plan for it.

They have great faith in their own power, and are worldly and careful. Asking for no mercy from anyone, they drive a hard, but not unjust bargain. They are extremely gifted in finding solutions to the most difficult problems and are very successful as troubleshooters.

They desire money, because theirs is a long-lived sign. They fear being dependent on others when they are old. This need for security may cause them to have frugal instincts which might make them stingy. They are old when they are young and young when they are old.

Capricorn represents the principles of hard work, perseverance, integrity and determination. Earth signs are tenacious, and have stable reserves of energy. The symbol of the Goat is often used to explain the particular brand of Capricorn tenacity, climbing ever higher, not stopping to take in the view until they reach the top of that mountain.

You have amazing ambition and are prepared to work to see it fulfilled.
You have older people, or respected role models around you.

You understand that nothing happens in this life without self-discipline.
You respect hierarchies and structures.

This sign helps you take the job seriously, and no matter what else may be going on in your life, things will always come back to your work! Your Capricorn planets lend you ambition, organising ability and patience. It makes you resourceful and in control. It gives you, above all other things, a reality check. It's an aid to accomplishment, no matter how high you aim.

Sometimes, looking at the career paths of certain Capricorns, it's difficult to imagine how they got here from there. If you have a planet in this sign, you stand a better than average chance of pole-vaulting way, way above the place you started from. There are many Capricorn influenced people who have rags to riches life stories. There are also those who have seemingly achieved the impossible – gone from actor to director, or from employee to CEO.

With a Capricorn planet, you like attaching yourself to people who can teach you something. Part of the reason for this is your ruler, Saturn, is the wise elder. Your guide may be male or female, but this person will inevitably be more experienced than you. You may feel that you have a lot to live up to with them, or that you must test yourself as you struggle to meet their standards or expectations. It is seldom an easy process, but then Saturn, your ruler, has never been known for producing easy learning experiences.

The positive qualities of Capricorns are leadership, patience, persistence, efficiency and practicality. They are ambitious and willing to work hard for what they want. There is strength and integrity in the higher type Capricorns. They are dependable and confident, and give confidence to others.

As Capricorn rules time and clocks, I am always tickled when I speak to my Capricorn friend and ask her: "How long have we been talking on the phone today?" Quick as lightning, she'll say, "21 minutes and 17 seconds!"

You identify with: organisers, directors, bosses, workaholics, traditionalists, older people, people in history books.

You're an authority on: age, experience, structures, traditions, taking the controls, handling inhibitions.

You need: a realistic job description, the big picture, order and organisation, continual work, high status, control, space to delegate to others, a solid professional structure.

Capricorn Symbols:
Saturn, Ambition, Structure, Stone, Rock, Sculpture, Bones, Skeletons, Pyramids, Directors, Employers, Age, Experience, Old Age, Senior Citizens, Mentors, Guides, Tradition, Classics, Organisation, Patience, Caution, Fear, Watches, Clocks, Time, Goats, Professional, Foundations, Industry, Maturity, Commitment, Consistency, Discipline, Timing, Earth, Work, Mountains.

Famous Capricorns:
Martin Luther King, Muhammed Ali, Mao Tse Tung, Joseph Stalin, Conrad Hilton, Elvis Presley, Isaac Newton, Helena Rubenstein, Elizabeth Arden, Paramanhansa Yogananda.

Aquarius ♒

January 20th – February 18th

"Vices are sometimes only virtues carried to excess!"
Charles Dickens (writer) Aquarius Sun

"I only go out to get me a fresh appetite for being alone."
Lord Byron (poet) Aquarius Sun

"There are persons who, when they cease to shock us, cease to interest us."
F H Bradley (philosopher) Aquarius Sun

"A new gadget that lasts only five minutes is worth more than immortal work that bores everyone."
W Somerset Maugham (writer) Aquarius Sun

Personal Creed: I know
Positive / Masculine Sign
Symbol: The Water Carrier
Element: Air
Energy: Fixed
Rulers: Uranus, Saturn
Body parts: The circulation, calves, ankles

People with an Aquarius Sun sign are generally:
Playful, friendly, spontaneous, open-minded, caring, devoted, liberal, understanding, tolerant, benevolent.

On the other hand they can also be:
Unreliable, cold, aloof, mean, self-centred, unable to commit, judgmental, fickle, intractable, contrary, unpredictable.

Aquarians love:
Good conversation, a boss who is more like a good friend, thinking outside the norm, fringe culture, independence, witty banter, committing to a cause, their friends sometimes more than their family.

They cannot stand:
Soppiness, bores, predictability, conventionality, tackiness, commitment, suburbia, people who try to be stereotypes, their privacy being invaded, popular culture in general.

Aquarians are the one sign that you cannot lump together as having lots of similar characteristics. In fact what makes them uniquely Aquarian is that they are all "one-offs." They are so different from each other – and they take pride in these differences, because after all Aquarius is ruled by Uranus, which is the planet of innovation, newness and sudden change.

Individuals born under the sign of brotherhood and fraternity have as their symbol the water-bearer, who spills out to mankind life force and spiritual energy. Since the planet Uranus rules Aquarius, friendship and companionship are extremely important to Aquarians. Those whom Aquarians befriend have their unswerving loyalty.

Born under a Fixed sign, Aquarians have eccentric temperaments and are determined and stubborn. They sometimes feel that those who are listening to them are unreceptive and incapable of comprehending their ideas, and they tend to become annoyed when people fail to understand them. Then Aquarians argue, and when they do, they stir up opposition from others.

Aquarians long for material possessions but are not greedy. They are disinclined to engage in sports as a rule, except as observers. Their pursuits are more intellectual than physical.

Aquarians are radicals and they like to think outside the box. They are known for their open-minded approach to life and people. They make it their business to be accepting of all people and cultures. They are generally attracted to a more liberal, humanitarian brand of politics, and if they are interested in politics, they will throw themselves into it.

Aquarians cannot stand commitment and will do anything to get out of confirming a time or a place.

Like Virgo, Aquarius can be a bit squeamish about bodies, and would prefer to live in the monastic cleanliness of their minds. This makes sharing space with others a little confronting for Aquarians. My aunt was an Aquarius Sun sign, and she married my uncle because he was the first man she met who didn't "maul" her.

They love the idea of people, but as long as it is only in the abstract. They may be attracted to the idea of living in a commune, but the reality of all that shared space, especially the bathroom, can be too much.

You will find Aquarians doing whatever they can to differentiate themselves from the crowd. Actors, dancers, artists, transvestites, fashion designers, writers — anywhere out there on the fringes is where you'll find Aquarius.

You have a wide circle of friends and contacts.
You refuse to conform or compromise if it means selling yourself or other people out.
You enjoy your own eccentricities.
You follow up every flash of brilliance that comes your way.
You are unusual, independent and well-intentioned.

It is in the nature of Aquarius to have sudden insights and to make innovations and discoveries which will help you to stand out from the pack. It is the things which are most unique about you — even if they are a little eccentric — which you need in order to feel confident enough to express yourself. If you have planets in Aquarius you are, above all, an extreme individualist.

Aquarius is a sign that often makes people feel uncertain, or unsafe. One of the biggest challenges for you is finding a way to accommodate your own unique ideas, opinions, life and values in a way that other people can accept. Most of the time, this live and let live approach will work successfully. However, it is in the nature of this, the maverick eleventh sign, to be stubborn. Aquarius — like Leo, Taurus and Scorpio — is Fixed. The freedom that you crave to be yourself, and the changes and new ideas that you long for may never happen unless you can find some kind of bridge that will lead you to the rest of the population. Your Aquarian side absolutely detests compromising and faking it, smiling politely and falling into line. But a small amount of this social oil — even a token gesture – will be necessary if your intense individuality is going to be allowed to breathe.

Your Aquarian side is always living in the future. Mostly, Aquarius planets are always a few decades ahead, and quite unknowingly. Your Aquarian side will "get" things before the rest of the population even knows they are desirable. Bear in mind that sometimes you will be too far ahead of your time.

Barry Humphries, also known as Dame Edna Everage, is an Aquarius Sun. Barry has channelled pure Aquarius through his beloved Dame. There is no other titled, transsexual celebrity on television apart from her.

Your Aquarian side expresses itself most strongly through what you don't do. Here are some other Aquarian refusals that I've jotted down over the years:
- not driving
- not eating meat
- not collecting the mail
- not wearing lace-up shoes
- not wearing anything red
- not having a TV set
- not carrying change
- not cooking
- not wearing a watch
- not paying parking fines

The things that your Aquarian side actually does do are probably just as personalised. I know an Aquarian who carries an alarm clock in her handbag. Another Aquarius Sun washes her underwear by wearing it in the shower.

Your Aquarian side can be quite perverse. It can desire change when hardly anybody else sees the need for it, and absolutely refuse to change if there is a sense that you are being pressured or forced. You are a reformer at the same time that you are quite a stubborn defender of your own position.

You identify with: eccentrics, rebels, visionaries, radicals, humanitarians, renegades, innovators.

You're an authority on: friendship, networking, new ideas, your own opinions, the future, a better world.

You need: the freedom to be eccentric, a flexible routine or no routine, special rewards for your flashes of genius, an ethical workplace, honest work relationships, your own dress code, long lunches with friends.

Aquarian Symbols:
Lightning, Electricity, Inventors, Innovation, Freedom, Liberation, Uranus, Friends, Groups, Tribes, Clubs, Associations, Shocks, Eccentrics, Change, Choice, Rights, Rebels, Outsiders, Computers, Technology, Science, Genius, Invention, Originals, Perversity, Experiments, Causes, Outcasts, Equality, Astrology, Circulation, Brilliance, Futures, Tomorrow, Revolutionaries, Humanitarianism, Surprises, Trailblazers.

Famous Aquarians:
Wolfgang Amadeus Mozart, Paul Newman, Thomas Edison, Abraham Lincoln, Franz Schubert, Charles Darwin, Lewis Carroll, Oprah Winfrey, Charles Dickens, Yoko Ono.

Pisces ♓
February 19th – March 20th

"A daydream is a meal at which images are eaten. Some of us are gourmets, some gourmands, and a good many take their images precooked out of a can and swallow them down whole, absent-mindedly and with little relish."
W H Auden (poet) Pisces Sun

"We should take care not to make the intellect our god; it has, of course, powerful muscles, but no personality."
Albert Einstein (physicist) Pisces Sun

"How boring moviemaking is…you work for one minute and then sit around for three hours."
Elizabeth Taylor (actress) Pisces Sun

Personal Creed: I believe
Receptive / Feminine Sign
Symbol: The Fish
Element: Water
Energy: Mutable
Rulers: Neptune, Jupiter
Body part: Feet

People with a Pisces Sun sign are generally:
Mystical, enchanting, emotional, loving, devoted, reverent, creative, easy-going, sensitive, instinctive, affectionate, submissive, unselfish, altruistic.

On the other hand, they can also be:
Escapist, idealistic, secretive, vague, weak-willed, easily led, needy, lazy, manipulative, confused, depressed, irresponsible, inarticulate, goal-less, indecisive.
Pisces love:
Romance, feeling appreciated and needed, stability, being encouraged to dream, sharing thoughts/dreams, having their input valued, a role model

They cannot stand:
Feeling vulnerable, feeling alone or unloved, being ignored, crude behaviour, noisy scenes, having no dreams, having no sense of structure.

You escape from the world through poetry, music, art, film or literature.
You listen to your dreams and take them seriously.
You regularly serve huge dollops of sympathy, sensitivity and soul – to people or animals.
You're in touch with something spiritual, special or unseen.

Pisces is a sensitive sign and those born under it are extremely responsive to the thoughts and feelings of others. They unconsciously absorb the ideas and mental outlook of those around them.

The Pisces temperament varies from being strongly optimistic to being acutely pessimistic. This can be irritating to those who are absorbed in the material world and cannot understand how people born under a sensitive sign can get lost in the business of living.

Generally, Pisceans are not ambitious for material or monetary acquisitions.

Neptune sensitises Pisces to the whole of human suffering. Thus, they sincerely want to initiate healing and relief. Many of them choose to work in the most sordid conditions or accept anything that will lighten the load for others. Pisces from all walks of life devote their strength and time, with no thought of personal reward, to the sick and desolate.

When Pisces are themselves, they are unselfish, lovable, devoted and eager to sacrifice themselves for those who surround them. The Pisces consciousness craves to reach out and become a part of all life, and the emotions are extended with compassion and tenderness to others. Pisceans are blind to all defects in those they love and trust. My Pisces friend recently lent a large sum of money to a friend that she "felt sorry for." Her Taurean husband was most displeased, as he didn't think they would ever get it back. Sadly, they have not had the loan repaid. This is another example of the Pisces idealistic, but impractical trusting nature of others. She also cries at the drop of a hat if she sees an animal in distress or hears a baby crying. There is always that empathy with the suffering of another.

Understanding the Piscean character is as frustrating as trying to catch silverfish in your hands. The idea that Pisces is the final sign before we are reincarnated into an Aries again has often been used to describe the faraway look in Pisces's eyes and their tired disposition. They have simply had it with this physical reality, they are dying for a cup of tea and a lie down in the spirit world – or maybe a shot of adrenalin in Aries.

Pisceans can be very indecisive and lack motivation if they need to do or get anything for themselves. They have been known to put up with terrible eyesight for a very long period of time before they will get around to buying a pair of glasses. The truth is, Pisceans would rather save their energy and resources to do things for other people.

If they are doing something for someone else, they find surprising reserves of strength. They will go to any lengths to give someone a hand. There is no sacrifice too large for them to make.

Pisceans can allow themselves continually to be taken advantage of. They know it is happening, but believe the reward for being open-hearted and trusting is worth it. They can appear to be gullible, but this is not correct, as Pisceans are never naïve. They are rarely surprised by the depths to which humanity can sink, and can see most things coming from a mile off. But they just heave a big sigh and get on with it.

The have a great capacity to feel, and sometimes that can be quite overwhelming. Fellow Water signs Cancer and Scorpio can protect their sensitivity with a hardened shell, even though they may be crying underneath. Pisces has no such defence. This is why some Pisceans find relief from the world in drugs or escapist cults.

Pisces can have strange relationships with possessions. They usually need many things around them, and can hoard like crazy, though they suffer a great deal of guilt collecting such symbols of materialism. Shopping soothes them, but they find it difficult to justify buying a few things for themselves.

Animation and website design are particularly Pisces careers. They are essentially lone pursuits with an enormous scope for creativity and fantasy. Pisceans can usually visualise anything, and if their intellect is strong they can imagine themselves in the most complex problem. Einstein, a Pisces Sun, was said to imagine himself as part of an atom in order to think about a problem. He also considered his sleep very important and would sleep for 10 or 11 hours each night before a big thinking day.

As Pisces rules the feet in astrology, Pisceans put themselves in other people's shoes. As a result you are hopelessly sentimental and easily moved and are frequently involved in helping others. This side of Pisces comes from your ruler, Neptune, which dissolves boundaries and increases your sensitivity. You "just know" what is going on in other people's heads, or behind an animal's eyes and you really feel for them.

At what point does a Piscean type cease being a saviour and turn into a victim? Is it a happy and healthy state of affairs to be a martyr to anything? This is one of the most baffling areas of Piscean experience, and astrologers often find themselves grappling with the contradictions. The two fish in the Pisces glyph do not swim in opposite directions for nothing. The contradictions in the victim/saviour patterns that you will experience in your lifetime are rather like those fish.

You may be a meditator, a lifelong wisher, a mantra-chanter or even a spell-caster. Pisces describes the unseen and the non-material world. There is something deeply mysterious about this area of Piscean experience. What you perceive as part of your Piscean experiences may be a result of your sixth sense, or a sense beyond that. Your Piscean side has an extreme sensitivity to all that cannot be measured, charted, or tested in a laboratory. Sometimes it is impossible for strongly Piscean experiences to be articulated, just because they lack this measurable, material quality.

Many Pisces-influenced people feel drawn to the esoteric, mysterious side of astrology, and have little interest in sceptics demanding proof and data. Some of the best astrologers I have known have Pisces planets because they bring intuitive gifts to the field. They also have a rare ability to sympathise and empathise with their clients, and to feel their way round a chart.

The myth surrounding Neptune, your ruler, involves several images of sacrifice. When astrologers look at Neptune in a personal horoscope, they associate sacrifice with the area of life occupied by that planet. Neptune in the 4th House, for example, describes a sacrifice made in connection with one's family, and perhaps one's homeland or house. In the 2nd house, Neptune describes giving up money and possessions.

With Piscean planets, both the idea and reality of sacrifice will be an important part of your story. What has been given up by you, or lost by you, may be totally involuntary, or it could be a fully conscious and personal decision. A

Pisces planet, however, lends the sacrifice a kind of depth and richness as well. There is less a sense of things having been mindlessly forfeited or thrown away, as a conviction that the sacrifice makes sense in the context of your whole life.

We have now come through the entire zodiac. We could say that: Libras will tell you the truth that you want to hear; Scorpios will tell you the truth because that is what you need to hear; Sagittarius will tell you the truth inadvertently; Capricorn is the master of tact and discretion; Aquarius knows the truth, so why wouldn't you want to hear it? Then we come back to Pisces, who are so tired of looking for the truth they suspect it doesn't exist. So we return to Aries, where we rejuvenate our energy and look at things afresh. The cycle begins anew.

You identify with: dreamers, artists, musicians, mystics, actors, poets, healers.

You're an authority on: the human condition, animals, dreams, imagination, mysteries, the arts, sacrifice.

You need: a space and a place to dream alone, low pressure or better still no pressure, a gentle atmosphere, subdued lighting, flexible hours so that you can escape when you have to, something to draw and doodle on, rewards for your imagination, birds on the windowsill, a stray animal to feed.

Piscean Symbols:
Neptune, Fish, Sacrifice, Fog, Mist, Oil, Water, Drowning, Rescue, Saviours, Saints, Martyrs, Alcohol, Hypnosis,

Clairvoyance, Oceans, Seas, Floods, Lakes, Eyes, Vision, Haze, Deception, Lies, Photography, Illusions, Film, Poetry, Escape, Impressionism, Paintings, Illustrations, Fiction, Liquids, Myths, Dreams, The Collective Unconscious, All Creatures Great and Small, God/Goddess, Spirituality, Ghosts, Feet, Shoes, Atmosphere, Intuition, Virtual reality, Addiction, Fantasy, Faith, Instinct, Camera, Turquoise, Violet.

Famous Pisceans:
Albert Einstein, Frederic Chopin, Michelangelo, Steve Jobs, Enrico Caruso, Helen Clark, Gordon Brown, Lisa Minnelli, Maurice Ravel, Julie Walters, Victor Hugo, George Harrison.

Chapter 4

"The Cosmos is a vast living body, of which we are still parts. The Sun is a great heart whose tremors run through our smallest veins. The Moon is a great nerve-center from which we quiver forever. Who knows the power that Saturn has over us, or Venus? But it is a vital power, rippling exquisitely through us all the time.

D H Lawrence – writer

The Ascendant or Rising Sign

The Ascendant is technically the exact degree of the Rising Sign on the eastern horizon in a birth chart. The Ascendant is the gate through which we most directly confront the outer world. It symbolises our individual approach to life itself. However, it may appear more dominant and authentic when the rest of the chart harmonises with it. When the rest of the chart is not particularly attuned to the qualities and energy of the Ascendant, it may then appear more superficial, a relatively artificial mask that may be quite at odds with the rest of the person's nature.

Although the Ascendant is of deep importance for each individual, there is no denying that it must be related to the rest of the chart and especially to the Sun Sign, in order to understand it thoroughly. The Sun is the core identity, the very centre of consciousness, the way we assimilate much of our experience, whereas the Ascendant – although it varies in importance from person to person – is not as central to the person's nature. It shows, among other things, the approach to life; but the Sun shows life itself!

The Ascendant modifies the expression of the Solar energy. For example, a Gemini rising will always give a more socially lively and intellectually curious approach to life to any Sun Sign. It will even speed up a slow Taurus Sun, make a Scorpio Sun more social and less secretive, help a Capricorn Sun to be less defensive and more communicative, and encourage a Cancer Sun to be less shy!

Another useful tool for understanding how a person's Ascendant and Sun Sign interact is to compare the Elements of the two factors. For example, a Cancer Sun Sign person with a Fire sign Rising is usually far more extroverted, forcefully expressive, and confident than a Cancer Sun individual with, say, a more conservative, self-protective Earth sign Rising. Another example is an Air sign Sun person with a Water sign Rising. They may appear much more emotional than they really are, whereas a Water Sun sign person with an Air sign Rising may appear far more detached and less emotional than they truly are.

Some people do not identify very much with their Rising Sign. The Ascendant is a factor that can be consciously developed over time and consciously utilised to aid one's self-expression. I have known people who were relieved to find out what their Rising Signs were, since it finally gave them a way of identifying a very deep but only semi-conscious tendency in themselves. In some cases, the qualities and abilities symbolised by the Ascendant were just beginning to emerge and learning the astrological keys to this factor helped personal development greatly. Perhaps more than with most other factors in the chart, the early environment can encourage or suppress the expression of the Ascendant's energies, since it is a primary channel with which one interacts with the outer world.

Very often, your Rising sign is not the real you, unless it is the same as your Sun, Moon, Mercury, Venus or Mars sign. In actual fact, it's often a very good mask. It's your outer style – the bit of you that people see at parties, job interviews and in any first-impression situation. Margaret Thatcher has Scorpio Rising and as the only female Prime Minister in the history of England she had to be secretive, intense and powerful. Every time she stood up in a dress and heels, people were reminded of her sexuality and so was she. That's her Scorpio Rising.

It's crucial to have your accurate time of birth in order to calculate your Ascendant. If the Rising sign doesn't make sense to you, look at the one before and the one after it. If one of these fits like a glove, that's probably it.

Aries Rising

You need action in your life and lots of it. You have an immediate and direct approach to life – you hate beating about the bush. Very few Aries Rising people like waiting around. You are certainly not lazy and you want to get out there and keep moving. You need to feel the earth moving underneath you in more ways than one. There is a strong sense of enthusiasm, and patience is something you will learn as you go through life.

You love a challenge and you like to find ways to solve it. Physically you need to exercise and move your body as you need a physical outlet for all your energy.

You can be abrupt, ambitious, restless, impatient – in a hurry to rush through life. There can be an abrasive quality to you at times. If Mars is in Pisces, Cancer or an Earth sign, these forceful qualities can be somewhat moderated. The blunt directness of Aries Sun that can seem offensive, insensitive and inconsiderate to others is often toned down in many people with Aries Rising.

You take on the role of leader, so invariably you act first, decide what's to be done, and get things moving. You are uncomfortable with having to wait things out, or with letting things develop outside of your initiative. You need to learn tact and diplomacy. Good in mechanical endeavours and physical activity. Keen, alert and quick reflexes.

Taurus Rising

You look for stability as well as financial security. You may find that you are put in financial high and low situations where you must work out a different sense of values each time. Nature, shopping and making money will all have importance to you as will the sensual world. Your sense of visual and musical appreciation is vital to your enjoyment of life. There are usually artistic or creative talents and also a strong feeling for design, form, colour and shape. Because sensuality and the aesthetic are so important to you, you may find that nature has given you an attractive exterior, or the skills and time to develop one.

You prefer to go out into the world rather slowly, in your own time, with the calm and steady movements that this Rising sign is famous for. You just won't be pushed.

Methodical, controlled, measured movements and a strong aesthetic and pleasure-motivated streak are in your nature. You can be lazy or steadily productive, but will insist on doing everything your own way and at your own pace. Venus' sign position strongly affects how ambitious or dynamic you will be. Taurus Sun more often seems lazy than Taurus Rising and Taurus Sun seems to be more predictably possessive. Both want to enjoy everything they do, and therefore refuse to rush anything. You have an extremely physical and sensual approach to life and a strong need for closeness, affection and security.

You are very much the creature of Nature and the physical senses, exuding an aura of permanence and constancy. No matter how you actually look, there is a tactile feel to you. A deeply committed relationship is definitely the fodder for you, the type of partnership that can endure quite heavy conflicts or tests of fidelity.

Gemini Rising

You are likely to spend your life in the world of words before anything else. Your enjoyment of good books and good conversation will be a big part of the journey. You'll be on the move a lot too, and will become one of life's jugglers. Education and learning new skills will always be a part of your life. You are well-informed and information and loose news always seems to follow you around. You are a mine of information with a quick and lively aura. The mental processes with Gemini Rising are always emphasised: anything from memory, to peace of mind, to concentration.

You are highly intelligent and communication is a vital part of your life. You want to share what you learn with others and you are constantly looking for new things to learn on your way.

The most inquisitive and friendly Rising Sign, but also the one most inclined to be worried about yourself all the time. Usually you are very intelligent and curious, and have a tremendous need to communicate verbally. The superficiality often seen in Gemini Sun is not usually as evident in the Gemini Ascendant, but the tendency for one side of the mind not to know what the other side thinks or says is even more extreme in Gemini Ascendant.

You approach life in the spirit of enquiry, like the eternal student. You love making connections between one thing and another, without necessarily having to feel any sense of where it is all heading or what it all means. You are a keen maker of contacts, priding yourself on being acquainted with all types of individual and scenes.

Friendly, adaptable, witty and clever. Very highly strung. Temperamental. People make you nervous but you love an audience as you love to talk.

Cancer Rising

You may become involved with property, housing, environment or accommodation issues in your life. Your journey involves finding a sense of place on a national level and working out what it means to be patriotic, or identified with your country of choice.

There may be several dramatic homecomings in your life. By travelling away, you better understand what it is to be home. Playing Mother is a natural Cancer Rising journey. Not every person with Cancer Rising has their own children, however, you are there to nourish people. Family members will exercise a great deal of influence in your life and in the choices you make. Your relationship with your mother and all other "mother" figures will be particularly vital.

You learn to be careful with the resources you have and you learn to stockpile provisions.

A sympathetic, mild demeanour, but the sensitivity and sympathy are often directed just as much toward yourself as toward others, often being oversensitive to slights and hurts. Cancer Rising seems to exhibit a more superficial type of empathy for others than Cancer Sun, whose feelings tend to go deeper and whose sentiment is more personally touching. Cancer Ascendant often seems even more reserved and private than the Cancer Sun person, who by virtue of his or her great acting ability can often seem quite social and outgoing. The Cancer Rising person is usually a strong introvert, although I have seen cases where the Moon was in Leo or a similar extroverted sign and the more outward-oriented tendencies were predominant.

You are all "feelers", picking up the emotional climate around you with instinctive ease. It can seem at times that you are purely responsive and reactive to whoever you are with and wherever you are. This can result in your not being at all sure whether it is your feeling or someone else's.

Leo Rising

The Leo Rising journey is about encouraging others. Because you will be confronted by people who seem to be looking to you for advice, or silently hoping for an example, you will have to respond properly. Leo Rising is about recognising that you must take command because no one else is willing or able to. It is about handling life in an elegant and graceful way after the occasional mistake. In this way, you win permanent respect.

You are a great organiser and good at delegating tasks. You seem to find a way to get people to do things and at the same time to feel good about it. You have the ability to dramatise the ordinary and elevate the mundane. You have a fierce kind of loyalty and you refuse to desert or bolt no matter what the situation.

A Leo Ascendant often seems to motivate you to try hard to express your best self. That is not to say that the pride of the sign Leo is completely absent from those with Leo Rising, but it does appear that they have less need to "lord it over" other people than those with Leo Sun. The Leo Ascendant seems to encourage an especially authentic expression of the person's Sun energy, whereas the Leo Sun person often displays a more self-conscious dramatisation of his or her deeper feelings. Bigheartedness, often said to be a trait of Leo, seems to be a more reliable quality in those with Leo Rising than Leo Sun, which so often insensitively manipulates others for personal gain. Leo Ascendant can, however, demonstrate an extremely aloof bearing and, because of their inordinate need for respect and a show of dignity, often seems to lack the spontaneous humour and playfulness of Leo Sun.

Like a king or a queen you express yourself with apparent confidence and style, with a regal air that names the game and sets the rules.

Virgo Rising

Your journey is about working hard, using your brain, communicating and maintaining good health. You have an orderly thinking style and lists are probably a big part of your life. You will be put in touch with your body by whatever means possible. This may happen because you enter a career, or an interest area, where bodies are the centre of existence. You go out into the world looking for a kind of purity – in your diet, in the sea, in your blood.

You will attempt to find order in the middle of chaos. You are on the path of the perfectionist. You also look to do something that will be of value and to make a real contribution in whatever you undertake.

Virgo Rising people often have a higher level of self-confidence than Virgo Sun people, and oddly enough, their humility often seems more authentic in at least one way: those with Virgo Rising always acknowledge that they have more to learn and further to go to improve themselves. The self-criticism that so often defeats and depresses Virgo Sun people is sometimes, but not nearly so often, found in the Virgo Ascendant. It is as if the Virgo Ascendant more often "works off" their doubts rather than just dwelling on them. The conservative and conventional qualities found in abundance in Virgo Sun are not nearly so deep-seated in the Virgo Rising person, who may appear aloof, severe or withdrawn but whose appearance may hide a much wilder nature. The Virgo Sun person is usually better with detailed analysis than is the Virgo Ascendant although both often display craftsmanship skills.

You approach life with a view to improving the quality of it in some way. Consequently, you are almost constantly on the go – there is always something or someone that needs seeing to from where you stand.

Libra Rising

Having a partner in your life – either intimate, business, soulmate – will probably be a big part of your journey. You are always looking for harmony between people. You go out into the world wanting people to accompany you and travel with you. You are a natural Public Relations expert. You know how to establish social harmony, and how to smooth things over between people. Ugly atmosphere, violent feelings or vulgar behaviour affects you most.

The Libra Rising journey involves righting wrongs. The only time you will break your famous rule of smiling and smoothing, is when you realise you have to declare war to get peace. It rankles when you believe that you or others have been unfairly accused. Your feeling for colours, textures, sounds and forms will be an integral part of what you do with your life.

Although a Libra Ascendant often tends toward a somewhat narcissistic self-centredness more often than is the case with Libra Sun, it must be stated also that the Libra Rising person is sometimes genuinely kinder and sweeter than the Libra Sun, who often relates to others in a more detached way, realising that life is not all sweetness and light. Libra Rising lends a personal tone to the way all other energies of the chart are expressed. Although close relationships are of central importance to those with Libra Sun, the need for "the other" is sometimes even more crucial for the Libra Ascendant, whose entire life often seems focused on the primary relationship of their life (or the lack of such a relationship). When there is no partner, the Libra Ascendant person sometimes loses all sense of direction and can feel a serious lack of initiative and physical energy. Libra Ascendant seems to retain a romantic view of life longer than the often cynical Libra Sun.

You want to make yourself out to be an agreeable and sociable person. Having a partner in life is more important for you than for any other Rising sign. Furthermore, you are willing to bend over backwards, make all sorts of compromises, and endlessly groom yourself in order to achieve this end.

Scorpio Rising

Your Scorpio Rising journey will tend to involve you quite intensely in your own physical wants and needs. Your path is also about keeping secrets. You will be confronted with the most sensitive and delicate issues and you will learn how to keep confidences.

The kinds of crises you encounter are transformative in nature. The Scorpio Rising journey is often about survival. The survival of the spirit after a literal or symbolic death experience is something you may end up appreciating in an intense way. Your life journey is associated with incredible passions and desires – not always physical, often professional or vocational. You have the capacity for total involvement with your goals.

Always known for intensity, those with Scorpio Rising are very often associated with the healing arts, exploring other people's motives, or exploring the unknown or esoteric. Although Scorpio is often described as courageous, what is usually not mentioned is how greatly fear is the element motivating their actions. For Scorpio, the best defence is a good offence. Those with Scorpio Rising are constantly on the defensive to a degree not usually seen in the Scorpio Sun.

Scorpio is a sign of emotional extremism, and it is therefore easy to find a powerful negative expression of Scorpio Ascendant for every positive expression. Scorpio Rising has in fact gained a rather negative reputation over the years, one which is not entirely undeserved. No other Rising Sign can rival it for vindictive, ruthless, jealous behaviour. Vengeance is often a strong motivating factor in their behaviour, as is sometimes a paranoid obsession with self-preservation. This often takes the form of a reluctance to let go of anything – money or emotions. There is a great fear of letting go and losing control. Those with Scorpio Ascendant tend to be perceptive into others' deeper feelings and motives, when not projecting their own motives onto others. They can be extremely resourceful and often intensely dedicated to a difficult challenge or life mission. The negative traits mentioned above are sometimes greatly ameliorated in Scorpio Sun people, who can be very loyal to those whom they allow into their "inner circle" of friends. Also, the tendency to undermine oneself seems much less common in Scorpio Sun than in Scorpio Ascendant. In considering the ruling planet of the Ascendant, the Mars sign is always more important than the sign of Pluto, and a positively directed Mars can help channel and transform the often self-destructive Scorpio energy.

Your persona is like a probe, seeking out whatever lies beneath surface appearing to satisfy your hunger for secrets, intrigues and powerful emotions. At the same time you cloak your own feelings and intentions, becoming as impenetrable as you are penetrating.

Sagittarius Rising

You go out into the world wanting to take more of it in. It often describes a life journey where space and freedom are the most basic guides. Because life will often throw you in a box, you will spend a great deal of your time trying to get out of it, not only physically but also mentally.

You have a lot of enthusiasm, good humour and optimism. You make a great warm-up person, coach or enthusiastic supporter. You might find yourself trying to burn the candle at both ends – this comes from your basic instinct to open your arms to all life has to offer.

Finding something, or someone to believe in will be a key part of your journey. You will develop a moral or ethical code which is far-sighted and all-encompassing.

The optimism, buoyancy, enthusiasm, and broad-mindedness that are often, but not always, seen in Sagittarius Sun people are almost uniformly expressed by those with Sagittarius Rising. Virtually every Sagittarius Rising person I have ever seen could be described as perpetually "up beat", even in the face of continued disappointments or obstacles. Although the tendency toward forcefully preaching one's personal beliefs as universal truth is present in Sagittarius Rising as well as in Sagittarius Sun, the Ascendant expression of this tendency is usually more tolerant and inspiring, while the preaching of a Sagittarius Sun person is often experienced as being hit over the head with "The Truth". In other words, self-righteousness seems considerably more flagrant in those with Sun in Sagittarius. Also, Sagittarius Ascendant people almost never show the aimless, drifting discontent that is so often seen in those with Sagittarius Sun. Sagittarius Rising seems more inclined toward definite action in line with an ideal, whereas Sagittarius Sun is sometimes limited to mental or theoretical activity alone.

Like the superior being that you are inclined to present yourself as, you express yourself with a larger-than-life sense of confidence and apparent self-assurance.

Capricorn Rising

Your life journey involves a quest for solid foundations. Faced with disorder, you will have to create order. You will be ambitious and will have a sense of responsibility in all your dealings. You like structure in your world – you need to know where you stand, what has worked before, so that you can repeat the process and actually end up getting somewhere. The Capricorn Rising journey is about establishing and securing – not leaping off in the dark.

You will be asked to find reserves of patience – often at the really crucial times in your life, because much of what you encounter will ask for a steady, thorough kind of understanding. The waiting games will repeat themselves throughout your life.

When faced with financial lows and crises, you develop amazing abilities to use what you have, and make more of the resources that are around you. When you have financial highs, you will still find shrewd ways of handling the options.

Capricorn Rising often expresses itself with extreme negativity and scepticism, more often than Capricorn Sun does. However one should understand that in both cases this apparent cynicism and disdain for the new is often a protective cover for a more inquisitive, vulnerable, even spiritually open nature. Capricorn simply does not like to have time wasted on unproven ideas, but practical and logical proof even of unorthodox realities will often be enough to capture their interest and eliminate their automatic scepticism. Although Capricorn Sun and Ascendant are both extremely concerned with outer form, appearances, and reputation, the Capricorn Ascendant seems to be far more fearful of public opinion, often going to great lengths to appear normal, conservative and "safe." Capricorn Sun seems to have a greater drive toward achievement and authority and a more determined approach to worldly success. Capricorn Ascendant sometimes seems satisfied merely with being secure. Both are so impersonal that relations with others are often problematical, although Capricorn Sun more often than Capricorn Ascendant finds it hard to relate on an even one-to-one level.

You approach virtually everything and everyone in a tactical, businesslike manner; you certainly do not lead with your feelings. You generate an aura of material awareness and if anything needs organising you'll be the first to offer – or rather start doing so without even being asked. Life to you is something to be managed and controlled, so when it comes to emotionally relating or social interplay you're not exactly one to let rip and let your hair down. Dependability and respectability are what you have on offer, not passion and drama. That is not to say that you have no sense of fun, but even that would have a certain limit placed upon it.

Aquarius Rising

Your life journey will involve your friends and fellow travellers, but also your own space. Your life will be an utterly original expression of yourself.

Faced with too many constraints, you will have no option but to pursue changes in your life. When you are surrounded by the mundane and the everyday, you will have to kick out. New ways of doing things and devising a blueprint for the future are important to you. Your journey involves reform and change in all kinds of ways. It can be as exciting to you as it is occasionally alarming to more conservative souls around you.

You respect the right of others to be as free as you want to feel. You are unconventional and have a strong sense of the humanitarian. You want to be of help, to innovate and to bring about changes for the better.

An unconventional, rebellious streak pervades the personalities of both Aquarius Ascendant and Aquarius Sun people, but these traits go much deeper in those with Aquarius Sun. They are usually lifelong aficionados of the new, the imaginative, the revolutionary, even if they don't express it overtly very often. Those with Aquarius Rising often seem a bit eccentric; indeed, they often feel rebellious, but there is usually a stronger attunement to convention in them that is seen in most Aquarius Sun individuals. Both types usually exhibit an immediacy or perception and understanding, a thinking speed and rapidity of learning, that can be startling to their slower friends. Both exhibit a cold detachment that is frustrating and often shocking to more emotionally sensitive people; Sun in Aquarius seems to be more aloof and impersonal than Aquarius Rising. The traditional Saturn rulership seems to be stronger than the modern ruler Uranus in many people who have Aquarius Rising. But the house and sign position of Saturn is always important for all Aquarius Ascendant people.

Your approach is cool but friendly. A person's intellect and social or political viewpoint is what appears to interest you most, for you engage on that level first and foremost. Emotional and sexual vibrations are generally kept beneath the surface.

Pisces Rising

Your life journey will involve some wonderful dreams and escapes as you slip in and out of the real world as only Pisces Rising can. There will be real compassion for others as this is a healing journey.

Because life is full of signposts, maps and instructions, you will enjoy getting lost. There is something dreamy, ethereal or hard-to-catch about you. Sacrifices will be made on the pathway. Giving up or giving in seems to come with the territory. Water images are very appropriate for you and very soothing for your soul.

You need time alone to recharge your batteries and also to find your own boundaries. You empathise so much with other people that you can find it hard to detach at times.

Because the Sun is weak in Pisces, thus allowing Pisces Sun individuals to be strongly influenced by all of the other factors in their charts, there seem to be more types of Pisces Sun individuals than Pisces Rising people. Those with Pisces Rising are almost uniformly sensitive, compassionate, emotional, imaginative and helpful. There seems to be a strength of character in the Pisces Ascendant that is sometimes lacking in the Pisces Sun, who is so often passive, evasive, escapist and irresponsible. Probably it is the ancient ruler of Pisces, Jupiter, that accounts for the strength of character and buoyancy that is especially evident in so many Pisces Ascendant people; sometimes that is far more apparent than the influence of the modern ruler Neptune.

One should always look to the Jupiter sign and house of Pisces Ascendant people for key insights to their nature. Besides being able to empathise with and help those who are having difficulties, Pisces Rising people are also often philosophical and surprisingly unperturbed when they themselves experience misfortune. Like Virgo Ascendant (its opposite sign), Pisces Ascendant people don't feel the need for credit or public acknowledgement for all they contribute to others.

Chapter 5

"Astrology is assured of recognition from psychology, without further restrictions, because astrology represents the summation of all the psychological knowledge of antiquity."
C G Jung - philosopher

The Planets

Table of Planetary Powers

Planet	*Ruler*	*Detriment*	*Exaltation*	*Fall*
Sun	Leo	Aquarius	Aries	Libra
Moon	Cancer	Capricorn	Taurus	Scorpio
Mercury	{Gemini {Virgo	{Sagittarius {Pisces	Aquarius	Leo
Venus	{Taurus {Libra	{Scorpio {Aries	Pisces	Virgo
Mars	{Aries {Scorpio	{Libra {Taurus	Capricorn	Cancer
Jupiter	{Sagittarius {Pisces	{Gemini {Virgo	Cancer	Capricorn
Saturn	{Capricorn {Aquarius	{Cancer {Leo	Libra	Aries
Uranus	Aquarius	Leo	Scorpio	Taurus
Neptune	Pisces	Virgo	Cancer	Capricorn
Pluto	Scorpio	Taurus	Pisces	Virgo

The above table of "Planetary Dignitaries" is one of the most important for you to memorise. On this rests all your understanding of how the energies of the planets mix together. In some signs the power of a planet's energy is able to project itself without any hindrance as it is functioning in a field harmonious to its own nature. In other signs a planetary energy is blocked by being in a sign that is incompatible with its nature and therefore its full expression is hindered. You will find the ability to judge the power of a planet very necessary in interpreting birth charts.

When a planet is in the sign it rules, it is said to be dignified because it is powerful in its own sign, and can express itself freely.

Planets in opposite signs to the signs which they rule are in their detriment. Their power is lessened by being placed in signs that are uncongenial to their own nature. For example, Saturn rules Capricorn and the sign opposite it is Cancer, so Saturn is in its detriment in Cancer. The mothering, nurturing, emotional sign of Cancer is not a good place for the cold, practical, unemotional sign of Capricorn. It constricts and inhibits Cancer.

It is easy to remember the tables of detriments if you know the signs the planets rule. The detriment is the opposite sign. Planets in their detriment are regarded as unfavourable and weak.

Every planet has one particular sign apart from the one it normally rules in which it seems able to express its nature harmoniously and to the best advantage. This is its sign of exaltation. Here we see the expression of the energy in its highest form. Exaltation may be regarded much the same as a powerful and favourable aspect.

Planets that are in signs opposite to their exaltation are in the sign of their fall. It brings disappointment to the concerns of the planet and to a certain degree, those of the house in which it falls.

When a planet is placed in an angle (near or in the 1st, 4th, 7th, and 10th houses) it becomes very important. Hence because of its place and not because of its sign, it is accidentally dignified.

A planet in its own sign is similar to a person in their own home. You have the authority to entertain as you see fit. On the other hand, a planet in its detriment is like being in someone else's home. You are not free and cannot do exactly as you please. Someone else has the power so you are limited. A planet in its exaltation is similar to someone who is not only able to entertain freely in their own home, but has plenty of substance so you have no limitations whatsoever. A planet in its fall is like someone who has neither the substance nor the home in which to entertain. You have to go to work and earn it.

When you study the planetary dignities along with the qualities of the signs, you can see how the nature of a planet is either dampened or invigorated by the sign it is in. For example, Saturn, the planet of limitation, clashes with the impulsive, devil-may-care Aries energy. Jupiter, the planet of expansion, is constricted in Capricorn, the sign of measured progress. Uranus, the planet of freedom and innovation, finds full expression in the penetrating and uncompromising insight of Scorpio.

The Planetary Cycles

The Earth orbits the Sun in approximately 365.25 days – one year
The Moon orbits the Earth in 27.32 days
Mercury orbits the Sun in 88 days
Venus orbits the Sun in 225 days
Mars orbits the Sun in 1 year 10.5 months
Jupiter orbits the Sun in 12 years
Saturn orbits the Sun in 29 years
Uranus orbits the Sun in 84 years
Neptune orbits the Sun in 165 years
Pluto orbits the Sun in 246 years

The Sun ☉

Rules Leo.

Keywords for the Sun:
Positive: Strong-willed, determined, dignified, confident, reliable, vital, loyal, poised, optimistic, powerful, courageous.
Negative: self-willed, cruel, austere, arrogant, wilful, aggressive, dictatorial, egocentric, overbearing, pessimistic.

You can see the Sun's influence in Leo's ability to be the catalyst. Their personalities tend to dominate a group, but in a life-giving way. Leo's Fixed Fire energy has the ability to bring people along with them, to feed people's egos and make them believe that anything is possible if you have the courage to take it on.

More than anything else in the chart, it shows the Will, Man's highest expression.

What the Sun means in your chart

The Sun is the largest body in the sky and it is where all life comes from. It is a very important planet in astrology and is given a great deal of weight. It is our motivation and our life force.

The Sun sign is the placement that people with the most rudimentary knowledge of astrology will know you by; but it is not necessarily how they will know you. It takes a long time for your Sun sign to become evident in your external appearance, and many people will assume you are more like your Ascendant (which is your conscious self, that is, what you would like to be rather than what you are). Your Sun sign gives you clues as to how you can really let yourself shine.

How to read the Sun in your chart

The sign in which the Sun falls describes the unravelling journey of your life. You may not even recognise your Sun sign yourself until you are much older, because it shows you where you want to be and what your life preoccupations will be. It is your vitality and your life force and, ultimately, your sense of self. Like the Sun when it rises, overriding everything else in the sky, your Sun sign colours the influence of every planet in your chart. So the Sun is your ego and the catalyst for your behaviour.

The house in which the Sun falls shows where you want attention and admiration. It will also show where you really shine, where you feel most comfortable and at ease with your ability to take on the tasks at hand. For example, if your Sun is in the 3rd House, the house of communication, you are known as a good communicator and it is important for you to be recognised as such.

Sun – Likes and dislikes

Sign	Likes	Dislikes
Aries	Action, coming first, challenges, the spur of the moment	Waiting around, no action, admitting defeat
Taurus	Stability, natural things, time to think, comfort, pleasure	Disruption, synthetics, being pushed or hurried
Gemini	Reading and talking, being on the move, the unusual, variety	Mental stagnation, being tied down, no education
Cancer	Kindness and tenderness, solitude, reassurance	Bluntness and direct confrontation, uncertainty
Leo	A good time, respect and appreciation, style	Repetition, being ignored, losing face, drabness
Virgo	Order, making lists, being helpful, natural methods	Sloppiness, making mistakes, being a martyr, crudity

Libra	Pleasing surroundings, peace, a partner/friends, gentleness	Conflict, violence, injustice, no social feedback
Scorpio	Total involvement, rooting out hidden causes, meaningful work	Superficial relationships, demeaning tasks, flattery
Sagittarius	Freedom and space, travelling, getting on with it, philosophy	Being constrained, domestic ties, details, glib theories
Capricorn	Being worldly, knowing your limits, order and control	Feeling groundless, feeling helpless, the untried
Aquarius	Good friends, rebellious causes, future, dreams, originality	Excessive loneliness, the ordinary, imitation
Pisces	Dreamy solitude, mystery, getting lost, creative expression	Criticism, the obvious, feeling lost, know-it-alls

The Moon ☽

Rules Cancer

Keywords for the Moon:
Positive: protective, magnetic, psychic, creative, kind, sympathetic, imaginative, domestic, maternal, flexible, sensitive, receptive.
Negative: materialistic, smothering love, emotionally unstable, passive, moody, changeable.

What the Moon means in your chart

The Moon represents your intuitive, emotional response to your environment. Just as the Moon reflects the Sun's light and the Sun is concerned with action, the Moon is concerned with reaction. In childhood, we are largely reactive. Without control over our environment or our emotions, we are raw in our emotional responses, crying out in pain when something hurts us and laughing until our bellies ache when something really tickles our fancy.

Looking at the Moon's sign, house and related aspects can be very instructive in showing us how we dealt with things when we were children – whether we were painfully shy, or cheeky and naughty, whether we had a natural compassion for others, or we struck out in hurt at those around us. These patterns of behaviour re-emerge throughout our lives, sometimes in the most painful ways. Looking at the placement of the Moon in your chart can help when trying to unlearn seemingly innate behaviour.

The Moon represents all that is innate and subconscious, our natural habits, including eating habits, our views on the past, our moods and the imagination.

How to read the Moon in your chart

The sign in which the Moon falls describes the way you innately react to your environment and the intensity of your moods. For instance, Moon in Aries indicates a short temper, but one that blows over quickly. It also means someone who is instinctively independent and rejects being "mothered" too much.

The house in which the Moon falls describes your instinctive needs. For instance, the Moon in the 3rd House would mean you find emotional security in learning, whereas the Moon in the 2nd House would mean you find emotional security in material gains. This also represents where you want to make your home.

Moon – Likes and Dislikes

Sign	Likes	Dislikes
Aries	The chase, new experiences, leading, honesty, outdoors	Inactivity, being told what to do, emotional confinement
Taurus	Material security, quality, extravagance, predictability, ownership	Change, waste, letting go, the unknown

Gemini	Variety, mental stimulation, being in the know	Predictability, being lost for words
Cancer	Your own patch, secure home, peace and quiet, a family feel	Feeling insecure, unkindness, being uprooted, carelessness
Leo	Being centre of attention, parties, romantic involvements, children	Feeling self-conscious, boring relationships, going 2nd class
Virgo	Order and plans, making lists, wholesomeness, cleanliness	Uncertainty, squalor, health hazards, sloppiness
Libra	Sharing, social situations, being agreeable, fine things	Coarseness, vulgarity, feeling misjudged, inhospitality
Scorpio	Intimacy, soul mates, profound feelings, moving experiences	Superficiality, being controlled, dragging things out, lying
Sagittarius	Freedom and adventure, honesty, extremes, travel and outdoors	Restrictions, small thinking, prejudice, pretentiousness
Capricorn	Strong people, steadiness of purpose, organisation, structure	Feeling out of control, having no purpose, feeling insecure

Aquarius	Being unique, openness, the unusual, keeping cool	Being ordinary, over-emotionality, emotional ties
Pisces	Highs and lows, music and poetry, romantic quests	The commonplace, the obvious, confronting reality

Mercury ☿

Rules Gemini and Virgo

Keywords for Mercury:
Positive: agile, adaptable, analytical, active, brilliant, alert, articulate, versatile, precise, aware, efficient.
Negative: irresponsible, mentally unstable, indecisive, restless, verbose, nosy, sceptical, imitative.

What Mercury means in your chart

Communication, intellect, and awareness are Mercury's calling cards, as are logic and reasoning, our manner of thinking, and how we create and express our thought processes. Mercury is the planet of conscious intelligence, and it will reveal how our memories work and how we choose to communicate conscious memories. It also tells us on what level we find communication satisfying, whether we speak only because we have to and would prefer to express ourselves by more tangible means, or whether we take real joy in having a good old chat.

Talking, thinking, sharing are the three words that best sum up the action of Mercury. Because this planet implores us to express ourselves, when Mercury goes retrograde (that is, when it appears to loop backwards across the sky), our communications will be challenged.

Body language is ruled by Mercury and its placement will tell you if you are a gesticulator whose heart is shown in an open sitting stance, or whether you stand in a closed stance and don't give too much away.

Mercury is never more than 28 degrees from the Sun, so the sign Mercury is in is more than likely to be in the same sign as your Sun. It is neither masculine nor feminine energy and assumes the gender of the sign it is in. It is the only planet that has this capability and is thought to bring reconciliation between the two sides of the personality. If you are peace with Mercury, you are at peace with the communication within yourself. This is a very powerful thing – if you have the ability to understand why you do things, you have the ability to control your destiny.

How to read Mercury in your chart

The sign in which Mercury falls describes the way you think and communicate, for instance, Mercury in Taurus, would mean that you think with purpose and with the view to coming up with considered and careful judgments.

The house in which Mercury falls describes where you choose to express your intelligence and communication. For instance, Mercury in the 10th House would mean you express your intelligence through your career. In the 4th house, it would mean that you communicate best in a family situation.

Venus ♀

Rules Libra and Taurus

Keywords for Venus:
Positive: beauty, love, art, sociable, feminine, gentle, cooperative, harmonious, devoted, refined, attractive, considerate, courteous.
Negative: indolent, sentimental, ostentatious, superficial, flirtatious, oversensitive, indifferent, evasive.

Venus combined with the element Air, as it is in Libra, means beauty with the flirt, which gives some idea of the Libran social whirl. You could call it the party-double. A dinner party with a Taurean host will guarantee you excellent food, but a Libra host will make sure you never stand alone.

What Venus means in your chart

Like its goddess namesake, Venus is the planet of love, beauty, art and indulgence, and about what we want. Venus has many similar qualities to Jupiter, the planet of fortune, but with a more material bent.

In childhood, the placement of Venus will reflect how we make friends and mix in school. Later in life it will become more about what we find beautiful and enjoyable and what we find attractive in a partner. By looking at Venus in your chart, you can see where there may be problems in forming relationships, and strategies for avoiding these problems.

Venus also shapes the personal appearance, the personality, and the degree of success in the social world and in love. It dictates your ability to attract and hold admirers, your general popularity and your capacity for spending money. Someone with Venus in a challenging position in the horoscope might be indulgent to the point of vice, quarrelsome, or on the run from creditors for their frivolous extravagance.

How to read Venus in your chart

The sign in which Venus falls describes the way you seek enjoyment or pleasure and the way you seek romance. For instance, Venus in Leo would see you seeking pleasure in the drama of life, and you would enjoy having a relationship in a very dramatic way with torrid door slamming arguments and passionate make-up embraces.

The house in which Venus falls describes where you find pleasure and romance. For instance, Venus in the 9th House means you seek romance in exotic people and are attracted to people from other cultures. It means a love of learning, although it doesn't necessarily mean you will sit down and do the study. Venus in the 9th house finds pleasure in trips to beautiful places and exotic things from foreign countries.

Mars ♂

Rules Aries

Keywords for Mars:
Positive: energetic, dynamic, impulsive, courageous, expressive, independent, practical, forceful, enthusiastic, spontaneous, heroic, fearless.
Negative: dominating, defiant, violent, combative, foolhardy, aggressive, sarcastic, cruel, destructive.

Mars is the embodiment of masculine energy and so fits the sign Aries like a hand in a glove. Aries is full of positive, Cardinal energy anyway, so probably doesn't need much more encouragement, but it is Mars that directs the drive for success.

Mars' influence over Scorpio is less pronounced than over Aries because Scorpio's prime ruler is Pluto. It is Mars' ruling of sexual energy combined with the watery Scorpio charm that can be deliciously dangerous, for the opposite sex at least. Rather than Scorpio's emotional ways and Fixed energy being doused by Mars' Fire, its power is enhanced by being harnessed in this way.

What Mars means in your chart

Mars is the "red planet", fiery and energetic, with passion and determination to spare. Mars shows your general energy level – whether you are a can-do, will-do or a gonna-do kind of person. If you are feeling weary all the time and it's an effort to get out of bed in the morning, then you have issues with Mars. But you will also have complications in other areas in your life because of this lack of energy. By looking at Mars you can really tease out what is making you feel apathetic and begin to fix the problem.

Mars also represents the instinctive survival mechanism of fight or flight. Mars must be understood in conjunction with Venus. Venus is what we want, but Mars is how we get there. So Mars symbolises all those things that help us achieve our aims in life. It is the catalyst to all our behaviour, the energy that inspires us and keeps us motivated. Mars' energy can be constructive or destructive. As the God of War, Mars could be brutally violent. While this energy still emanates from the planet, it can be harnessed for stamina, ambition, courage and achievement.

Mars still rules the military, our sexual energy and weapons. In medical astrology it rules fevers, accidents and surgery – in short, all childhood disasters. Its exuberance and energy for life is similar to that of a child's.

How to read Mars in your chart

The sign in which Mars falls describes the way you assert yourself. For instance, if you have Mars in Capricorn, you have a deep reserve of energy that you use to best advantage. Mars is at its best in a sign like Capricorn, where the energy is focused and consistent but still undiluted and powerful. If you have Mars in Aries, you assert yourself impulsively. Mars is at home in Aries, so its effect is magnified. This means that although Mars in Aries means extra energy, it also means very little staying power.

The house in which Mars falls describes where you find your motivation. For instance, if Mars is in the 10th House, you concentrate your energy on your career, which is where you feel most energised and powerful. If Mars is in the 2nd House, you are motivated by a desire for possessions and to make your own income.

Jupiter ♃

Rules Sagittarius

Keywords for Jupiter:
Positive: generous, benevolent, confident, optimistic, humane, merciful, idealistic, philanthropic, devout, reverent, faithful, radiant, charitable.
Negative: impractical, extravagant, indulgent, fanatical, bigoted, cynical, pompous, gullible, indolent, formal.
Jupiter gives Sagittarius its lucky aspect, its search for deeper meaning and the desire to travel.

Jupiter's influence over Pisces is less pronounced than over Sagittarius because Pisces' prime ruler is Neptune. Jupiter gives Pisces its emphasis on wisdom and the deeper, universal concepts of life.

What Jupiter means in your chart

Jupiter is the lucky planet, a symbol of aspirations and hope. As the largest planet in the solar system, it represents expansion and expansive behaviour. Wherever it falls in the chart will be in an extravagant manner.

Like its namesake the King of the Gods, Jupiter is a benevolent planet overseeing life and wisdom. Optimism, generosity, good luck, humour and opportunity are all associated with this planet, as well as sports, games, pets and leisure time. Jupiter is also the guardian of the abstract mind, rules higher learning and is our catalyst for exploring ideas, both intellectually and spiritually. Jupiter forms our ideology and religious preferences, our ethics and morality. It will search far and wide for answers as Jupiter also rules long-distance travel. It also addresses our sense of optimism.

However, the largesse of this planet can deteriorate into laziness and sloth, and a difficult Jupiter placement could mean weight gain and a lack of motivation.

How to read Jupiter in your chart

The sign in which Jupiter falls describes the way you seek personal growth and wisdom, and the way the benefits flow to you. For instance, if you had Jupiter in Scorpio you would seek growth in all things hidden and mysterious. You would be attracted to professions such as the priesthood or private investigating. Jupiter in Scorpio also gives you luck in dealing with other people's money and resources, and in having these available when they are needed.

It takes Jupiter about 12 years to circle the zodiac so people born in the same year as you are likely to have the same positioning as you do. Primary school teachers will tell you there is such a thing as a studious year (Jupiter in

Virgo or Capricorn) and a year of the chatty (Jupiter in the sociable Libra). This has a lot to do with the planet Jupiter.

The house in which Jupiter falls describes where you choose to expand your world and where you have confidence. For instance, Jupiter in the 5th House would mean confidence in romance, creative endeavours, socialising and gambling. It is the planet of largesse in the house of magnanimity, so there is a danger of feeling so over-confident that you take one risk too many.

Saturn ♄

Rules Capricorn

Keywords for Saturn:
Positive: cautious, serious, sincere, stable, patient, self-disciplined, humble, responsible, thrifty, diplomatic, respectful, enduring, structured.
Negative: fearful, severe, miserly, pessimistic, stern, rigid, obstructive, destructive.

Capricorns get their planning ability and their control fetish from Saturn. Capricorns often give the impression of being mature before their time, and this is old man Saturn's influence.

Saturn's influence over Aquarius is less pronounced than over Capricorn because Aquarius' prime ruler is Uranus. Saturn gives Aquarians their innate wisdom. Its domain is knowledge and social structures, both major concerns of the Aquarian. Aquarians also like to keep a bit of distance from the world, which is how Saturn likes to rule, like a disciplinary professor.

What Saturn means in your chart

Saturn is where we feel hindered or blocked. It is where we find great challenges, and if they are overcome, there are great rewards to be had. Saturn is the planet that inspires the most fear and loathing of any of the ten, because the house in which it is placed will be where you have cause for frustration and concern. But the kind of disappointments Saturn brings are also the source of the greatest motivation.

For instance, you might think having Saturn in the 10th House would be the cause of great woe, as this is the house of career and ambition. But it doesn't mean that you will spend the rest of your days wrapped under a newspaper on the park bench in a sorry state of destitution. Oprah Winfrey, Bill Clinton, Pablo Picasso and Albert Einstein all had Saturn in the 10th House and all worked hard to make sure they were successful.

That is the gift of Saturn. Look carefully at what is happening in your chart with Saturn and you will find that, although you have had difficulties in this area in the past, you have made quite a bit of progress and will continue to do so until you are really achieving what you want.

Saturn governs old age and the lessons it teaches us. It represents our attitude towards authority figures, tradition and wisdom. Structure and order in the way we conduct our affairs are all ruled by Saturn. The consolidation of assets is important here and it does rule the old age pension and superannuation. Saturn concerns itself with karma and the lessons past experiences might bring.

How to read Saturn in your chart

The sign in which Saturn falls describes the way you feel safe and secure and, by process of elimination, where you feel inadequate. For instance, Saturn in Sagittarius means you need to know everything about a situation to feel secure. If the information is incomplete, you cannot just roll with it, you have to wait until all the facts are in front of you.

The house in which Saturn falls describes where you feel blocked. For instance, Saturn in the 5th House can mean you feel blocked in creativity. It also means you feel restricted when it comes to fun and games. You take romance far too seriously and are generally told to "chill out" a lot.

Uranus

Rules Aquarius.

Keywords for Uranus:
Positive: independent, original, unconventional, idealistic, intuitive, progressive, inventive, spirited, perceptive, resourceful, individualistic.
Negative: radical, rebellious, erratic, eccentric, detached, fanatical, over-impulsive, irresponsible, combative.

Aquarius embodies the Uranus ideals of independence and an unhindered intellect. Its emphasis on society as a whole is from the Uranian concern for humanitarian issues.

What Uranus means in your chart
Through the signs, Uranus moves so slowly that its effect is more on your generation than on you as an individual. It will show how your generation will shake up the establishment, and where it will be inventive in its thinking. If there is undue emphasis on this planet, there will be more influence on you as a person.

How to read Uranus in your chart

The house in which Uranus falls can give you insights into where you will rebel against the establishment or where you are different. A strong Uranus presence in your chart will mean a desire to disassociate yourself from the masses, who you will see as brainwashed by the flickering eye of television. A strong Uranus will lead you to think very clearly and carefully about why you do the things you do and lead you to question their validity at times. These people can be very cynical of advertising, media hype and almost impossible to hypnotise.

Through the houses, Uranus shows you how you differentiate yourself, and in what area your genius lies. For instance, if you have Uranus in your 7th House, you would choose to have a less conventional marriage (if you got married at all).

Neptune ♆

Rules Pisces

Keywords for Neptune:
Positive: sensitive, inspirational, compassionate, clairvoyant, sympathetic, creative, visionary, peaceful, devoted, impressionable, imaginative.
Negative: dreamy, fearful, over-sentimental, self-indulgent, chaotic, unreliable, confused.

Neptune can be seen in Pisces in their dreamy qualities and their weakness for drugs or escapism. Pisces is the only sign to be ruled by Neptune and that is the planet that carries us over from this life into the next.

What Neptune means in your chart

Neptune is the higher octave of Venus, meaning it takes Venus's concerns to a more spiritual level. It is the desire for spirituality, to search longer and harder for evidence of another realm.

Neptune is the planet of illusion and dissolves worldliness; it is concerned with fantasy, escapism, drugs and spirituality. It is the desire for greater perfection in the world, and its placement will show where you seek that perfection. In essence, Neptune is creating an illusion, of what is enchanting on the outside, and captivating within. This includes drugs, alcohol, trances and hypnosis, delusion, hypochondria, abnormality, sleep and dreams.

Neptune rules the oceans. Poetry, music and dance are among the trance-like activities this planet favours. It also rules movies, television, theatre, fashion and all forms of glamour. Animation is a very Neptunian art form.

How to read Neptune in your chart
The sign in which Neptune falls describes the way we attain our dreams and whether we are successful. Neptune spends roughly 14 years in each sign, so its effect is generational and it usually signifies the grand illusion of each generation.

For example, the baby-boomers (born 1942-1957) have Neptune in Libra. This signified an intense desire for peace and love, but also a lack of motivation. Libra is the sign of romance, and so the baby-boomers have very idealistic and sometimes unrealistic expectations of love, and this has manifested itself in a huge upsurge in the divorce rate. The next generation born (1956-1971) with Neptune in Scorpio sought rebirth through drugs, and thus the hedonistic 70's were born.

The house in which Neptune falls describes where you are required to have faith and trust, as well as where you may encounter confusion and loss. It is through these events that you gain greater spirituality and insight.

It is also where we turn a blind eye and dream. For example, if you have Neptune in your 2nd House, the house of material goods, you are haphazard about your possessions. You probably don't think you really deserve your possessions and would be much better off pretending they belonged to someone else – you would then take better care of them.

Paradoxically, you are also very skilled at dreaming up get-rich-schemes (Neptune is the planet of imagination), but holding on to your hard-won gains is a different story.

Pluto ♇

Rules: Scorpio

Keywords for Pluto:
Positive: transformation, power, renewal, strength, transmutation, submission, construction, rebirth, integration.
Negative: death, annihilation, destruction, intensity, struggle, obsession, wilfulness, disintegration, darkness.

Pluto's influence can be seen in Scorpio's obsession with sex, death, birth and rebirth. Pluto embodies the issues that the Scorpio mind loves to tackle. Water gives Scorpio its emotional capabilities and its Fixed quadruplicity its stable nature, but Pluto gives Scorpio its simmering rage and obsession with answering the big questions in life.

What Pluto means in your chart

Pluto takes the energy of fiery Mars to a more intense and spiritual level. This planet is about transformation, regeneration and rebirth, death, sex and obsession. When you consider the time that it was discovered, in the first year of the Great Depression and at the beginning of the events that led to World War II, you get an idea of where Pluto is coming from.

These events were tragic, but (you would hope) society has learned some big lessons from them. Whatever Pluto does, it provides us with massive change and asks us to transcend what we know, redeem ourselves in the process and come out stronger as a result. Pluto relies on the fact that we will find a will and a way to survive.

There are two sides to Pluto. One side is interested in universal welfare and in cooperating with others for the greatest good of all. Psychic abilities and the ability to extend one's consciousness throughout the universe fall into this realm. Pluto beseeches the masses to look inward (and to their subconscious) to see what's there. It revolutionises the thinking of a whole generation and ensures that each generation leaves its mark and tries to make the world a little better.

On the other side, Pluto rules destruction, death, obsession, kidnapping, coercion, viruses and waste, atomic energy, crime and the underworld, along with many forms of subversive activity like terrorism and dictatorships.

How to read Pluto in your chart

The sign in which Pluto falls describes the way you regenerate, and because Pluto takes such a long time to pass through a sign (because of its eccentric orbit, this can take anywhere from 12 to 21 years), it is a generational sign. In fact, along with Neptune, it could be considered the sign of the generation gap. Often when a generation has the most productivity in its youth, the regeneration is not apparent, but as the generation grows older and takes over positions of power, its impact becomes imbued in the fabric of society.

For instance, the last generation that had Pluto in Gemini undermined the established wisdom and replaced it with new ideas about communication and energy (Freud and Jung in psychology, Einstein and Planck in physics, Picasso in art). But it wasn't until this generation grew up that its ideas became part of the norm.

The house in which Pluto falls describes where your greatest influence or obsession is. For instance, with Pluto in the 3rd House your words can heal or kill. This placement gives your communications great power. Therapists or salespersons often have this placement.

Chapter 6

"Courteous Reader, Astrology is one of the most ancient Sciences, held in high esteem of old, by the Wise and the Great. Formerly, no Prince would make War or Peace, nor any General fight in Battle, in short, no important affair was undertaken without first consulting an Astrologer."
Benjamin Franklin - Statesman

The Houses

A house is a term used by astrologers to define the twelve sectors of the sky that clearly delineate the twelve main areas in our life. Each planet will fall into one of these houses. You may have many planets in one house, and many houses without planets, or they may be beautifully spread across the whole chart. The empty houses have a meaning as well. So, when you are looking at a chart, you will be looking carefully at the position of the planets and noting which house and sign they are in.

From an interpretative standpoint, the houses represent the various departments of life. Through them the characteristics of the individual revealed in the signs and planets are expressed in the activities of daily life. The lines separating these houses are called cusps.

The four Angular house cusps: 1st, 4th, 7th, and 10th are considered the most important and most sensitive positions in the horoscope. These are called Angular houses.

Next come the Fixed or Succedent house cusps: 2nd, 5th, 8th and 11th houses, followed by the Mutable or Cadent house cusps: 3rd, 6th, 9th and 12th houses.

The houses below the horizon relate to individual, personal, hidden, subjective, private and family oriented experience. The 6th through to 1st houses correspond to the period of darkness from sunset to sunrise when the Moon reigns supreme. The houses above the horizon correlate with other people, objective situations, and the public view. The 12th through the 7th houses cover the period from sunrise to sunset when the Sun illuminates what we do for all to see.

The following lists pairs the polar meanings of the day and night houses:

Night houses (6,5,4,3,2,1)	**Day houses** (12,11,10,9,8,7)
Night	Day
Self	Others
Private	Public
Subjective	Objective
Individual	Group oriented
Local environment	World at large
Mine	Yours

To understand the function of the various houses, it helps to think of them as 6 pairs of polar opposites, each representing a day and a night mode of manifesting experience.

Night houses
1st house
I
Self
Me
My body
My physical presence
Initiator
New beginning
What I decide
Individuality

2nd house
My resources
My values
My talents
My possessions
My income
My money

3rd house
Short trips, visits
Kin, neighbours
Concrete knowledge

Gossip, rumours
Early education
Classroom teaching
Mundane communication
Neighbourhood
Writing, reporting

Day houses
7th house
You
Other
My partner, my opponents
Your body
Where I remove to
Antagonist
Immediate outcome
Agreements with others
Bonding with others

8th house
Your resources
Your values
Your talents
Your possessions
Partner's income
Money that I can borrow

9th house
Long trips, travels
Foreigners, strangers
Abstract thought; world view
Wisdom, prophecy
College, University
Public lecturing; seminars
Religion, philosophy
Distant lands
Publishing, disseminating

4th house
Family
Familial authority
Mother
Home
Foundation, roots
Domestic matters
Heredity, ancestry
Personal base of operation
Real estate, land
Natural disaster

5th house
Personal enjoyment
Recreational sex
Children
Offspring
One's own children
Inventions
Pregnancy
Speculation, gambling
Self-gratification

6th house
Service to others
Sickness
Physical Illness
Servitude/servants
Self-regulation
Distress
Work, labour
Attention to detail
Small animals, pets

10th house
Career
Government
Judge, administrator
Executive, president, ruler
Business
Pinnacle of success
Relations with outer world
Status in the community
Place in the community
Structure of society

11th house
Friendship, socialising
Humanitarian concerns
Group associations
Acquaintances, peers
Stepchildren
Modern technology
Hopes and wishes
Counsel, advice
Altruism

12th house
Spirituality
Hospitalisation
Mental Illness
Confinement/Slaves
Regulation by others
Sorrow, grief
Charity, welfare
Escapism, undoing
Large or wild animals

Adjustment   Secret enemies
Tenants, lodgers   Prisoners
Craftsmanship   Sorcery
Daily work   Spiritual experience

The polarities between opposite houses allow us to appreciate the houses' deeper connections. The 12 houses consist of four groups, each group made up of three houses (an Angular, Succedent, and a Cadent house linked to each Element.) Within each such group, the three houses are in trine aspect with one another. Each set of trines corresponds to one of the classical elements: Fire, Earth, Air and Water. Houses in trine relate harmoniously.

I shall outline the basic qualities of each house in numerical order first, and then will look at the houses in relation to their particular Element in more detail.

1st House
What you look like
Yourself
The present
Your personality, appearance, disposition and manner
Your outlook on life
The window through which you view the world

2nd House
What you own; your resources
Financial standing, money possessions
Peace of mind
How you meet your obligations
Your own earned income and spending capacity
Your values

3rd House
What you think
Your ability to relate to your environment
Early education and early surroundings
Siblings, acquaintances and neighbours
Short journeys
Writings, news, communications, gossip
Memory, perception, speech
The synthesising powers of the conscious mind

4th House
Your base of operations; your home
The hidden depths of the self
Domestic affairs
The nature of your home
End of matters; latter part of life
Real estate and property
Parents and family

5th House
Self-expression
Things that distinguish you from others e.g. children you create, books you write, affections you show
All emotional and romantic tendencies from the heart
Children
Love affairs
Speculation, gambling, investments, stock market
Entrepreneurship
Dramatics, theatre, films

6th House
Work and health
Food, clothing, comforts

Domestic pets
Service to others
Working conditions
Employers, employees, personnel

7th House
The house of others as opposed to self
Relationships
Marriage and partnerships – both love and business relationships
All one-to-one relationships
Cooperation or lack of it
Open adversaries

8th House
The house of generation, degeneration or regeneration
Death and rebirth
The psychic, the occult
Inheritances and legacies
Other peoples' money and resources

9th House
Superconscious mind
Philosophy, religion, higher thought
Long journeys
Expansion of horizons both mental and spiritual
Worldwide contacts
The in-laws

10th House
Prestige, honour and standing in society
Professional career, reputation
The public arena

Success through hard work
Politics, governments, structure in society

11th House
Goals and objectives
Friendships
Hopes, wishes and dreams
Associations, clubs, groups of people
Humanitarian ideals

12th House
The subconscious; that which is hidden
House of charity, given or received
House of Karma – the law of cause and effect
Hospitals, prisons and institutions
Service or suffering
Limitation and confinement
The 3rd house rules the conscious mind; the 9th house rules the superconscious mind and the 12th house rules the subconscious mind.

The first six houses are more under the personal control of the individual than the last six houses. They are related to others and are more under the sway of other people. For instance, physical health (6th house) is under your control and largely dependent on your own actions. However, 12th house matters are beyond your control, in that they comprise frustration and even loss of personal liberty dependent on the way others react towards you and the sort of things that must be endured if they cannot be cured.

The houses can be divided into four trinities:

Trinity of Life (Fire)
1st House: Body
5th House: Soul
9th House: Spirit

Trinity of Wealth (Earth)
2nd House: Possessions, property and resources
6th House: Comforts, such as food, clothing, employees and health
10th House: Honour, prestige, business or professional standing

Trinity of Association: Relationships (Air)
3rd House: Brothers and sisters
7th House: Marriage and partnerships
11th House: Ties of friendship, close associates and advisors

Trinity of the Psychic (Water)
4th House: The environment in each stage of life especially in relation to old age
8th House: The influence of others on your environment especially in relation to death and inheritance
12th House: Service to those limited and restricted or suffering. Influences that can slow or accelerate growth

The Fire (life) houses are 1, 5, and 9.
The Earth (substance) houses are 2, 6, and 10
The Air (relationship) houses are 3, 7, and 11
The Water (emotional) houses are 4, 8, and 12

The Sun is the key symbol of the Element Fire. The Element Fire represents the enthusiasm, vitality, confidence and optimism of the self projecting into the world. The Fire houses (1, 5, and 9) show how these factors play out in the life of the individual. The 1st house represents the self, the 5th house the self's creative activity, and the 9th the self's expansion through contact with others.

Saturn, the earthiest of the planets, is most representative of the Earth houses, 2, 6, and 10. Saturn stands for structure, building, substance, gravity and the practical use of matter for tangible, concrete results. The Element of Earth is solid, dependable, careful and hard-working. The 2nd house represents the native's talents, the 6th his or her practical use of those talents in work, and the 10th the structure that is built from the labour and toil of the 6th house.

The next Element is Air, and Mercury is the quintessential Air planet. The winged messenger of the gods, Mercury constantly communicates and creates relationships among people or things. He is an intellectual planet and reflects the preference of the Air houses (3, 7, and 11) for ideas and relationships as opposed to concrete reality. The 3rd house signifies relationships in the immediate family, the 7th relationships with a significant other, and the 11th relationships with humanity.

Finally, the Moon is the most watery of the planets. She is sensitive, receptive, passive, protective, motherly, intuitive and emotional. The Moon reflects the light of the fiery Sun. The Moon and Water represent the mother principle (yin) just as the Sun and Fire represent the father principle (yang). The Moon symbolises the predilection of water houses (4, 8, and 12) for merging, fusing, receiving, transforming, nurturing, and connecting emotionally with others.

Water has its hidden undercurrents and signifies all that is hidden, secret, occult, and psychic. The 4th shows our merging with mother in her womb and with our mother earth in the grave. The 8th shows our fusion with a significant other in sexual intercourse and a sharing of our substance with the other for the procreation of children. The 12th reveals our mystical fusion with God and the universe.

The Fire Houses – 1, 5, 9

1st House
Angular
Ruler: Aries
Body parts: Head, face

The 1st House corresponds to the pioneering first sign Aries. Starting at the Ascendant, it symbolises the rising Sun. Mars, ruler of the 1st house, stands for your individuality, leadership, purposeful initiation, self-assertion, and important personal interests.

This is also the house of personal appearance, it is how you want to be rather than how you are. It is associated with the sign Aries and the planet Mars. This house is usually referred to as the house of the self. It sits in the east and was where the Sun rose on the day of your birth, so it is the house of sunrise and new beginnings. This is focused on the individual: the self and the voyage of discovery that defines every personality, looking at such questions as who are you? What will you become? How will you realise your potential?

The 1st House shows your outward character traits. Any planet in the 1st House will give you outward traits of the sign that this planet rules. A planet in the 1st House will be instrumental in how you see yourself and how others see you. A planet in the 1st House is usually very evident in the childhood years, and what we believe our personality to be until we find the motivation of our Sun sign. For example, if your little Sagittarian child seems as shy as a mouse, is very secretive and would prefer to play alone, she probably has Pluto in the 1st House, which gives her the appearance of a Scorpio child. She will not bloom into her rough-and-tumble Sagittarian ways until her teens and often even later.

The ruler of the 1st House is also said to be the ruler of the whole chart. A sign in the 1st House is known as the Ascendant and is instrumental in the first impression we have of someone physically, their type of body, the shape of their face and so on. For example, you could be a Gemini with a Taurus ascendant, so instead of being born with the classic Gemini streamlined sporty body, you will have a Taurean model which will have a much slower metabolism.

The Sun in the 1st House gives you the traits of Leo. You like to be seen as dramatic and attention-loving and the centre of attention at all times. People will be attracted by your flair.

The Moon in the 1st House gives you the traits of Cancer. You like to be seen as emotional, moody and perceptive. People are attracted by your caring nature.

Mercury in the 1st House gives you the traits of Gemini and Virgo. You like to be seen as curious and communicative. People are attracted by your conversation.

Venus in the 1st House gives you the traits of Libra and Taurus. You like to be seen as artistic, fair and just a little self-indulgent. People are attracted by your charm and sensuality.

Mars in the 1st House gives you the traits of Aries. You like to be seen as the action person. People are attracted by your fiery energy.

Jupiter in the 1st House gives you the traits of Sagittarius. You like to be seen as optimistic, lucky and with a tendency to say the first thing that pops into your head. People are attracted by your happy smile.

Saturn in the 1st House gives you the traits of Capricorn. You like to be seen as ambitious, well-organised and cautious. People are attracted by your level-headedness.

Uranus in the 1st House gives you the traits of Aquarius. You like to be seen as independent, and intellectual and just a little bit eccentric. People are attracted by your unusual clothes.

Neptune in the 1st House gives you the traits of Pisces. You like to be seen as trusting, imaginative and dreamy. People are attracted by your liquid eyes.

Pluto in the 1st House gives you the traits of Scorpio. You like to be seen as intense, mysterious and intuitive. People are attracted by your emotional strength.

5th House
Succedent
Ruler: Leo
Body parts: Stomach, liver, heart, sides, back

The 5th House rules: Pregnancy, children, the health or sickness of a child, fun, pleasure, romance, recreational sex, creative self-expression, self-indulgence, enjoyment, sport, hobbies, gambling, speculation, personal agents or messengers, ambassadors.

This house rules our hobbies, creative activities, amusements, and places where one experiences pleasure, courtship, romances, love affairs, creative writing. This house rules recreational drug use done for the "high" it produces. When drug use becomes an addiction, we place it under Pluto in the 8th of obsession or Neptune in the 12th house of self-undoing.

The 5th house governs the operations of the law of chance. In financial matters the 5th house rules betting, gambling, and speculation, including stocks. It governs risk taking in general.

This house holds sway over love relationships that do not involve commitment such as dates, boyfriends, and mistresses.

Houses 1 to 4 have dealt with staying alive. This is the first house that says "Let's enjoy ourselves."

The Sun in the 5th House will always put love first. The creative urge is strengthened here. Lovers and the first child will be fiery and dramatic.

The Moon in the 5th House means your romantic interests will tend to be on the changeable side. This placement can attract "poor me" types in romance.

Mercury in the 5th House means you express yourself creatively through writing and speaking. You are likely to fall in love with a talker or chatterbox.

Venus in the 5th House means that your lovers are always charmers, and you are creative, artistic and self-indulgent.

Mars in the 5th House means that your outlet for energy is in the house of fun, so you will like sports and games.

Jupiter in the 5th House means more fun, confidence in romance, confidence in creative endeavours and confidence in gambling.

Saturn in the 5th House denotes caution in fun and games. Undue importance is placed on romance. Saturn can be very good for creative projects that take forever to do and require endless patience. This placement can often lead to having one or no children.

Uranus in the 5th House means an attraction to unusual types in romance and an innovative sense of the creative.

Neptune in the 5th House can make you fall in love with rose-tinted glasses turned onto the full spectrum. There is a tendency to find a "soul mate" on every street corner. Neptune here is very creative in the arts.

Pluto in the 5th House means intense relationships followed by periods of celibacy and a tendency to become obsessed with your lover. Games are never just games, they are taken very seriously. Games are also where you recharge.

9th House
Cadent
Ruled by Sagittarius.
Body parts: Hips, thighs, buttocks, anus.

The 9th House rules foreign interests and contacts, foreign countries, overseas voyages, long journeys, expansion of the mind, philosophy, religion, lawyers, dreams and visions, knowledge, science, learning.

The 9th House is associated with adventure, travel and freedom.

Anything that broadens the mind is located in the 9th house. Commonly this includes higher education, studying, international finance and trade, foreign communication.

The creative manipulation and organisation of ideas falls into the 9th house. This includes science, knowledge, the law, astrology as a system of knowledge, codes of ethics.

The 9th House is the house of formalising and legalising matters. Legal procedures and rituals that legalise like wedding ceremonies, probate hearings, adopting and christening a child are all 9th house matters.

Things that are high up or actually in the sky are located in the 9th House. This includes attics, high places, airplanes, space ships, UFO's, comets, meteorites, birds and space shuttles. The 9th house also rules locations and persons closely connected with flight such as flight attendants, airports and space stations.

The 9th House expands those activities that are found in the 3rd House of communications. The local meeting of the 3rd becomes the large convention of the 9th. The close kin of the 3rd correspond to the in-laws in the 9th. The trivial publications of the 3rd become the serious books of the 9th. The 3rd House teacher correlates with the 9th House professor or public lecturer. The Elementary School of the 3rd contrasts with the University of the 9th.

The Sun in the 9th House loves to shine in study and higher learning and gains a great deal from overseas travel. You have a greater than normal interest in philosophy and big picture issues, and prefer to deal with general principles rather than specific facts.

Moon in the 9th House means you tend to have philosophies based on principles of the heart rather than those of logic. There is a strong emotional need to travel and study.

Mercury in the 9th House likes to scrutinise life philosophies, take them apart and put them back together, but they have no emotional ties to them. To people with this placement, one idea is as good as the next.

Venus in the 9th House finds pleasure in study and travel but may lack motivation. You may find love overseas, or be attracted to a foreigner at home. You are not likely to travel anywhere dirty or ugly – Tuscany or Paris is more your choice.

Mars in the 9th House is a placement that can result in a crusader. You will have causes that motivate you and you will want to communicate this to the world.

Jupiter in the 9th House gives luck in long-distance travel and higher education. Just take off and see the world at your whim – the energies have conspired to protect you.

Saturn in the 9th House struggles with university as they are much better at learning in a hands-on environment. This placement will prefer a more conservative philosophy of life.

Uranus in the 9th House is anarchy in the house of beliefs. If you were raised by conservative Christians, you will love shocking them with your latest devotion to the doctrines of a way-out cult and you will enjoy venturing off the beaten track, ignoring all the advice in your guidebook.

Neptune in the 9th House is where philosophy and travel occupy your dreams. You are drawn to the sea for long trips.

Pluto in the 9th House means long journeys revitalise you and study is balm to your soul. You will enjoy studying anything that might be instrumental in solving hidden mysteries.

Earth Houses – 2, 6, 10

2nd House
Succedent
Ruled by Taurus.
Body parts: Neck, throat, voice

The 2nd House rules estates, fortunes, resources, money, income, wealth, profit or gain, loss or damage, movable goods, valuables, values. So too are intangible resources such as rights of ownership, copyrights, and royalties.

This house reflects your attitudes about the material world, your philosophy towards money, possessions, finances and your earning and spending capacity. It is associated with the sign Taurus and the planet Venus.

Planets that fall in this house indicate your attitudes towards wealth and material goods, whether you are a scrooge or a spendthrift. They will also indicate how and where you are likely to spend your money – on yourself, on your children or on setting up soup kitchens for the needy.

On a deeper level, this house also reveals your sense of self-worth. This house deals with what you value both within yourself and outside yourself. It signifies where your emotional and financial security lie, and its sign and planet will show you whether you value financial security or emotional security or vice versa.

The Sun in the 2nd House will focus the conscious awareness on money and possessions. In some cases possessions may be used to compensate for a lack of self-worth.

The Moon in the 2nd House will make money and the sense of self-worth fluctuate as if pulled by the tides – make sure you have put some aside when the tide is high.

Mercury in the 2nd House will mean that communication is important to your sense of self-worth and increases the chance that your income will depend on your communication skills.

Venus in the 2nd House is the planet of love in the house of possessions. Beautiful and artistic things are what you value, romance is where you find self-worth.

Mars in the 2nd House is easy come, easy go. Mars thinks money is for making and spending, not for hoarding.

Jupiter in the 2nd House gives you a happy-go-lucky attitude to money. That doesn't mean you will necessarily be rich, just that you know the money will turn up when you most need it, so there is no need to stress about it.

Saturn in the 2nd House is what you regard as important, so important that you might be fearful that you are going to blow it. With this placement you will fear poverty and will do anything in your power to avoid it.

Uranus in the 2nd House will ensure you never get paid in a usual way. Freelancers, actors, and people paid on commission often have this one, receiving lump sums and then nothing for months.

Neptune in the 2nd House dreams about being rich, but that is where the money generally stays – in their dreams. There can be a guilt associated with money as well.

Pluto in the 2nd House means, with this planet of extremes, that money is either an obsession or absolutely of no importance. You are either a millionaire or a tramp.

6th House
Cadent
Ruled by Virgo.
Body Parts: Intestines and nervous system.

The 6th House rules: service to others, work, health, sickness, employees, labour in general, small animals, tenants.

The 6th House is associated with the critical, meticulous, hypochondriac virgin of Virgo. The Virgo native loves purity and is dedicated to service and efficient functioning, and has an interest in health and hygiene. The 6th house is the house of service. It rules tradesmen, craftsmen, repair men, baby-sitters and anyone hired as a servant or domestic. The 6th house rules therapeutic activity and healing measures including medications and medical regimes.

The 6th House rules small domesticated animals that serve us. Animals in zoos, serving the larger community are found in the 12th.

Any planets that fall in the 6th House show how you like to work, what your work environment should be like for you to feel comfortable.

The Sun in the 6th House means that you have to shine in the workplace and you need recognition for what you do to feel good about your world.

The Moon in the 6th House means that you have an emotional need to work and your office will be a home away from home.

Mercury in the 6th House means work will involve speaking, writing or travelling, no matter what your career.

Venus in the 6th House means you need a pleasant work environment, and even if you work in an office, you will insist on a place near a window.

Mars in the 6th House is action and aggression in the workplace. You like to be up and about, talking and getting things done.

Jupiter in the 6th House is lucky in finding jobs and in health, but it also means that you are likely to become bored before you get the real benefits in a job.

Saturn in the 6th House can mean challenges in the workplace, such as being overlooked for promotions. It can also mean great success once these obstacles have been overcome. Work is very important to this placement and this position frequently gives excellent organisational skills.

Uranus in the 6th House needs independence in the workplace. You cannot stand having someone looking over your shoulder. High-tech jobs would suit you very well.

Neptune in the 6th House means you will be best working with people who are needy or in a job where you need to use your imagination. You can feel imprisoned in an office job and find yourself daydreaming a lot.

Pluto in the 6th House means you need to be obsessed about your work. Office jobs will probably result in office politics and power struggles.

10th House
Angular
Ruler: Capricorn
Body parts: Skeletal system, knees

The 10th House rules: Government, vocation, career, status, official office, any position of command or trust, integrity, dignity, kingdoms and empires.

The climbing, sure-footed, practical, ambitious goat of Capricorn is associated with the 10th House. As its opposite sign Cancer seeks security in the home, the 10th House ruler, Capricorn, seeks security in its position in the outer world. It shows public success, awards and honours as well as public disgrace and shame.

Because the 10th is the house of government, we locate bosses, presidents, superiors, employers, school principals, and administrators here along with the administration of any matter.

When choosing a career direction it is important to look at what is going on in your 10th House, as it will show where your ambition lies.

This house is power balanced with responsibility, and it will show how we manage both.

The Sun in the 10th House shines in public, and you are likely to do well in whatever profession you choose. You will gain an authoritative position as a matter of course.

The Moon in the 10th House means attitudes to your career go through phases, and that you may change your mind about your career periodically and have several different careers in your lifetime.

Mercury in the 10th House means mental stimulation is important in your career choice, as is the circulation of information. Short trips could form a part of your career path. Writing, public speaking and sales would make satisfying careers.

Venus in the 10th House means networking and public relations are skills you put to good use in your career. Art and design, beauty, jewellery and fashion are all careers ruled by Venus. Whatever you do, you will always look good doing it.

Mars in the 10th House means that whatever you do, you know you can do it better than the boss. Mars means rapid advancement in a career and will make you very ambitious. Careers involving energy, initiative and action will be satisfying.

Jupiter in the 10th House means work in the pursuit of your ideals will be the most enjoyable career for you. Luck is strong in your career, and you will find that success is likely to come to you.

Saturn in the 10th House means it may take you a while to get going in your career, but with your diligence and hard work, you will eventually succeed. You are organised and disciplined.

Uranus in the 10th House fits in perfectly with the technological revolution – turning up to work on a skateboard at 6pm to work into the night on cutting-edge projects on the Internet suits this placement entirely. Forget the corporate ladder, you need a place to express your eccentricities.

Neptune in the 10th House means you need a dreamy side to your career. Filmmaking, art, or fashion design would work very well, or areas like charities, medicine, prisons, nursing homes which Neptune also rules.

Pluto in the 10th House means you must attempt to match your career with your twin desires for power and to serve society. Politics, religion, the police, psychology and medicine (Pluto is the planet of healing) are all careers where you can synthesise these disparate desires.

The Air Houses – 3, 7, 11

3rd House
Cadent
Ruled by Gemini.
Body parts: Shoulders, arms, hands, fingers

The 3rd House rules: siblings, cousins, kin, neighbours, communications, immediate environment, local travel, short journeys, letters, rumours, news, intelligence, messengers.

The 3rd House association with Gemini reveals its dominion over communication, mental activity and transport of any kind. The 3rd rules transportation and the gathering of facts and information. It governs cars and garages, buses, walking, cycling, motoring, talking, visiting, newspapers and magazines, computers and software, telephones and tape recorders, tools and gadgets, brothers and sisters, messages and messengers, streets, literature, files and filing systems, radios, TV's, teachers, early education, local meetings, editorial work.

This house describes how you were educated in your early life. If you experienced a difficult time at school, have a good look in your 3rd House for complications. As it describes early schooling, it also shows how we now process language and how our brain retains information. It shows in what style you communicate, whether you are calm and lucid or frantic and confused.

The Sun in the 3rd House is where you want admiration, and this placement means you want it through communication. This will give you Gemini characteristics as well.

The Moon in the 3rd House means emotions are communicated easily. However, you will be very sensitive to criticism from others.

Mercury in the 3rd House is at home here. This will make you a good student with excellent verbal and written skills.

Venus in the 3rd House knows how to charm with words.

Mars in the 3rd House wastes no time telling it like it is so that they can move on to the next project.

Jupiter in the 3rd House means communications are cheerful and free-flowing, but there may be a tendency to talk big and tell too much.

Saturn in the 3rd House is cautious in communication and may have learning difficulties.

Uranus in the 3rd House tends to say off-the-wall things and come up with new and eccentric ideas.

Neptune in the 3rd House is imaginative in communication, especially gifted in artistic pursuits.

Pluto in the 3rd House gives your communications great influential power – be sure to use them wisely.

7th House
Angular
Ruled by Libra
Body parts: Hips, kidneys, lower back.

The 7th House rules: marriage, partnership, open enemies, wife, husband, girlfriend, boyfriend, lover, significant other, adversary in a lawsuit, opposing partner in war, quarrels, wars, legal battles.

It rules all kinds of partnerships and unions, the marriage partner, committed relationships, marriage as well as divorce, and significant others. It has general dominion over any other person with whom one has dealings.

All contracts, agreements and contractual relationships between equal partners are ruled by the 7th. A contract as a written document per se is ruled by the 3rd, but as a legal agreement by the 7th.

The Sun in the 7th House will give you a sunny partner with traits similar to Leo. There is a strong focus on partners and marriage with this placement, and you will feel more outgoing in general when you are in a good relationship.

The Moon in the 7th House may give you moody and changeable partners. You will find it easier to express your emotions while you are in a supportive relationship. You may tend towards mothering or being mothered in your relationships.

Mercury in the 7th House will give you an intellectual, talkative partner, who may be quite flirtatious. Talking will be an important part of your relationship.

Venus in the 7th House will give you a charming partner. You may find yourself becoming more self-indulgent after marriage.

Mars in the 7th House will give you an active, energetic partner. Married life will never be dull, with lots of activity interspersed with the occasional argument.

Jupiter in the 7th House gives you luck and confidence in love. You will grow and learn from your relationships.

Saturn in the 7th House people are often better off waiting to get married until they have established their own personality and have a very good idea of what they want from a partner. Saturn usually gives you an older partner.

Uranus in the 7th House may never marry, as you value your independence very highly. This placement favours an unusual partner or someone who is a genius.

Neptune in the 7th House gives you rose-tinted glasses when you look for a partner. This placement gives you a highly artistic, sensitive and romantic partner – or a drug-addicted bigamist. The unfortunate thing about this placement is that you will probably be the last to know which one you married.

Pluto in the 7th House is all or nothing. Love or hate your partner, your feelings will never be wishy-washy. Pluto will give you a very intense partner.

11th House
Succedent
Ruled by Aquarius.
Body parts: Circulation and legs to the ankles.

The 11th House rules: friends and friendship, fidelity or falseness of friends, hopes, wishes, trust, confidence, praise and criticism, counsel; the love and concord of friends and acquaintances.

It also rules, colleagues, social life, casual ties, clubs, societies, and group associations. Acts of friendship and friendly advice are found here along with counsel and counsellors in general. One's professional clients belong in the 11th House.

The detached, intelligent, eccentric, new age water bearer are the wavy electrical lines of Aquarius that are associated with the 11th House. This house is especially concerned with how you integrate yourself into the greater community.

This is the house of social conscience and will show your attitude to charities and helping others. This house can be thought of as an extension to the 5th House, which shows where we are creative in a personal way. The 11th House shows us where we are creative in the wider, social sense.

The Sun in the 11th House means you will have lots of friends and acquaintances and enjoy being in clubs and societies. You may have trouble forming close personal relationships.

The Moon in the 11th House means involvement in community politics is likely. You like taking a role in the large social groups you tend to move in. Your hopes and wishes tend to be changeable.

Mercury in the 11th House will not tolerate friends who cannot hold their own in a social situation, and will not suffer anyone who is too shy to speak up for themselves. Acquaintances tend to flit in and out of your life.

Venus in the 11th House means you find social satisfaction in a large and varied group of friends and acquaintances. You value taste and artistic ability in your friends.

Mars in the 11th House people are well-connected networkers who are superficially close to a vast amount of people – everyone seems to know them and love them. You will have equally assertive friends. You set your goals and you go for them without a second thought.

Jupiter in the 11th House makes you so charming in friendship that people clamour to be your friend. You will seem to receive all that you wish for – don't get complacent or your luck will run out. Your ambitions are very broad-based and you are comfortable enlisting help from your acquaintances where others would err on the side of politeness.

Saturn in the 11th House means you were painfully shy in your youth, so you have either overcome this obstacle to be very adept in social situations, or you have resolved to stick to your few very close friends. You have older more mature friends.

Uranus in the 11th House means unusual and different friends from a variety of walks of life. Your long-term ambitions are original and you probably have an unusual plan to achieve them by circumventing the normal channels.

Neptune in the 11th House has long-term ambition rooted in fantasy land, and goals tend to change with fashions. Friends will be artistic and gentle types. They may also drain you emotionally and take you for a ride. You may have difficulty in distinguishing real friends from the others. You tend to be shy in large groups.

Pluto in the 11th House means you find personal power in group situations and will have a natural ability for politics. You have only a few very close friends. Your hopes and wishes can become your obsessions – you will no doubt achieve what you set out to do. Make sure it is what you really want.

Water Houses – 4, 8, 12

4th House
Angular
Ruled by Cancer
Body parts: Breasts, stomach.

The 4th House rules: Roots, family, home, earth, foundations, lands, mining, agriculture, real estate, houses, the grave, towns and cities, ancient dwellings, gardens, fields, orchards.

The 4th has dominion over the weather, monuments and memorials, natural resources on or beneath the earth, the manifestation of natural forces such as earthquakes, floods, and storms. It also rules old age, museums, history and anything that has been preserved.

Ashes to ashes, dust to dust. In the 4th house our physical body returns to the earth from which it came. The Water quality of the 4th house symbolises our final merging with mother earth.

The relationship with the stronger parent figure is a major feature of this house. It could be either the mother or the father, but usually it is the parent who had the most influence over your growing up.

It is not only the family home, but it is about the home you set up for your own family, and the values you intend to pass on to your children. It shows the "feel" of your home and how you tend to act there.

The Sun in the 4th House rules the roost. The home is very important to you and your influential parent is likely to be outgoing and gregarious.

The Moon in the 4th House has a more potent power, because the Moon's home is here. Home is your refuge, and your family life is paramount. Your influential parent is moody and emotional.

Mercury in the 4th House means home is a hubbub of communications with radio, TV, computer, chatter and the phone ringing.

Venus in the 4th House means home life is harmonious and beautiful, filled with tasteful furnishings. Retirement will be comfortable.

Mars in the 4th House means that home is where you are most active, energetic and argumentative.

Jupiter in the 4th House means a large house with a great view, and a tendency to travel and study in your retirement. This is an extremely good placement for a comfortable life.

Saturn in the 4th House leads to a fear of domestic instability which makes you work hard to establish a stable, permanent home. This placement can mean that your childhood home was unstable and you determine this will not be the case for your family.

Uranus in the 4th House means your home and family life are probably a bit eccentric. You will become more eccentric as you get older.

Neptune in the 4th House means you would love to live by the sea. You were a bit different from your family and sometimes felt you didn't really belong.

Pluto in the 4th House means you can go home to recharge your batteries. You are strong at home, though home may also be a place of power struggles.

8th House
Succedent
Ruled by Scorpio.
Body Parts: Genitals and bladder.

The 8th House rules: death, transformation, joint finances, the estate of the dead, wills, legacies, fear and anguish of mind, danger, rebirth, loans, other people's money, garbage, elimination, butchers and surgeons, poisons, the partner's wealth or movable goods.

As we fuse with the earth in our final resting place in the 4th, we merge with a significant other in the sexual intercourse of the 8th.

The 8th governs occupations connected with elimination, injury and death. This includes undertakers, coroners, surgeons, santitation workers, garbage men and women. The dominion of Mars and Pluto over probing and penetration connect the 8th house to research, psychology, psycho-analysis, and the occult. Negatively, penetration relates to rape, murder, sadism, sodomy and other ways people pierce one another. The sex of the 8th is vastly different from the recreational sex of the 5th house.

In financial matters, the 8th rules the money of a partner, wills, goods of the dead, taxes, fees, bankruptcy, alimony, public funds, recovery of debts, mortgages, joint resources.

The Sun in the 8th House means a dramatic and intense approach to everything you do. A career in health, alternative healing, or finance would be fulfilling.

The Moon in the 8th House means emotionally you need to heal and nurture. This placement wants to accumulate its own money and possessions.

Mercury in the 8th House wants to teach and communicate the esoteric. That which is invisible, the occult, astrology, healing all fall into this placement of Mercury.

Venus in the 8th House enjoys possessions especially if they have been provided by someone else. There is a love of the occult and the paranormal.

Mars in the 8th House will be very interested in sex and will want to put a lot of energy into a partner on a very intense level. You will also put your energy into other peoples' resources.

Jupiter in the 8th House likes people of unusual and different cultures. People tend to throw money and resources at you with this placement of Jupiter. You need to be sure you can pay it back if required.

Saturn in the 8th House likes a planned sex life without too many surprises. You have a gift for managing other peoples' resources and finances.

Uranus in the 8th House loves to break the taboos and be a little different. You revel in breaking the social rules.

Neptune in the 8th House sees sex as a dreamy affair. Neptune puts the blinkers on when it comes to business partners in this house – make sure you are the one managing the books.

Pluto in the 8th House means sex can become an obsession. You are either celibate or promiscuous. There is no middle way.

12th House
Cadent
Ruled by Pisces.
Body parts: Feet

The 12th House rules: despair, confinement, imprisonment, self-undoing, Karma, the past, large animals, secret informers, those who maliciously undermine their neighbours; secret enemies not named, anyone committed to prison, captives, slaves, hostages; institutions of confinement, monasteries, hospitals, prisons, infirmaries, places of retreat.

Because mental and emotional problems involuntarily limit the individual, the 12th House rules alcoholism, psychosis, delusions, hallucinations, neurosis. It represents self-harm, suicide, sacrifice and basic limitations of the self. The law of Karma as it limits the individual is placed in the 12th.

On the other hand the possibility of release from confinement is also ruled by the 12th. The literal escape from bondage through parole, reprieve, rescue, liberation, pardon or getting out on bail is shown here. Release from mental or emotional bondage through psychotherapy, meditation, charitable work or other circumstances is also shown in the 12th House.

The 12th governs work done in seclusion or behind the scenes such as work done in a home office. In the 12th we find retreats and places of retreat, recluses, confidential matters, private activities, remote out of the way places, mysterious locations and conditions, undisclosed matters, and secrets. It also rules bondage, persecution, plots, kidnapping, assassination, treason, and the state of being hidden or invisible.

The Sun in the 12th House means privacy is treasured. You are very sensitive and need to retreat from the real world every now and then to recharge. You may be a night owl and have esoteric interests. You need to be encouraged to bring your insights into the wider realm.

The Moon in the 12th House means you are shy and sensitive, and often hide your emotions and mood swings. You prefer to do good works behind the scenes, with compassion and imagination. Your home is your refuge. You need to be encouraged to let your emotions show.

Mercury in the 12th House means you have little confidence in your ability to express yourself, which is a great pity, because your ideas are often carefully considered and mindful of the wants and needs of all parties. You need to be encouraged to speak out on issues close to your heart.

Venus in the 12th House can mean only a few friends and shyness in social settings. You need to be encouraged to be more open about your feelings to friends and let them into your confidence.

Mars in the 12th House tends to bottle up anger. You like to work behind the scenes. You need to be encouraged to speak up when upset or offended so that you do not hold your anger inside.

Jupiter in the 12th House can hide your joy. This placement brings luck in protecting you from physical harm. Often the religious or spiritual world is preferable to the real world. You need to be encouraged to laugh and enjoy with others.

Saturn in the 12th House suppresses grief, which only keeps it held inside. You fear the future and authority figures. You have to find ways to express your inner purpose and put your talents as a behind-the-scenes organiser to good use. This will help you to build self-confidence.

Uranus in the 12th House hides your eccentricity and genius. You have a wonderful imagination and yoga and meditation would be of great value to you. Probably reluctant at first, you will surprise yourself at your talent in these areas, and the benefits you will derive from them.

Neptune in the 12th House hides your dreamy, imaginative side. You should be encouraged to keep a dream diary. This placement is quite harmonious, as Neptune is at home here, liking his reveries hidden.

Pluto in the 12th House can mean hidden rage bubbling beneath the surface. Watch for this one as an escape valve must be found. Abilities in the healing professions are heightened. An interest in psychology or the occult could help you to uncover your hidden nature.

Chapter 7

"A physician without the knowledge of astrology has no right to call himself a physician."

Hippocrates – Father of Medicine

Interpretive Guidelines
Sun in Signs and Houses

Sun in Aries
Ignition key and pioneers of the zodiac.
Want to be first, don't like being on a team. First on the bus and first off, don't like wasting time. Fearless, heroic and enthusiastic. Dash into things especially when it's something new. Notorious for never finishing anything. Good starters but poor finishers. Great for inspiring other people, always on the attack, like to strike while the iron's hot.

Sun in Taurus
Practical and cautious. Can we afford it? Don't like change unless they initiate it themselves. Most Taureans will dig a hole and line it with velvet. Sign of earned income. Taureans like to have a "rainy day fund" because they need the inner knowledge that they can always provide for themselves if necessary. No joint accounts for Taureans. Don't like rubbish. Like quality and like to surround themselves with artistic beauty and peace. Noted to be possessive and can sometimes be over possessive with their children. Very generous. Presentation is important. They all believe in insurances and want to ensure that their

family is all right. They are often bankers – good at handling money, their own and other people's.

Sun in Gemini
Children and communicators of the zodiac. Dual personalities. Very independent. The "why" people. Will always be young at heart and be able to relate well to children asking questions because they remember their own childhood in their psyche. Make good teachers and students. Great communicators, very curious and love to talk. You will sometimes be lucky to get a word in. Good in the media. Sometimes a Gemini won't say anything but they can still be communicators either in writing or by phone. Good in transport.

Sun in Cancer
The mother of the zodiac. Always have to nurture. Many go into nursing and they sometimes go into the restaurant business. Moody. They are the most sensitive sign of the zodiac and are experts at hiding their feelings. When they feel threatened or upset they go into their shell. Very fond of babies but not so much of growing up children and can lose interest when they grow up because they feel locked out. Very good when a person is ill. Make good publicans and are born housekeepers, both men and women.

Sun in Leo
Have a good head of hair. Need to know they are loved and cherished; men, women and children. They get their own way in a nice way. Very good at organising and delegating. One of their faults can be their pride. They are very loving people and are very fond of showing their affection. Would definitely rather have gold than silver.

They can take the stage and love dressing up. Older Leos love live performances and theatre. Love to be in the front row of the circus. They do everything in a big way. Love to delegate and often find themselves in a position where they have to delegate. They attract high positions. Walk with their nose in the air. Sunny people who like the Sun.

Sun in Virgo
Workers and perfectionists of the zodiac.
Enjoy bringing order out of chaos but then let anybody touch it and there's trouble. They can spot a 50c piece at 50 paces. Always having baths. Make excellent secretaries, like everything in its place. Find it hard to delegate and take responsibility very much to heart. Like to be their own boss either on their own or within a large company so that they are responsible for the whole job. They only like one lover at a time but they do like a change. Don't like having to tell lies because it messes them up. Don't like the limelight, prefer to work in the background.

Sun in Libra
Peacemakers of the universe. Libra is the sign of marriage. They sometimes stick to partners even though all the joy and love has gone out of the relationship because they need someone to share their life with. Feel more comfortable with a partner than on their own. Sign of relationships which mean a lot to them. Need to relate. Sometimes find themselves sitting on the fence because they can see both sides to a problem. "Shall I, shan't I?" Like to beautify people, are often hairdressers, beauticians, dressmakers, anything which enhances. Presentation is important to them and so is colour. Things must be balanced out. They will go all out for a cause. Don't like

antagonistic atmosphere, they will walk away. Make good adjudicators.

Sun in Scorpio
The most intense sign of the zodiac. Very black and white, no middle road. Either in the police force or the mafia. Very magnetic people and people are drawn to them. If a Scorpio makes a friend of you, you are very honoured because they very rarely get close. Also the most secretive sign of the zodiac. Loyalty means everything to them. People are attracted to them and tell them all their business. They make good detectives because they won't leave any stone unturned until they find what they want. They are much maligned. They are extremely loyal. Also the sexiest sign of the zodiac but they can either be nymphomaniacs or icebergs. If they are married and there is unfaithfulness, the marriage is over. Sexual jealousy. Sign of blood and guts; often dentists, surgeons and butchers.

Sun in Sagittarius
Most jovial sign of the zodiac and also a natural teacher. Changeable and adaptable. Tend to bite off more than they can chew and so they burn the midnight oil. Don't know when to stop, tend to overdo things. Most religious of all the signs and may enquire into many religions. They enjoy telling people of their adventures and what they have done and love to travel far and wide, the further the better. The holiday starts as soon as they lock the front door behind them. They don't want to lie in the sun, they want to see what other countries are like and explore the world. Very rarely go back to the same place more than once.

Sun in Capricorn
Steady, hard worker of the zodiac. Status and prestige are very important. They are not born brimming with confidence. They are achievers. Will stay in a job until they get the gold clock. Want to prove that they can achieve by themselves. Very reliable and the sign governs time. They have clocks everywhere. They have pride. They never really make a fool of themselves because they always like to be in control. Control is their word. Don't like to show themselves up because of their status. Very reliable, always early, good workers, have a wry sense of humour. Sticklers for protocol, rarely dress outrageously, may wear the same kind of shoe all their life. Hate waste, they don't waste time and don't waste words.

Sun in Aquarius
Ruling planet of astrology. The loners of the zodiac. Before an Aquarian sounds off and gives an opinion, he likes to know the facts. They want to be sure that they know what they are talking about before they make a spectacle of themselves. Unconventional, loners except for friends, by whom they set great store. They make wonderful friends. They get more and more eccentric as they get older but they don't mind as they are working towards being an individual. Like to join groups of people, they are inventors, they are interested in anything new which would be more efficient and can be electronics engineers. Many are counsellors. They can distance themselves and give good judgment. Welfare workers, good organisers.

Sun in Pisces
Most restless of all the signs. Not only a Water sign but Mutable so that it trickles. If it comes to a rock it goes round it. They don't like making decisions but they can make them if they choose. Psychic, intuitive and most sympathetic. Will sit down and put their arms around someone. Not the blood and guts department but good at working in after care. Very fond of the sea, like a little flutter. Very sensitive but they don't like saying it. They answer a question with a question. They don't like ruffling the waters, like to be peaceful, they are extremely fond of music and the art world is their escape. Neptune, ruler of Pisces, is concerned with music, the realm of the tides.

Sun in Houses

1st House
Keynote: to be

Sun in the first house indicates abundant vitality combined with a strong will and intense self-awareness. Initiative, leadership, ambition, and self-determination, the desire to follow one's own course, are highly characteristic. These individuals possess great reserves of energy and strong recuperative powers that enable them to overcome physical afflictions and ailments of almost every kind. Distinction and esteem are of paramount importance to them, and they will work long and hard to achieve it. If the Sun is afflicted in the 1st House, the individual can suffer from excessive pride, egotism, compulsiveness, and the desire to dominate others.

2nd House
Keynote: to possess

The Sun in the 2nd House indicates how the individual uses money and other material resources. Here, the proper management and utilisation of money and property must be learned. The Sun sign position is a strong indicator of how income and resources are acquired and used.

If the Sun is afflicted in the 2nd House, there can be exaggerated concern with wealth and material gains at the expense of other values. These people may also frivolously squander their wealth in the name of self-aggrandisement and ego gratification.

3rd House
Keynote: to know

Here we see a strong drive to achieve distinction through intellectual brilliance and accomplishments. A strong, scientific bent may be indicated. Owing to their curiosity, these individuals have a strong desire to travel and are eager to investigate anything new, especially when it is related to matters ruled by the Sun sign and their particular field of activity. Brothers, sisters, friends, and neighbours are mostly likely to play major roles in their lives, and the ability to clearly express and communicate their ideas is very important to them. If the Sun is afflicted in the 3rd House, the individual may suffer from arrogance and intellectual snobbery with a tendency to impose his or her ideas on others.

4th House
Keynote: to establish

A secure home and family is extremely important to the Sun in the 4th House person. They tend to be proud of their family heritage and wish for their homes to be the showpieces by which they are perceived and judged. The first part of their lives may often be a difficult struggle to obtain the property they desire, with increasing prosperity and security coming later in life. The Sun in the 4th House indicates a strong interest in real estate, ecology and natural resources.

When the Sun is afflicted in the 4th House, there may be excessive family pride, conflict with parents, and a desire to dominate and even tyrannise the domestic scene.

5th House
Keynote: to express

Here we see a joyful love of life and a strong drive for creative self-expression. These individuals are highly competitive, inclined toward sports and artistic pursuits. They seek pleasure and romance with others, have radiant dispositions, and tend to attract many friends. They wish to be noticed and appreciated. They can, however, sometimes appear as egocentric, overly dramatic, petulant, and childish.

People with a 5th House Sun are ardent lovers, and falling in love can be all-consuming for them. In spite of their highly amorous natures, they are very capable of being loyal to one person. They have a great love of children, although, if the Sun is in one of the Fire signs, they may have few or none of their own.

6th House
Keynote: to improve

People with the Sun in the 6th House seek fulfilment and distinction through their work and service, in which they take great pride. Their self-esteem is related directly to their work. If their work is not outwardly recognised and appreciated, they can become resentful toward their employers. Employees with the Sun in this position will demand rights and privileges, while employers with the Sun in the 6th House can be exacting and authoritarian.

The Sun in the 6th House tends to indicate delicate health, with the need to pay careful attention to diet and exercise. If the Sun is well aspected, the individual has an intuitive understanding of how to maintain his or her health. There may even be an interest in a health-related career such as nursing or medicine. Good employment is rarely a problem, unless the Sun is afflicted, in which case long periods of unemployment can be the result.

7th House
Keynote: to relate

The Sun in the 7th House indicates a strong capacity for close personal relationships. The accent is on "we" and not "me." People with the Sun in the 7th House have to learn to adjust to the needs and demands of others. In marriage, the partner holds the power. When the Sun is well aspected, the individual attracts strong loyal friends and business associates. Marriage is of paramount importance and can add to greater success in life. When the Sun is afflicted, there can be a tendency to dominate or be dominated by one's partner, with a need to learn cooperation and respect for others.

8th House
Keynote: to transform

This points to an underlying interest in the mysteries of life, especially death and other ideas pertaining to the continuation of consciousness and the possibility of an afterlife. Spiritual growth and self-improvement come as a result of conscious will. It is likely that this person will have direct personal experience of a deeper reality beyond material circumstances, making them fearless in the knowledge of life's fundamental principles. Much can be required and much can be gained. On a more mundane level, there will be concerns with taxes, insurance, inheritance, and the finances and assets of other people. It can indicate inheritances and legacies, or, if afflicted, troubles with these matters, including divorce settlements.

9th House
Keynote: to understand

The Sun in the 9th House shows a dynamic interest in spiritual, religious, and philosophical pursuits. Their intuitive intellect is developed, active and capable of insights that can border on the prophetic. There is a keen interest in international affairs and foreign countries and their cultures, often accompanied by a strong desire to travel. If the Sun is in one of the Fixed signs, the urge to travel may be greatly reduced. If Leo is on the 4th House cusp, the individual will most likely end up living far from his or her childhood home.

10th House
Keynote: to achieve

The Sun here denotes strong ambition to attain positions of power and authority. Many politicians have the Sun in the 10th House. Along with the drive for power comes an enhanced sense of social responsibility. There is a strong desire for honour and recognition, and a capacity to work hard in order to achieve the desired success. Often, these people are born into families of high social standing and possess an acute sense of personal dignity and the importance of moral integrity. When the Sun is afflicted, the opposite is true; they can be ruthless and unscrupulous in their drive for power and subject to public disgrace.

11th House
Keynote: to transmute

Here we find an interest and concern with friendships and group relationships and activities. These people are attracted to scientific endeavours and inventions, as well as matters related to the occult. When the Sun is well-aspected, the individual will have many friends and be held in high esteem. Humanitarian feelings are strong, with a deeply rooted and impartial belief in individual dignity and human rights. If the Sun is afflicted, there can be a tendency to dominate others, often for selfish motives. The individual can also be easily deceived or led astray by others.

12th House
Keynote: to transcend

Here the will is directed toward exploring and understanding one's personal inner life, with a keen interest in psychology and psychic research. These people are often quiet and retiring, to the extent that they can be isolated and lonely. However, they can find fulfilment through service to others. If the Sun is afflicted in the 12th House, there can be excessive shyness, neurosis, and a desire to control others through secret or clandestine means. There may also be secret enemies lurking in the background.

Moon in Signs and Houses

The Moon in a horoscope indicates the person's subconscious and instinctive reactions to life, interpreted as behaviour, habits, mannerisms and moods.

The Moon in a chart is affected by the sign and house placements and by the aspects made to it by the other planets. For example, the Moon in the 6th house would show a subject who is interested in hygiene and health matters. Whereas the Moon in Gemini would show restlessness and mental activity.

The Moon's influence is particularly strong in babyhood and early childhood, when habits and reactions to the environment are being formed. Often a child will display its Moon sign to the apparent exclusion of the other planets. For example, a Moon in Leo baby will appear more sunny natured and gregarious than its own Sun in Capricorn would indicate.

Moon qualities are basically emotional and are shown as instinctive vulnerable withdrawal from aggressive forces.

This crab-like action of withdrawing into herself and of drawing people, things and experiences towards herself and holding them is typical of Moon traits.

The Moon relates to the unconscious, all things emotional and feminine and it represents what we put into our body in the form of nourishment.

Moon in Aries
"Now, now" cried the Queen, "faster, faster!"
Lewis Carroll

Inclined to have a volatile, emotional, impulsive nature. Not enough thought before taking action. Sudden flare-ups. Temper, but only temporary and soon forgotten. Prominent female in life. Very independent. There is a tendency to dominate others emotionally and also to take things personally. Hides a sense of insecurity behind an independent and aggressive exterior.

I've known people with Aries Moon leave angry notes for their pets! When you renovate or decorate, you do it in half the time that everyone else does, but you tend to start off enthusiastically, then lose interest. You are always dashing in and out.

Moon in Taurus

"Happiness is a good bank account, a good cook and a good digestion."

Jean-Jacques Rousseau

Exalted, strong. A need for financial and material security in order to attain emotional well-being. Good at handling financial affairs. Sees things through to the end. Fond of the good things in life. Must have stable home life. The Moon in this sign attracts wealth. Your emotions are generally steady and placid. Strong emotions. Tremendous desire for security. Good-natured and attractive personality.

You need security and certainty – unless you give up your money for an ideal, you'll opt for home ownership every time. A beautiful garden, home insurance, a financial safety net, a personal code of values, a good accountant.

Moon in Gemini

"The time has come" the Walrus said, "to talk of many things: of shoes and ships and sealing wax, of cabbages and kings."

Lewis Carroll

Your emotional nature is likely to vacillate. Quick-witted, resourceful, with the ability to come up with solutions to practical problems through rational analysis. Good at talking, always on the phone. Great deal of restlessness. Frequent short journeys and change of scene. Nervous and fidgety. Good at thinking up solutions to problems. Longing for knowledge. Spread themselves too thin and scatter forces.

You need people, books and magazines, radio and TV, pens and paper, a mobile telephone, variety, change, talk and opinion-sharing. Everything in the Moon in Gemini house leads back to the telephone.

Moon in Cancer

"I weep for you," the Walrus said, "I deeply sympathise."
                                                                Lewis Carroll
The eldest oyster winked his eye and shook his heavy head — meaning to say he did not choose to leave the oyster bed.
                                                                Lewis Carroll

Strongly emotional. Can sense the moods of others. Good home-makers and often fond of babies. Domestic security and marriage important for your well-being. Very sensitive to atmosphere. Tend to brood when hurt. Make good homemakers, parents and cooks. Everything experienced is held in feeling memory. Conservative. Can be psychic.

You need security, your own home, a family, or substitute family, a sense of place, privacy, female friends, trees, something to nurture or care for. Your home is the centre of everything you need. You want a signed document to say that the place is yours, above all other things, as the insecurity of renting is not really your ideal. Peaceful surroundings, or a door that slams on the outside world, are very important.

Many of you are enthusiastic cooks, or natural entertainers and have a fine appreciation of good food. Some of you may even make a career out of it. A strong Moon or Cancer emphasis in a horoscope usually describes a natural cook.

Moon in Leo

"Always star in your own movie."   *Anon*

"Everyone has a right to my opinion."   *Anon*

You will have a flair for the dramatics and can be quite proud. Often in the spotlight. Need romance and affection. Inclined to be stubborn. Always striving for improvement. Much vital force and courage. Extremely susceptible to flattery. Want your own way and will do your best to get it. Money more important to you than you might think. Keen and enthusiastic interest in life.

You need the spotlight, special treatment, luxury, authority, loyalty, a leading role, 5 star accommodation and first class tickets.

Your home is designed for parties, children or creativity or perhaps all three. Leo Moon homes always contain something grand, impressive, rare or expensive. You are house proud and really need a palace or a castle.

Moon in Virgo

"I have measured out my life with coffee spoons."
                                                                   T S Eliot

"It's the little things that bother us – we can dodge an elephant but not a fly."
                                                                   T S Eliot

Exacting and hardworking with a practical nature. Great regard for neatness and cleanliness. Particular about food and diet. Can be rather shy and retiring, preferring to work quietly behind the scenes, and happy to serve as a dedicated and thorough worker. Curious about work and welfare.

Reserved in expression. Very critical and analytical. Not necessarily very loving. Can be cranky and fussy about minor details. Very proper and conservative.

Likes pure food, without additives or toxins, white sheets, lead-free petrol, order and organisation, books, pens and paper, a doctor or health adviser.

You create order out of clutter. You know exactly where everything goes, and enjoy sorting it all out. You may develop an interest in health and healing, or a strong connection to your own body. Your experiences with illness, or more serious crises within your body, will be turning points in your life, because they bring the Virgo side into sharp focus.

Moon in Libra
"I'm giving you a definite maybe." *Anon*

"It isn't much fun for one, but two can stick together," says Pooh.
A A Milne

Strong reactions to the attitudes of others. Constant argument can make you ill. Charm and elegance in your personal appearance adds to your emotional well-being. Courteous and gracious to everyone as your self-esteem is largely dependent on the approval of others. Dislike coarseness and vulgarity. You are very gentle, ambitious, but dependent too. Need to be honest with yourself as well as with others.

You need peace, harmony and cooperation, a place for everything that is easy on the eye and above all else loving relationships. With Moon in Libra your home tends to be a setting for your social life. Appearances will generally be important and you may spend a long time selecting the colours, shapes and textures you prefer.

Moon in Scorpio
"What does not destroy me makes me stronger."
Nietsche

"The only way to get rid of temptation is to yield to it."
Oscar Wilde

Do not like defeat or interference from others. Will not accept people or things at face value. Can be courageous and firm. Take personal matters very seriously. Have definite motives for your actions. Very sensual nature with a strong pursuit of personal pleasures. You do not easily forgive or forget personal affronts. Can be stubborn and unyielding. Impatient and moody, easily hurt and can be jealous. Greatest need: to learn to forgive and forget. Strong physically. Needs to achieve an optimistic attitude toward life.

You need intensity, passion, dramatic and powerful music, emotional purges, mystery, secrets, sexuality with depth, a walk on the wild side, mutual obsession, privacy.

Moon in Sagittarius
"Climb high, climb far, your goal the sky, your aim the star."
Anon

"He wants to tie me and narrow me down but I want to expand by being in all horizons."
Stadler

Have an idealistic nature. Fond of travel. Move house a lot. Appear very optimistic, cheerful, adventurous and curious about the world, with a love of travel and meeting new people. Like to speak out freely about your thoughts and ideas. Tendency to over-indulge partners. Wants to feel free to roam. Not apt to have many close friends, but many acquaintances. Needs to learn to think before speaking.

You need wide open spaces, freedom to come and go, weekend getaways, overseas hauls, a belief system or sense of meaning, people who share your sense of humour, family or friends who make you laugh out loud.

You definitely need a room with a view and can become edgy if you feel too locked in. Bits and pieces from your travels end up in drawers and on shelves. You're optimistic and like taking gambles.

Moon in Capricorn
"To have what we want is riches, but to be able to do without is power."
George McDonald

"The secret of success is constancy to purpose."
Disraeli

Reserved and cautious nature. Good for business. Ambitious and hard working. Financial security very important. Great drive for success especially in the outer world. Often late bloomers, with success finally being achieved as a result of the many lessons learned during the long climb to the top. There is an emotional need to be organised and get the job done. Wants to win recognition as an important and powerful person. Not very emotional. Parental influence very strong.

You need people who are as organised as you are, a feeling of control at home and at work, friends or contacts in high places.

At heart, you're a home owner, not a renter. You need firm foundations, and the prospect of throwing everything into a removal truck every few years makes you depressed. You like good, solid construction and like it if you can see the plans. You like a workspace at home, too, and because you so often bring things home with you, will develop one part of your living space as a kind of floating desk or office.

Moon in Aquarius
"When you cease to make a contribution you begin to die."
Eleanor Roosevelt

"If this is coffee, I want tea. But if this is tea then I wish for coffee."
Anon

Sympathises with the needs of humanity at large. Will be friendly to all in an impersonal way. Seeks freedom of emotional and intellectual expression within relationships. Like to use their home for friendly discussions. May have unusual or nonconformist marriages. Not very emotional. Feelings are cramped and limited, and do not operate freely.

You need a room of your own, freedom, strange hobbies, your funny little ways, independence, mad clothes.

You have the most peculiar domestic set-up in the zodiac. Aquarius Moon homes which appear to be quite normal are based around something very…slightly…odd. It's hard to generalise about your house or flat, because this sign is so intensely individual. However – whatever your friends or family have, you don't want. Whatever the home and lifestyle shows tell you to do, you won't. The basic rule with the Aquarian home is that you need lots of space to yourself, and freedom to come and go.

Moon in Pisces
"I can't figure out where I leave off and everyone else begins."
Anon

"This is serious" said Pooh, "I must have an escape."
A A Milne

Romantic and sentimental. Tends to daydream. Moods of your surroundings affect you a great deal. Do not like to be alone for long. Strong psychic tendencies. Vivid imagination and often poetically, musically or artistically gifted. Kind, sympathetic and often love music.

You may have books on spiritual matters on the shelves in your home. Other books may reflect your favourite escapist interests. The Pisces Moon home is usually decorated in an inspired and imaginative way. If you can, you'll live near water, or have a pool or pond. All creatures great and small – in the garden, or indoors, will make a difference to you.

Your Pisces side probably found a place to breathe in your childhood, above all other times in your life. At an age when fairy tales are read aloud, picture books seem true, pets are cared for and imaginary friends made up, Pisces-influenced children seem quite well catered for.

Moon in Houses

1st House

You have an emotional need for personal recognition which makes you over eager to please. Then there is resentment if you are not appreciated. Apt to give too much for too little. Strong tie to mother. Needs to learn not to react to life through the emotions. Your identity tends to be influenced by others. You can be changeable and moody in response to your environment and you may lack a clear sense of direction and purpose. Other people are likely to become involved in your personal affairs.

2nd House

A strong need for financial security in order to make a stable home and family situation. Good business ability, especially to do with food, home and property. Your emotional well-being depends on material comforts. If the Moon is in a Fixed sign there will be a strong ability to make and hold onto money. Changing conditions in finances. Often makes money through the public. Shrewd and acquisitive.

3rd House

Your thinking is strongly governed by your emotions. There is an insatiable curiosity and you are constantly on the move. You may be prone to daydreaming. You soon tire of monotonous routine. Good for teaching. Can easily become involved with neighbours and people close by. Emotional type of mind. Sensitive and imaginative. Absorbs through listening to others. Easily swayed by the environment.

4th House

You cannot be happy without a meaningful home life. Family relationships will affect your whole emotional outlook. Good at cooking and housekeeping. In business can excel in goods used in the home, food and property. Parents, especially the mother, represent a strong influence. If well situated, financial prospects are likely to be better in the second half of life. Apt to insulate yourself from reality. Love of home very strong. Inner desire for peace but has to go beyond the personality to find it.

5th House

Your romantic attachments and pleasure will be heavily influenced by your emotions. Fond of enterprises and theatres. Very fertile if in a Water sign. Your family may interfere in your romantic affairs. Your affections may be changeable or capricious if there is emotional instability. Fond of children and may like a flutter. Constant search for pleasure. Has to learn how to cultivate the will. Desires attention because of a need to feel important. Great deal of charm. Strongly emotional where affections are concerned.

6th House

Your emotions may affect your health. Emotional stress can have a positive or negative effect on work and business relationships. You could change the type of work you do frequently. Diet and nutrition will be important. Fond of pets. Skilful in food preparation. Your emotional state will affect your work. Often have a delicate constitution. Need to watch your health. Should not eat when overtired or emotionally disturbed.

7th House

A tendency to marry for emotional and domestic security rather than for purely romantic reasons. Your family may influence your marriage. Could have lots of dealings with the general public. Will seek emotional fulfilment through relationships. Very sensitive and responsive to the needs of others. Wants mothering rather than a mate. Partner sensitive and moody. Changes in feelings where partnerships are concerned.

8th House

Intense emotional reactions and strong psychic sensitivity. Can be too vulnerable. Very sensitive to social currents and social demands. Must learn to sacrifice feelings and learn to live impersonally. Affection means more than sex. Concerned with insurance, inheritance and taxes. You will wish to share your thoughts and feelings with a close partner. You have a highly developed psychic sensitivity and an awareness of invisible forces that might lead to an interest in the occult.

9th House

Deep emotional attachment to religious, social and ethnic values. Will have many varied experiences that enable the personality to build a philosophy of life. Dreams and visions can be of great significance. Long journeys and foreign interests. You will recognise the need for strong moral values in family life. This is the house of higher mind, of reason and understanding. Could make your home abroad.

10th House

You have the need to achieve prominence and recognition by your own efforts. What others think is very important. Feelings often dominated by the desire for achievement. Highly self-protective. Many changes in career. Cannot live for self. Must make social usefulness primary goal. Mother figure could be a big influence. May end up with a job in public life, possibly politics. Proud of family and their achievements. May come from a family of high social standing and inherited ambition.

11th House

You will have a powerful emotional need for friends and group activities. Many friendships with the opposite sex will be of a purely platonic nature. Easy to make friends, but must guard against superficiality. Your goals and objectives fluctuate with your moods. You need companionship without ties for your emotional well being. Your homes are sometimes used for discussion groups.

12th House

You will be strongly affected by past experiences and have psychic interest. Very active subconscious, open to the feelings and instincts of others. Extreme emotional sensitivity can result in shyness and easily hurt feelings. Hypnosis can be a danger to you. You may be involved in clandestine love affairs. You are highly psychic and intuitive.

Mercury in Signs and Houses

Aries
Quick-thinking, outspoken, and the ability to produce original ideas. You like competitive argument and debate. You get impatient with opposition and delays so that to avoid a lengthy debate you will make decisions. Good motto for you: "where angels fear to tread."
Impatient, enjoys arguing a point, debating.

Communication style is assertive, your voice is strong. Writing out your emotions can be a great way of dealing with your anger.

Taurus
A practical steady mind which needs time to assimilate facts. Shrewd in business, but may be slow to form opinions, but once having done so, you will be difficult to influence. Generally cheerful and able to appreciate art and beauty. You have great powers of concentration, enabling you to shut out or ignore anything that might distract you from the object of your focus.

You are practical, sensible and methodical. You take your time and prefer to go for the hard facts. You do well in the Venus-ruled subjects like art, music, business, economics.

Gemini
An inventive and lively mind. You may give the impression of being well informed, but may only have a superficial grasp of a subject. Good and persistent talker, sometimes lacking in emotion. More concerned with facts than attitudes. Clarity of expression. Highly sensitive nervous system.

Very intelligent, good at English, likes debating, chatty, witty.

Cancer
Keen memory and powerful imagination which should have some creative outlet. Strong tendency to live in the past and to harbour resentment. Usually extremely kind and thoughtful. Highly susceptible to attitudes and opinions of those around you. Much of your thinking is centred around your home and family.

You tend to form study habits – both good and bad. You like subjects about people, first and foremost: the humanities or people-related sciences will appeal most.

Leo
You have a strong will and fixed opinions. Thoughts are expressed optimistically and in a kind-hearted way. Good organising ability. Capable of focused concentration. Your mental self-confidence makes you positive in tackling and resolving problems. You have a strong desire to be regarded as an expert in your chosen field. Lots of ambition, but can be lazy.

Virgo
You have an analytical mind and great practical reasoning ability. You require accuracy that may appear trivial to others. You appreciate orderly surroundings and efficiency around you. Very intellectual and discriminating. Good at painstaking research. Meticulous but could become obsessional.

Literate, good with details, modest, intelligent, you pick up on your teachers' mistakes.

Libra
You have an intense curiosity about human relationships. You are easy to communicate with because of your interest in other people and their ideas. Good reasoning powers and the ability to see both sides of the question. Slow to make decisions, tending to wait and see. Very strong sense of justice. You are highly sensitive to the odours, personal appearance and mannerisms of other people.

Gentle and considerate in communication, you can be stern where principles are involved.

Scorpio
You have an intuitive mind and are capable of profound insights. Your mind is so sharp it can cut straight through muddle or distractions to the kernel of truth. Able to solve difficult problems. Very conscious of the darker side of life. You do not mince your words and you say exactly what you mean or will keep silent. Must watch tendency to pass judgment.

Penetrating research is your trademark. You like subjects which revolve around human passion and survival. Everything from literature to psychology – or head straight for the serious money subjects.

Sagittarius
You have a constant need to widen your intellectual horizons. Generally broadminded. You demand the right to voice your opinion. Mental freedom is essential to you. Possibly an aptitude for foreign languages. You are concerned with ideas rather than facts and are often insightful in your understanding of social forces and the subsequent unfolding of events.

At times, there is a preoccupation with distant goals and lofty ideals, which can make you oblivious to what is going on under your nose.

Capricorn
A rational serious mind that can be cool and calculating. May have scientific and mathematical ability. Sound grasp

of logic. Practical, ambitious, shrewd and organised. You are patient and disciplined and have good management abilities. Can be manipulative. Not especially optimistic. Realistic rather than idealistic.

You work extremely hard and like subjects where there is a right answer and a wrong answer. You can procrastinate, but you're shrewd, too. Having Mercury in Capricorn puts you on a learning curve. Often you gain strength from hardship. With this placement of Mercury, you are in the unique position of being able to use your hard-won experience to fuel something bigger and altogether better for yourself.

Aquarius
An original, inventive mind with good intuition. Your mind is totally open to new experiences. Thoughts are expressed in a friendly, kindly manner. There can be a special appreciation of astrology, astronomy, new technology. Unbiased and objective. Truth must come first and you will have little concern with tradition. Due to your objectivity, very little surprises you and you readily accept what others might find incomprehensible.

You are subject to flashes of brilliance, good with computers, not good with stuffy, boring or overly bossy teachers.

Pisces
A flexible, highly sensitive and easily impressionable mind. Forgetfulness and absentmindedness may alternate with deep intuitive insight. A vivid imagination and the ability to visualise thoughts and memories. Sympathetic to those in

need, but at times your emotions are too easily played upon. Your extreme sensitivity can result in great literary, artistic and visionary abilities.

You are imaginative, vague with facts and figures, artistic, brilliant at mimicking teachers or other kids, and have an ability to soak up favourite subjects without being conscious of it.

Mercury in Houses

1st House

Usually more than average intelligence. Curious and inquiring outlook on life. Very little escapes your attention. You are aware of everything happening in your environment. Your actions and self-expression are based on logic and reason. Willpower and mental initiative are the hallmarks of Mercury in this position. Good writers, journalists, scientists, researchers and scholars because of your intelligence and innate ability for self-expression.

2nd House

Excellent business ability and good bargaining powers. Your primary preoccupation will be with business, money, and that which produces practical and concrete results. An interest in finance could lead to a career as a persuasive financial adviser. Economists, entrepreneurs, business advisors and corporate planners often have this placement of Mercury. May earn money using communication skills e.g. writing, sales, media.

3rd House

Good intellectual ability. Interest in all forms of communication. Good writer or speaker. Strong ability in communication in any variety of forms, with much mental ability and originality. Adept at finding practical solutions to problems. You need constant mental stimulation and are apt to have an itch to be on the road. Curious about everything. Good position for teachers, journalists.

4th House

Likely to study or do mental activity in the home. Shows forethought and rational attitude to family matters. Intellectual disputes possibly with members of your family. The home is more than likely to be the centre of educational activity as well as the place of work. Your home may have a large library, and you may spend much time with your family in educational pursuits. Often many changes of residence and worry about domestic affairs. Need to learn to relax and not let the inconsequential details worry you.

5th House

Powerful mind. Good at expressing yourself. Romantic attachments must be mentally stimulating. Confident, broadminded and good at giving orders but may leave an impression of arrogance. Good position for teachers. Great position for writers in general. Often romantically attracted to those they find intellectually exciting and stimulating.

6th House

Excellent placing for those who organise other people's work. Interest in alternative medicine. Methodical and efficient in handling details. Good for medicine and engineering. You will not tolerate disorder in your work. You are particularly sensitive to any disorder or chaos in your environment. Concern with duty, work, personal hygiene and appearance.

7th House

You are concerned with other people's opinions and views. A lively attitude towards marriage and business partnerships. Partner must be intellectually stimulating. Need for intellectual rapport. May look for a younger partner. Make a good counsellor or in a job where diplomacy is required. Skilled in public communication and often successful in law, public relations and sales. This can indicate marriage with an employee, coworker or even a relative.

8th House

Strong penetrating mind. Intense mental activity, especially about other people's finances and deep subjects such as birth, death, rebirth, sex. May have interests in insurance, inheritance and marriage guidance. Your job may require you to keep things highly confidential. You thrive on mystery and intrigue and are particularly gifted in uncovering secrets and exposing the hidden motivations of others.

9th House

Emphasis on in-depth study and there can be a flair for languages. Broadminded and free thinking. Curious about higher education. Love to travel to faraway places. Make good teachers or preachers and are interested in how the law works. Decisions are based on ethical and moral considerations as well as practical ones. Prophetic insight into the nature of things to come.

10th House

The career must be intellectually stimulating, otherwise restlessness can inhibit progress. A career in the field of communication would be sought. Politically astute, able to communicate effectively with the public, and have considerable executive ability. Serious, deep-thinking and well-organised mind. Capable of making deliberate plans and achieving specific goals. Very dependable.

11th House

You will be keen to exchange all kinds of ideas with friends and you have the ability to think originally. Very good at organising and you will have strong humanitarian ideals and goals. Compassionate and insightful of the broader social issues. Dearest hopes and wishes may be about writing and teaching. A love of truth, impartiality and the ability to judge objectively.

12th House

Thinking is strongly influenced by unconscious memories and habits rooted in past experiences. Conclusions and decisions are often based on feelings and impressions rather than on logic. Might be quite shy and hesitate to say what you think for fear of hurting other peoples' feelings. Communicates with disadvantaged people e.g. as a prison visitor, therapist etc. May have secrets that must be kept hidden. Good intuitive powers.

Venus in Signs and Houses

Aries
You confidently pursue the objects of your desire. You can be competitive in seeking the attention and affection of others. Interested in finding new ways of enjoyment. Your outgoing personality helps you to be the life and soul of the party. Love at first sight. Need excitement in your relationships and a lot of personal attention. May be inconsiderate of others without being aware of it. The lesson needed with this placement is the ability to put yourself in the other person's shoes.

Taurus
Loyalty and steadfastness may be coupled with jealousy if emotional security is in any way threatened. Sensual and tactile. Demonstrative and affectionate as well as passionate and extremely possessive. You enjoy physical contact with your loved ones as well as comfort, luxury, good food and nice surroundings. Can give constant

lasting affection. Kind and pleasant. Appreciate good manners. Good taste and make good sculptors, painters, antique dealers and art collectors.

Gemini
A strong desire for varied experience and an innate curiosity about people. You seek variety in your love and social life. Great charm, wit and expressiveness. An entertaining companion, but not one to be taken too seriously. Hard for them to decide on one love when there are so many from which to choose. Often two important loves in life, though not always at the same time. You are not naturally predisposed to settling down in a steady relationship, although you are capable of sustained devotion. Given your wit and conversational abilities, you are attracted to agile minds and strong intellects. Dislikes coarse behaviour.

Cancer
Deep sensitivity where romantic feelings are concerned, along with a strong desire for both emotional and financial security. Gentle, receptive, changeable and forever seeking security. The basic need is security, either in persons or possessions. Your extreme sensitivity can make you easily hurt, and your moods can be fluctuating and unpredictable. You require open demonstrations of affection in order to feel loved and secure. Always like to help others especially if they are in trouble. Like to mother others.

Leo
Ardent and constant in love. Born romantics, you love courtships that are dramatic and exciting. You are warmhearted, outgoing, and affectionate and are likely to

have a fondness for children. You are deeply loyal to those you choose as worthy of your royal affection and you tend to be proud of your partner, with a desire to show them off and put them on a pedestal. Dramatises emotional experience to the hilt. Very attractive. Colourful personality.

Virgo
You tend to analyse emotions and be highly critical of loved ones. You often seek partners with whom you can share your work and intellectual pursuits. However, Venus in this sign can indicate those who remain single due to their highly critical and exacting standards for a mate. You are capable of being very sympathetic, with a nurturing instinct which makes you skilled at tending to the sick. You may make sexual conquests in order to give you confidence. Strong desire to serve. Inclined to put off marriage because they see so many imperfections. Harmonious in their work.

Libra
Marriage and harmonious social relationships are of paramount importance to you. Refined and artistic. Keen sense of colour. Cannot function in a discordant atmosphere without their health being affected. You have a strong desire to please and a deep consideration for others, along with a sense of justice and fairness in all of your relationships. Although romantic and affectionate, like all Air signs, you seek mental stimulation in a partner. Disagreements are very distasteful to you and can make you ill if you are overly exposed to them. Often gifted musically. Able to make money by pleasing and helping others.

Scorpio

Your emotions and sexual desires are strong and passionate, often jealous and secretive. You take much pride in sex and romance. There can be emotional extremes and excesses. You can be very passionate and yet extremely inhibited. If slighted or rejected, intense resentment and bitterness can be the result. The strong emotions and desires of Venus in this sign can make for a vivid personality, with an aura of mystery and intrigue. Once a relationship is broken it can never be restored.

Sagittarius

You are vivacious and sociable, outspoken and frank. Demonstrative and friendly in affection. Not always dependable where affections are concerned. Good intuition. This is the placement for a gambler and someone who is extravagant. You may gain emotional satisfaction through sports, outdoor activities and travel. Often, people with Venus in this sign marry foreigners or those of a different race. Freedom in your relationships is a necessity. You are extremely generous and may have short-lived romances.

Capricorn

Wealth and material status are necessary for emotional security. Reserved and dignified, you dislike overt, public displays of emotion and affection. There is a fear of giving too much of yourself, and a desire to shield yourself from hurt. Although not openly demonstrative in your affections, you are loyal and steadfast to your loved ones. You may seek an older partner. You like to help friends and partners get ahead.

Aquarius

Your romantic partner must be a friend as well as a lover and understand the Aquarian need for freedom, variety and mental stimulation. You dislike jealousy and possessiveness. Romantic attractions can be sudden and casual as opposed to stable and lasting. Intellectual stimulation is important in a romantic partner, and you are often attracted to eccentric types. You are capable of sustained and dedicated loyalty to someone you truly love and admire.

Pisces

The love principle reaches its highest manifestation on the evolutionary scale of the zodiac with this position. The experience and knowledge of having passed through all the signs of the zodiac enable the soul to identify and sympathise with all of humanity. You are sensitive and romantic. You marry for love and love only. You require clear and demonstrative expressions of love and affection in order not to feel lonely and unappreciated. You have an innate ability for inspired artistic expression.

Venus in Houses

1st House

You have personal grace, pleasant manners, and a friendly disposition. This placement is especially beneficial to women, for it bestows physical beauty. You are fond of anything that enhances your personal appearance, from fine clothes to expensive hairdos. Your ability to mix well socially provides you with both business and romantic opportunities.

2nd House

This indicates a love of wealth and all the things that money can buy, including social status. You may seek romantic and marriage partners who are wealthy and able to provide material comforts and luxuries. You are talented in matters of business, especially those involving the arts or beauty. You might be extravagant when entertaining.

3rd House

A strong interest in artistic and cultural pursuits, with a special love of literature and poetry. Communication skills, especially speech and writing, are well developed. You have a tendency to intellectually analyse both your romantic and social relationships. You communicate well with your partners and friends and have good relationships with those around you.

4th House

This placement denotes a strong attachment to the home, where you prefer to entertain romantic partners and friends in a warm and intimate domestic environment. You are likely to be close with your parents, through whom much happiness, as well as inheritance, can come. Venus in the 4th House holds the promise of being surrounded by beauty and comfort in old age.

5th House

This shows a romantic nature and a love of pleasure and life in general. You tend to be popular and a lover of, and talented in, the performing arts. You are very pleasure-oriented with a sunny outlook on life. You are likely to have many romantic opportunities and be very popular. There is often a love of children and if you have children, they may be very beautiful and artistic.

6th House

Friendships and romance are more than likely to come about through work. Working conditions and relationships tend to be pleasant and harmonious. You are likely to have a love of beautiful clothing and often ability in dressmaking and fashion design. Although not necessarily robust, your health tends to be good and often improves with marriage. You will seek to be of service to your loved ones.

7th House

Marriage and close friendships are important. Marriage is sought in the name of romantic fulfilment, and if Venus is well aspected, the marriage will be happy and harmonious. The 7th House Venus openly expresses love and consequently receives it in return. You tend to be very popular because of your pleasant demeanour and consideration for others.

8th House

This placement often indicates financial gain through marriage and partnerships. This can lead to an inheritance, unless Venus is afflicted, in which case, marriage can be motivated more by financial gain than love, or there can be an overemphasis on sex and sensuality. You have a very sensuous nature with intense emotions. Loyalty is essential on both sides of the relationship.

9th House

There is a basic love of philosophy, art, religion and travel. Marriage partners and friends are generally met through universities and religious groups, as well as through travel to foreign countries. You have strong ideals regarding love and may attempt to convert your loved ones to your own beliefs. Generally, you will be well educated with a strong interest in artistic and cultural history.

10th House

There is both social and artistic ambition, and if you do possess artistic talent, there is a strong likelihood of achieving recognition and success. Marriage will probably be sought with someone who can bestow wealth and status. Relationships with employers will generally be good, and Venus in this house grants success in dealings with the opposite sex, who will help in advancing your career.

11th House

Friendships and other relationships resulting from group activities are indicated by this placement. Kindness shown will mean kindness received, adding greatly to the likeliness of hopes and ambitions being realised. Many friendships will be made with members of the opposite sex. Friends can become romantic partners, and romantic partners, friends.

12th House

You love quiet and solitude, and your relationships will tend to be secretive or at least of a highly private nature. This also applies to love affairs. Your shyness can result in loneliness and unrequited love. Artistic inspiration can come from being deeply attuned to the unconscious mind, and you are highly sympathetic and compassionate toward others.

Mars in Signs and Houses

Aries
This shows uncontainable energy that must find an outlet in which to channel its intense initiative, courage and impulsiveness. There is a strong drive to get things done, with a great desire to be first. Staying power and sustained enthusiasm, however, may be lacking, so that projects are not seen through to their conclusion. You can be headstrong and very independent with little to no tolerance for opposition or interference. Lots of physical stamina.

Taurus
This produces a strong desire for money and material possessions, with much energy and focus channelled into the practical means for acquiring them. You may be slow to act, but have great determination and perseverance once action is taken. You are gifted with patience and precision, and you may be very good with your hands to create objects of beauty and solidity. Although usually peaceful, if pushed beyond your patience, you can be a strong fighter.

Gemini
You have a highly active and critical mind, with a love of debate and mental contest. You may also have some mechanical or manual skills. Restlessness is characteristic of this position, implying that there may be many changes of occupation or working at more than one job at the same time. Ingenuity and resourcefulness are typical characteristics. You make good reporters and journalists.

Mercury, the ruler of Gemini, was the Italian god of commerce and your Geminian side is adept at either finding bargains, or running a sales pitch.

Cancer
There is a strong tendency for you to be intensely emotional. Moodiness and anger can be the cause of discord and strife in domestic relationships. Suppressed emotions can lead to psychological ailments, along with ulcers and other stomach problems. You have a strong desire to dominate the domestic scene and to own or build your own home, which also makes you very handy and possibly a good carpenter. You may have challenges with parents in early life. You will tell your family and friends what's best for them.

You burn off energy doing housework, gardening or home repairs. You like outdoor pursuits and a bath afterwards!

Leo
This bestows great energy, willpower, creativity and charisma, and much of it will probably be expressed dramatically through the arts. Proud and high-spirited, you have a strong desire to be in the forefront or the limelight.

You may have strong and unswerving beliefs, which can inspire opposition from others. Your desires are fixed and passionate, which means you are ardent in love, but can also be possessive. There is a very strong attraction to the opposite sex. You do things in a big way.

Virgo
Mars here indicates great skill and energy, precision, and methodology in whatever work you do. Your actions are systematically planned and carefully executed. Virgo is the sign of health, and Mars rules sharp instruments, so that quite often surgeons have Mars in this sign. There is a strong tendency toward perfectionism, which might make you quite fastidious. You have an active intellect and are always on the lookout for interesting new things.

Libra
Libra gives grace and refinement to the otherwise selfish and aggressive tendencies of Mars, and their combined energies gives you a strong urge for balanced action within a social context. You have a strong desire to be noticed and appreciated by others. Although Mars is here softened and tempered by Venus, you become very angry when your sense of justice is violated. You may seek an aggressive and energetic partner.

Scorpio
This confers powerful desires and emotions along with relentless courage and drive. It can represent the heights of spiritual development and achievement or the lowest depths of moral degradation. With steadfast courage, determination, and resourcefulness, Mars in Scorpio will rise to the occasion in the face of adversity. You can be

uncompromising, with an all-or-nothing attitude, and prone to making either devoted friends or enemies in your dealings with others. You are at your best in a crisis.

Sagittarius
There is a love of sports and outdoor activities. You desire to be a leader in law, religion, philosophy or education, but with a tendency to follow traditional paths. Your love of adventure and desire to attain far-reaching goals can cause you to scatter your energies and neglect the practical matters of your immediate surroundings. Your attitudes are direct and open and you are a natural teacher.

You love most outdoor activities. You are a natural crusader and when you are on the attack or defence, will take a morally superior, crusading stance. You'll lean hard on a belief system, philosophy or ideology to back up your point.

Capricorn
You have a great capacity for hard work and are patient and persevering. You are ambitious and have a strong sense of responsibility and discipline. Your actions are carefully calculated to achieve concrete results – usually the acquisition of money and power. Mars in this sign confers a high degree of self-control along with great pride in doing a job well. You expect the same discipline and obedience from those under you.

Aquarius
Mars in Aquarius demands absolute personal freedom to pursue unconventional courses of action, often having to do with reform of the status quo. You do not work well

under authoritarian direction. For you, teamwork, rather than individual effort, is far more likely to achieve results, which can be considerable, especially in the fields of science and humanitarian endeavours. You must be allowed to do things your own way and learn by your own mistakes.

Pisces
Excess emotional sensitivity can stand in the way of your self-confidence. You may act secretively in order to avoid direct confrontation with your opposition. There is a strong need for periods of quiet and solitude in order for you to come to terms with your feelings and rejuvenate your energies. If Mars is well aspected, it can enhance artistic or musical expression and be beneficial for those who work in psychology. If afflicted, you may cry easily and manipulate others by requiring attention for physical and psychological problems.

Mars in Houses

1st House

You are likely to be robust, outgoing and have an abundance of energy and physical stamina. Ambitious and hardworking, you are capable of reaching great heights of achievement if your courage and strength are matched with intelligence and self-discipline. You insist on absolute freedom of action and will not tolerate any interference. You are not content to be a bystander in life.

2nd House

This points to the active pursuit of wealth and material possessions. You have good earning abilities, but may tend to deplete your resources through impulsive spending. You have a strong desire to own and run your own business rather than work for anyone else and are always out to prove your capacity to make money by surpassing the competition. Personal property is important to you and you will fight to protect it.

3rd House

You have a highly active and resourceful intellect, with the ability to think quickly in emergency situations. You tend to be intellectually assertive in order to both acquire and deliver information. Many newspaper reporters, for example, are likely to have this placement of Mars. You might be quick to jump to conclusions. You are direct in speech and would be successful in anything connected with communications.

4th House

This placement predisposes you to dominate the domestic scene and direct much energy toward the home in general, including the acquisition of property. There is often an inheritance of land or property from parents or relatives. A need for domestic harmony is important. If well aspected, it can indicate that you work hard to improve your surroundings, not only on the home front, but also in terms of environmental and ecological concerns. There is a tendency to have a strong constitution which you sustain into old age.

5th House

Love, pleasure, sex and romance are actively pursued. Leisure activities will be very important to you. If Mars is afflicted, you might find yourself involved in quarrels about sexual jealousy during courtship. This is often a placement for athletes, for it conveys a natural love of competitive sports of all kinds. It can also entail a fondness for working with children. There is an ability to become an excellent teacher who inspires enthusiasm and devotion in your students.

6th House

This makes for hard and energetic workers, with little to no patience for those who are lazy or apathetic. This position of Mars is often found in the horoscopes of mechanics, engineers, and surgeons. Great skill and precision is shown in work, with personal esteem being derived from a job well done. If Mars is afflicted, irritability, ill health, or job related injuries can result from overwork. Perfectionism and fussiness with details can lead to the neglect of major issues and concerns.

7th House

Mars here emphasises the importance of partnerships or working with the public. You will prefer to work and act with a partner, and much can be accomplished if Mars is well aspected. If Mars is afflicted, there will be disagreements with associates, conflict and possibly divorce, along with a tendency to compete rather than cooperate with others. There is a great involvement in all types of one-to-one relationships.

8th House

This is a powerful position for Mars. You have very strong desires and emotions, along with a powerful sex drive. You will have great energy and perseverance in accomplishing goals. There may well be an interest in the occult, psychic phenomena, and spiritualism. You may have a specific interest in joint finances. Actions are often carried out in secret, both for good and bad purposes.

9th House

There will be a strong interest in travel, sports, and social and philosophical issues and causes. You might be a passionate crusader in the name of your ideals and beliefs, expressing yourself in terms of action rather than with mere words. If Mars is well aspected, your broad understanding and concern for humanity can inspire genuine reform for the good of all. You are a seeker of adventure and experience, which often leads to travel to foreign countries.

10th House

There is a strong desire for power and fame. You are gifted with initiative and executive ability that enables you to achieve practical goals. Highly driven and competitive, you are likely to achieve fame or notoriety in your chosen field.

You have a strong drive to reach the top of your profession. This is a powerful placement for Mars as it is exalted here. You would make a good political leader.

11th House

Your overriding concern and focus are friendships and group activities. Often these friends and associates are instrumental in assisting you to achieve your business and professional goals. You will have an aptitude for new technology, especially computers; and a desire to improve conditions for everyone. If Mars is afflicted, disagreements and conflicts with friends are likely. There could be good mechanical ability and a gift for inventiveness.

12th House

Desires and actions are strongly influenced by the unconscious. You tend to be highly secretive about your desires, purposes and actions. You may also have secret sexual involvements. Many of your activities will be carried out in seclusion. You may work in a large institution in order to lose your personal identity. It is important to be open and honest about your anger.

Jupiter in Signs and Houses

Aries

This placement confers great abilities for leadership and innovation in art, education and other social, and cultural endeavours. Jupiter in this sign bestows great powers of creative and spiritual regeneration along with an acute understanding and respect for it. You have great energy and are inspired and inspiring, arousing those around you to confident and enthusiastic action. You have a positive and optimistic attitude.

Taurus
This indicates the ability to attract wealth, along with an awareness of the correct and beneficial use of money and material resources. Money and material goods are regarded as a form of energy that simply flows from one person to another for the good of all. You are concerned with enjoying the good things in life and have a strong desire to share the wealth you naturally accumulate as a matter of principle. You enjoy advising others about their finances.

Gemini
Here is found a broad understanding and love of philosophy. You are mentally and physically restless and are prone to much travel and delving into many areas of study. You have strong abilities in writing, teaching and lecturing. Social contact is very important to you and your mental restlessness makes you curious about people and situations. You are a multifaceted person with an acute understanding of social, political and historical trends.

Cancer
This often indicates a good family background, not necessarily of wealth or standing, but one in which moral and religious principles, kindness and generosity are instilled from an early age. You seek to establish a secure, comfortable and friendly home environment for yourself and your loved ones. You are kind and generous to family

and friends. You may have a strong maternal instinct and wish to mother everyone. You tend to be emotionally idealistic, with a true belief in human kindness and honesty.

Leo
You are blessed with abundant energy, strong constitution, optimism and self-confidence. Dignified and inspiring leaders, you are benevolent and generous, although you do demand admiration and appreciation in return. You like to do things on a lavish or opulent scale. With your warmth, generosity, and affection, your unselfishness can win the admiration and love of others, often enabling you to find fulfilment in romance. This position can give an aptitude for gambling and stock market speculation, along with business success in entertainment, the arts, sports and education.

Virgo
Here, honesty and integrity in work and business can make for congenial relationships with coworkers, employees and employers. You will probably find yourself in pleasant working conditions and you tend to be paid well for your services. You might be interested in charitable pursuits involving mental and physical health, hospitals and educational institutions. You zealously demand absolute integrity in every detail and are able to readily distinguish truth from error or falsity.

Libra
There is an overriding concern for justice and moral principles in partnerships, marriage, friendships and other close personal relationships. Marriage will tend to be based

on shared spiritual values and a sense of cooperation that go beyond sexual attraction. Your generosity and consideration of others means that you are popular and well liked. You deal well with the general public, making excellent mediators, psychologists, fundraisers, diplomats and peacemakers.

Scorpio
This strongly suggests dealings with joint or corporate finances, insurance, taxes, legacies and the like. You are prone to acquiring, as if by magic, secret information about the private lives of other people and can yourself have friendships based on hidden motivations. There is a chance of receiving inheritances as payback for favours rendered. You might have an interest in the occult and communication with the spirit world.

Sagittarius
This points to a love of philosophy, education, travel and foreign cultures. You have a strong need for a moral system of some kind that governs personal conduct, relationships and way of life. Jupiter is well placed here and there will be an interest about the nature of man's consciousness and the meaning of life. You like to teach about the experiences you have had. You have an innate respect for other belief systems and an almost prophetic insight into the future.

Capricorn
There will be a deep concern with the letter of the law rather than with its spirit. If well aspected, Jupiter in Capricorn can confer great integrity in moral conduct and business and political ethics, especially in relation to the

responsibilities of high office. You have a strong drive to attain power and status, which can be based on either personal ambition or an acute sense of social responsibility, or a combination of both. Great wealth is often attained as a result.

Aquarius
You insist on social and moral values that are impartial, democratic and universal. You are open to all of humanity without biases toward class, race or religion and are intolerant only of intolerance. Tolerance, acceptance, respect and cooperation are for you the essentials of any social order and interaction. Independent friendships are important to you. You will share your ideas with people from all walks of life.

Pisces
This confers emotional depth, understanding, and compassion along with mystical tendencies and deeply felt religious or spiritual convictions. There is the danger that others will take advantage of your sympathy and generosity, and it is often necessary for you to learn discrimination, and that others must, at a certain point, take responsibility for their own lives and learn their own life lessons. You have acute psychic abilities and an intuitive perception of spiritual realms.

Jupiter in Houses

1st House

This indicates an optimistic and sociable nature. You are honest, trustworthy, benevolent and amicable and tend to be very popular. Your optimism and confidence inspires the same in others. You are dignified in your bearing and manner, especially as you get older. Generally you are fortunate throughout your life. You appear to be blessed by some kind of divine protection or guardian angel, who often appears right at the 11th hour.

2nd House

There is substantial business ability and good fortune regarding money and property. Those with this placement of Jupiter often engage in businesses involving real estate, food, domestic products, fund-raising, publishing and travel. Other professional pursuits might be related to psychology, education, hospitals and other similar institutions. If afflicted, money is likely to disappear as fast as it appears. You must be careful of over spending.

3rd House

This makes for congenial relations with neighbours and people around you. You are optimistic and philosophical, with a strong intellectual interest in trends in social thought and communication, especially expressed in speech and writing. There is also a fondness of travel. You are interested in mental expansion. You have an inner vitality which puts you in contact with many favourable influences.

4th House

This shows good family relations and domestic comfort and security. You are likely to come from a family that is financially secure, with good standing in the community, and thus enjoy many social and economic benefits. There will be good fortune in your second half of life, with the likelihood of inheriting property from parents or relatives. If Jupiter is afflicted, family members may become burdens emotionally, or financially or both.

5th House

There is likely to be involvement with the arts, sports, education and all aspects of dealing with children. You would make a good teacher, counsellor, or advocate. This usually indicates good fortune and happiness in romance, often with someone of wealth or status. Business endeavours can often involve the stock market, investments, the arts, entertainment or education. Many movie and theatrical producers have this placement of Jupiter.

6th House

There is an active and dedicated interest in service, driven by a desire to serve others and contribute to society in a practical and constructive way. Work related to mental and physical healing can be fulfilling here, for you have an innate understanding of the mental and emotional states as they affect physical health. Usually you are well liked and respected in your work and enjoy good relations with coworkers, employees and employers.

7th House

Here there is openness, friendliness, along with a sound moral sense in relationships with others, often leading to good fortune through marriage and other partnerships. You have a strong sense of justice and are fair and honest in your dealings with others, and you expect the same in return. You may marry someone of wealth or social standing. Business partnerships usually prove fruitful, owing to good judgment in choosing associates. You will have abilities in law, public relations, sales, negotiation and mediation.

8th House

This indicates a strong chance of benefits through inheritance, insurance, and joint finances. You might be attracted to businesses involving taxes, corporate fundraising and insurance. You believe that fair play always pays off. You will have an interest in life after death and other matters pertaining to spiritualism and healing. Unless Jupiter is afflicted, you can look forward to a death in later life that is peaceful and brought about by natural causes.

9th House

You have an innate love of philosophy, religion or spiritual matters and higher education. You make an excellent teacher and might be associated with institutions of higher learning. Generally you are broadminded, learned and tolerant. This is an exceptionally favourable placement for Jupiter. Long journeys will give you great pleasure and help to expand your mind. You want to spread your experiences and ideas to everyone.

10th House

This placement indicates professional achievement, prominence and acclaim, usually in the latter part of life. You are a consummate professional, known for your personal standards of excellence. You have considerable professional ambition, along with honesty and reliability. You will derive great satisfaction with whatever you achieve. You get along easily with others and have a good sense of humour.

11th House

This achieves its goals through friendships and social relationships based on shared interests and concerns. Favours are rendered and returned, as you are kind, well-liked and tend to attract friends who are generous and helpful. A spirit of mutual cooperation and consideration enables you to successfully carry out large and constructive enterprises to the benefit of all. Business may relate to social organisations, science and inventions.

12th House

There is a need for seclusion, solitude, introspection and meditation in the search for life's spiritual truths. Intuition and mysticism tend to be prevalent with this placement. There is a deep empathy and sympathy for the less fortunate and humanity in general, and you gain emotional satisfaction from helping others. You are a natural peacemaker, with the ability to make friends out of enemies. Humility and sincerity are features of this position of Jupiter.

Saturn in Signs and Houses

Aries
You may be forced by circumstances to acquire initiative, patience and self-reliance in order to provide for the necessities of life. By being obliged to develop your own resources, you develop strength of will and character. Saturn represents the laws of cause and effect, the consequences of action, and Aries, the primary impulse to action. In Aries, a new cycle of experience is just beginning, and consequences are yet to be felt and their lessons learned. As a result, you may be lacking in sufficient awareness of social justice and the rights of others in terms of the effects of your actions. On the other hand, Saturn in Aries can provide resourcefulness, initiative, and creativity, enabling you to bring new concepts and innovations to your chosen field. The test of Saturn in this placement is that of self-centredness.

Taurus
You have a strong need for financial and emotional security. Material possessions, upon which your sense of security is often based, are only acquired through discipline and hard work. A well-aspected Saturn bestows patience, endurance, practicality, and an adherence to principles. You may be attracted to banking, business management and insurance as a career. You cannot be at peace if your finances are in chaos. You are very practical in business,

but also rather cautious. Great persistence and stamina. Saturn tests the power of ownership in this placement. There is a tendency to be over-possessive.

Gemini
You have a logical, well disciplined and practical mind. You have great reasoning ability to solve problems and express ideas verbally and in writing. You judge ideas according to their practicality and proven value. You like things to be clearly defined down to the last detail, especially with contracts and agreements. Honest communication and dependability are of utmost importance to you. You are disciplined in all forms of mental activity and may excel in science and mathematics or any work requiring concrete implementation or expression of ideas. The test of Saturn lies in learning to have faith and optimistic viewpoints in life as there is an inclination to be negative.

Cancer
This placement can cause repression of emotional expression and estrangement from family members, resulting in emotional and psychological isolation. Early relationships with parents and siblings may have been cold or austere. The need for respect for both the individual and the family is felt deeply by you, and you often hide your emotions in order to preserve your dignity. You may feel inhibited about expressing yourself freely. You will strive to create harmonious feelings in your own home. Ambitious and shrewd, with material things having great importance. Pyschic tendencies strong. The test of Saturn is the need to learn the value of responsibility and empathy.

Leo
This gives a strong desire for power and leadership. You may have an almost compulsive need to personally control your environment. You require the recognition and respect of others and can be very demanding of attention. Security is sought through autocratic means. Extremely strong willed. Can be reserved and cautious. Very often, parents with this placement are strict and severe disciplinarians with their children. Professionally you may be interested in education and business management, which could involve the entertainment industry. Saturn tests for true humility and lovingness in this placement.

Virgo
You are extremely practical, hardworking, and exacting in your concern for efficiency, detail, precision and accuracy. A tendency to worry about inconsequential details needs to be overcome. The lesson is to learn discrimination between what is important and what is not. You may be drawn to such fields as health and medicine, scientific research, and detailed record-keeping professions like accounting. You may appear to be austere owing to the weight and responsibility you feel about your work. It is important that you learn how to relax, develop a sense of humour and enjoy yourself once in a while.

Libra
This indicates a strong concern with the responsibilities and rules concerning contracts between people, both in marriage and business. Saturn in Libra recognises mutual agreement, cooperation, commitment, and justice are essential to creating enduring human relationships, whether it be marriage, business, or close friendships.

Since this placement of Saturn rules contracts, these agreements are often of a karmic nature, based on past debts and responsibilities. This may also indicate marriage later in life or marriage to someone with serious business or professional obligations. You may be attracted to a career in law or as a mediator. The test in this placement is the ability to relate to all living beings.

Scorpio
This indicates a heavy responsibility in dealing with financial affairs, especially the finances and property of others, which can include corporate resources, a partner's finances, taxes, inheritance, and insurance. You tend toward perfectionism in your work and can be a hard taskmaster both on yourself and others, with no patience for laziness or lack of diligence. Much energy and discipline will be exerted in the name of achieving practical goals. Responsibilities are taken on with a serious steadfastness. Persistence, thoroughness, and a grim determination are characteristic of this placement of Saturn. The will for power and authority is very strong, you will struggle hard to realise your ambitions whether the means is fair or foul, depending on how Saturn is aspected. The test of outgoing desire is found in this placement of Saturn. There is the ability to love greatly or hate bitterly. Not a weak character, but can be destructive.

Sagittarius
This placement indicates someone who has strict moral codes. You are probably intently serious in your pursuit of philosophy and higher education in your search for the truth and constructive values that guide personal behaviour. You have a fierce intellectual pride and a deep

need for the kind of intellectual, philosophical, or spiritual achievement that brings distinction and recognition. Your personal reputation is extremely important to you, and you have an acute fear of disapproval and criticism of any sort. This placement of Saturn involves the lesson of understanding. Physical exercise is very important as there can be a lack of circulation in the lower extremities.

Capricorn
Here there is a strong ambition to achieve worldly power, status and authority. You are possessed by a driving need to make significant achievements in your career. Whatever endeavours you undertake will have a practical purpose and reward. However, you are not a risk-taker. You will protect your security while pursuing your ambitions, gaining the prominence you desire without putting either in jeopardy. There is a tendency to be conservative in both business and politics and obedient to your superiors. When you do reach a position of power, you will take it upon yourself to teach others to help themselves. The test with this placement lies in the use of power.

Aquarius
This signifies a mind that is impersonal and scientific, with a paramount concern for the truth in all matters. You possess great powers of mental concentration. You are intellectually ambitious as well as original, often working hard to make some scientific breakthrough or discovery. You possess the ability to visualise form and structure, often of a geometrical nature, and are gifted mathematically. This confers an acute sense of justice and responsibility in relationships, making you loyal to both the

friends and groups with whom you work. The test of Saturn in Aquarius is that of responsibility.

Pisces
This is the karmic planet in the karmic sign. You have a tendency to become trapped in your memories of the past. A fearful and overactive imagination can create anxieties and neuroses of all types, imagining slights and problems where none actually exist, and it can become difficult to deal with the demands of the present. On the other hand, this placement can confer a deep emotional understanding, a strong sense of altruism, and the willingness to work hard in the name of helping the less fortunate. Humility and psychological insight into others, along with a profound spirituality, can be Saturn in Pisces' special gift. The test here is of severance – letting go and letting God.

Saturn in Houses

1st House

You are serious-minded and hardworking, accepting responsibility and tending to neither speak nor act without definite purpose. If Saturn is close to the Ascendant the birth has been a difficult one; the soul was reluctant to come in. You will work long and hard to achieve success and power. However, limitations on the fulfilment of your ambitions can cause a hidden hostility and resentment making you prone to covert scheming in order to take advantage of others. Shy and introverted. You need to cultivate self confidence and a sense of your own self worth as an individual. The lesson of Saturn in the 1st

House is to learn to love, trust, and cooperate with others. Then, success and fulfilment will be achieved.

2nd House

Great ambition and hard work to acquire money, material possessions and status are characteristic of this placement of Saturn. Generally you will have to work hard to achieve your goals, but you are shrewd in your business dealings and are able to store away your money. Caution and frugality, though, can result in stinginess, which can hinder business expansion and mean that opportunities could be lost. You need to learn to be more fluid in your business dealings, that to make money, money must also be spent and risks taken. You do not gain inner peace unless you have learned to share what you have with others. Real estate or anything to do with land will be a good investment. This house rules peace of mind and this depends on where your values lie.

3rd House

This gives patience and methodology to the thinking processes, and there is great mental discipline and practicality through which ideas are judged according to their useful application. Serious and penetrating type of mind. Capable of deep concentration. Keen sense of justice. Tendency to despondency needs to be overcome. Education may be interrupted, but you are an "eternal student" and will go on seeking knowledge all your life. This placement often indicates a slow and deliberate way of speaking, and scientific and mathematical abilities. You may be attracted to work in publishing, printing, and other communications media. You would make a good accountant, researcher, writer and teacher. You are careful with agreements and wary and thorough when it comes to signing contracts.

4th House

You may have had to take on heavy responsibilities from an early age and you may have had to struggle for domestic security. You will work very hard to provide for your home and family. Your professional and business interests may revolve around real estate, building, farming or the manufacture of domestic goods. Care must be taken in managing the home, property and inheritance. You may become a recluse in later life or be restricted to your home by force of circumstance. There can be gain through real estate or land. Often a strong mother complex and a tendency to cling to the past. Needs to get away from home. Appears independent but fears to leave home. Will be happier away from place of birth.

5th House

Self expression and creative ability can be inhibited. This can indicate heavy burdens and responsibilities concerning children. In a woman's chart, it can show difficulties in childbirth. Often children are denied. Not wise to adopt children with this placement of Saturn. More sorrow than joy would result. Psychological block where sex is concerned. Teaching or working with young people would be a constructive use of a 5th House Saturn. Romantic involvements may entail burdensome obligations, and you may be involved with older, mature partners. A well aspected Saturn in this house can bestow a desire for power and leadership through artistic self-expression. Business and politics can also provide creative outlets. You would make a good investor and stockbroker. Must learn to forget self and care about others.

6th House

Here heavy responsibilities are incurred through work or service. An ability to work hard and efficiently is indicated, with work taken very seriously and requiring some kind of specialised skill. There is also a serious attitude toward health and hygiene. You are inclined towards a career in medicine, science, engineering, and other fields that require skill and precision. A well aspected Saturn means that you will be respected by your employers, employees and coworkers. If afflicted, there can be low vitality as a result of overwork and worry, and work relationships can be strained and stressful. Can be a nagging person and get irritated far too easily. Work isn't as important as the attitude toward it.

7th House

This house corresponds to Libra, the sign in which Saturn is exalted, thus conferring a strong sense of justice and responsibility in all important relationships and transactions. There is a tendency to either marry later in life or marry a mature, serious-minded and career-oriented person. If Saturn is well aspected, the marriage will be stable and long-lasting. If afflicted, marriage and partnerships will be problematic. There is a separative tendency deep within that makes it difficult for you to relate to others. You must learn to cooperate with others. Marries for security rather than love. Extremely sensitive but tends to hide from the world. You are capable of working hard and responsibly in cooperation with others, upholding your side of all agreements. You are likely to have a keen interest in law and are skilled in formulating contracts and in business management.

8th House

Strong sensuality needs restraining. Lesson to learn where sexual attitudes and appetites are concerned. There is often too much or too little sex. Can be psychic. This indicates involvement with partners' resources and finances, and the subsequent responsibility this involvement naturally entails in terms of being accountable for other people's money and property. An afflicted Saturn can mean litigation, losses, and other troubles involving other people's money and property. Marriage may entail a financial burden, and there may be restrictions on fulfilling career ambitions due to lack of income or capital. If Saturn is well aspected, money can be made through skillful management of a partner's resources, and you can attain deep spiritual insight into the meaning of life's mysteries.

9th House

Saturn's best positions are in the 3rd and 9th Houses. The 3rd House steadies the conscious mind and the 9th House stabilises the superconscious faculties. This points to a serious interest in philosophy, and higher education, with a concern for their practical value in governing action and behaviour and contributing to the betterment and stability of society. Education, especially at some acclaimed institute of higher learning, will be sought for the status and professional advancement it can bring. Your moral standards will tend to be conservative, and you are extremely concerned with your moral reputation. If Saturn is afflicted, you can be narrow-minded, rigid, and authoritarian in your attitudes and views. You will seek and desire personal distinction through some achievement you gave gained through hard study.

10th House

Pride is the great danger here. A rise to the top followed by a fall. This only happens if the lesson of humility has not been learned. This house corresponds to Capricorn, which Saturn rules, so this strong placement indicates great ambition and an enormous drive to achieve professional status and success. This will become paramount after the age of twenty-nine. A well aspected Saturn means that hard work and integrity will bestow power, authority, and wealth, especially in later life. Farsighted organisational and managerial abilities are indicated. This is very favourable for politicians and executives. An afflicted Saturn can mean that obstacles, lack of opportunity, and just bad luck can stand in the way of achieving success. You will exercise caution concerning your principles, because your social standing is very important to you. Self-reliance and ambition strong. Often lack of father image in life.

11th House

Great care, consideration, and responsibility in relationships with others, both personal friendships and group associations, are indicative of Saturn in the 11th House. Important and influential individuals will be sought out as a means of advancing your career and status, and with friends you will enjoy an equal exchange of loyalty and good advice. Shared interests will provide opportunities to gain knowledge and grow intellectually. If Saturn is afflicted, you and your friends may use each other for personal gain. A well-aspected Saturn means that you hold a sense of equal justice for all in your friendships and group associations, from which everybody benefits. Often these friendships and associations are karmic in nature. There is a strong likelihood of friendships with older individuals who provide wisdom and guidance as well as opportunities for advancement. It will be hard to obtain goals and objectives but they can be attained if you are willing to be patient and to work hard. You have to earn everything with this position of Saturn. If it is done the rewards are great, and life gets better as it advances.

12th House

This often means recognition will be hard to obtain, unless Saturn is favourably aspected to the 10th House or its planetary ruler. You will probably spend much time in seclusion or working quietly behind the scenes. An afflicted Saturn here can impart loneliness and depression. There is a craving for solitude. A well-aspected Saturn in this house means that you can escape your psychological challenges by working vigorously and serving others in a constructive way that energises you and gives you a greater purpose. You will not like to acknowledge authority figures. Serve or suffer is the keynote here and you can choose which way you will take; but choose you must.

Uranus in Signs and Houses

Aries
Freedom of action is of paramount importance to you. Courageous, daring and resourceful, you have the potential to be a groundbreaking pioneer in science and social reform. Blunt and outspoken, this generation demands change and the adoption of new lifestyles. There is a spirit of adventure and the constant search for new experiences. You can be rebellious and you will want the freedom to act in your own way. Inventive ability is strong. Note the positions of Uranus and Mars, and the aspects between them to know how this position of Uranus will operate in the chart. If both planets are in harmony this can be someone who is a genius and has healing powers. It is the pioneering spirit backed by enough energy and individualism to bring new concepts and new ideas down to earth. Action is quick and impulsive. If Mars is afflicted to Uranus there is difficulty due to rebelliousness and compulsiveness.

Taurus
Taurus deals with the world of matter, and Uranus is not interested in material matters. It belongs to the intuitive and higher realms of thought. It is in the sign of its fall in Taurus. When Uranus went into Taurus the USA went off the gold standard. The banks were closed. The depression set in and the values inherent in materialism were challenged as never before in the USA's history.

Those born with this placement of Uranus have new and innovative ideas about the use of money and resources and often seek economic reform based on humanitarian principles. You are endowed with a strong sense of purpose and determination. If afflicted, you can be stubborn and unyielding. If well-aspected, it can bestow considerable artistic talents, especially in music.

Gemini
Though this position makes a nervous restless temperament, it is a good place for Uranus. The emphasis is on the mind and as Uranus is the higher octave of Mercury it steps up the ability of the mind to grasp new concepts and ideas quickly. Education is very important. When Uranus went into Gemini the whole emphasis on education changed. Many more people were able to go on to college and university.

The generation with Uranus in Gemini is gifted with brilliant and intuitive minds; they are the progenitors of new ways of thinking, pioneers in science, literature, education and communication. They can, however, be prone to extreme restlessness that can make it difficult for them to bring things to completion. Self-discipline is necessary for the concrete fruition of their ideas. Given their restlessness and curiosity, they tend to travel a great deal, meeting new people and discovering new ideas.

Cancer
During the time Uranus was in Cancer, books dealing with the subconscious began to appear. The irrational world of feeling began to be explored. The old fashioned mother who stayed in the home and reared her children all but disappeared. She wanted to be an individual in her own right.

You seek freedom and excitement through emotional expression and independence from the restrictions of family life and parental authority. You desire an egalitarian relationship with your parents and try to make your parents into friends. There may be an interest in communal living or in untraditional ideas of family.

Leo
Here the rebels have been born. Strong will and determination are the labels of these people. There is tremendous vitality and forcefulness. Leo rules gold and Uranus in Leo has disturbed the gold standard and the end is not yet in sight. Leo rules dictators and governments. Dictators came and went in these years. Uranus always upsets the status quo. New nations were born and went through the birth pains inherent in any birth into freedom.

You seek freedom in love and romance. You have untraditional ideas and morals about courtship and sex and may be advocates of free love. You are a born innovator, with strong willpower and creativity and are capable of developing new concepts in the arts, theatre and music. You refuse to conform to the standards of society, and instead create and live by your own rules. You can be stubborn and incapable of compromise with others and insist on going your own way at any cost. You like to encourage others to try out new ideas.

Virgo
Interest in natural means of maintaining health was strong in those born with Uranus in Virgo. The power of the mind in regard to healing the body was promulgated. The

civil rights movement is part of the effect of the Uranian change that began with Uranus in Virgo.

Many technological inventions were born during the period of Uranus in Virgo, that have revolutionsed business, industry and communications. This confers ingenious and highly practical approaches to science, technology and health care. This is the generation designated by the zodiac to bear the burden of the hard work required to lay the practical foundations for the new Age of Aquarius. You have an unusual talent for business and are diligent and resourceful workers. There are likely to be many disruptions and upheavals in business as we have seen with the dotcom boom and the collapse of the technology bubble. You will create new and unique ways of working.

Libra
Those born with Uranus in Libra bring in new forms of harmony and beauty. Uranus is the esoteric ruler of Libra. There may be many upsets in relationships and marriage due to the fact that these souls are individualists that want freedom. Unless it is given, the relationship will be broken.

This is a group of people with distinctly new ideas about marriage, partnerships and the rules of social conduct. In marriage, the integrity of the relationship and individual freedom are far more important than any binding legal contract, which you regard as superfluous. Concerned with individual freedom, you may be prone to experiment with open relationships and communal living. You will have a keen insight into other peoples' motivations.

Scorpio

This is a powerful position for Uranus. Tremendous will and persistence has to find an outlet, whether it be constructive or destructive. This placement makes a fine healer, psychologist or surgeon as they have the ability to probe deeply into the cause of distress. Can be a devil or a saint and are capable of the highest or the lowest where morals are concerned. Self will or God's will; the choice would have to be made in this sign.

Those born with this placement of Uranus are destined to see the destruction of the old order, out of the ashes of which the new order is born. You have highly charged emotions and believe in taking swift and decisive action. You have no tolerance for any form of laziness, procrastination, or inactivity and tend to possess great scientific ingenuity. You are not easily influenced by other people. You have strong psychic tendencies and are extremely resourceful.

Sagittarius

There is an inner optimism with a strong desire to expand horizons, whether inwardly through knowledge of the higher planes or outwardly through travel.

You will have an interest in foreign cultures and systems of belief and will wish to travel widely and often. Travel to far away places or taking up residence in another country is common to this placement. You will seek out new concepts about philosophy and higher education. During your lifetime, there is likely to be a period of scientific, social and spiritual change. You may wish to be instrumental in leading those changes for the betterment of mankind.

Capricorn
Uranus is the planet of change and Capricorn hates change. So there is conflict. One side clings to the past while part of the individual is trying to go forward into the future.

You are likely to affect important changes within the power structures of both government and business, with a strong desire to change and improve the status quo in order to secure a prosperous future. You are concerned with bringing ideas into practical and concrete actuality. You seek constructive change, building the new on the foundations of the old, and therefore never fully do away with the past. You are ambitious, with a strong will to succeed, and are able to take old ideas and develop them in new ways.

Aquarius
Uranus rules Aquarius and is therefore powerfully placed when in this sign. You have an overall concern for the good of humanity. Your humanitarian traits often extend to clairvoyance and a deep intuitive understanding of scientific as well as universal truths. You are open to new ideas and seek social reform through work with groups and organisations. Independent and strong-willed, you insist on making your own decisions and drawing your own conclusions. Objective and impartial, you will readily discard any ideas that do not stand up to scientific scrutiny. You have an independent strong nature that cannot be pushed but can be reached through logic and reason.

Pisces

This confers strong intuitive abilities coupled with a keen scientific and psychological interest in the workings of the unconscious. Your great motivating drive is to liberate the mind from the emotional influences and shackles of the past, to overcome the limitations of materialistic concerns, and to seek a higher spiritual understanding and identity. You may have strong religious inclinations that can border on the mystical. Many of your ideas and insights come to you through dreams. You need to learn to relax physically and emotionally. There is an inner longing to be free of earth and its complexities. You are very psychic and interested in helping humanity.

Uranus in Houses

1st House

Very strong individuality. You must follow your intuitive sense, whether for good or for ill. Very original methods of working. Erratic and sudden impulses not always understood, not only by others but by yourself. Must surrender the willfulness inherent in this position of Uranus. Unrest and isolation will always be felt until the will becomes willingness. Not a conformist and apt to be too direct and blunt in opinions.

You are driven by an irrepressible desire for personal freedom. You are restless and crave constant change and excitement, often preferring a life of risk and adventure to one of settlement and security. You will have little regard for conventional behaviour. A routine existence is an anathema to you. You may be seen as eccentric and exceptional, and you tend to possess intuitive and unique talents in the arts or sciences. You are interested in the new and inventive. You often act the opposite of what is expected of you.

2nd House

This placement of Uranus creates sudden and unforeseen circumstances where finances and income are concerned. There are ups and downs in money conditions. Not a fixed income. You will have a great desire for independence and so do well in your own business. Not good for speculation if afflicted. Inventive where business ideas are concerned.

You can be impulsive and reckless with your money and can spend it as fast as you make it. However, you can also have an unusual talent for making money, especially through businesses involving inventions, electronics, and other scientific fields. You have a great desire to be financially independent. Also, as Uranus is ruled by Aquarius which rules astrology, you may earn your money through new ways of presenting and teaching astrology.

3rd House

You must learn to accept the home environment in early years. Upsets in home life in growing up can cause suffering especially if Uranus is afflicted. There is great mental restlessness. Sudden and unexpected urges to travel. You have a keen and alert mind, but are often lacking in concentration. You have to be willing to give up self will.

You are free thinkers with unusual and intuitive minds that are prone to sudden insights. Your thinking is not subject to the influence of other people, and your ideas are based on direct experience and scientific fact. Impersonal and impartial, you are open to new ideas and always investigating the undiscovered and the unusual. Many inventors and scientists have Uranus in the 3rd House. You may also be involved in the media, especially radio and television. You need lots of mental stimulation.

4th House

There are upsetting domestic conditions unless Uranus is well aspected. Not a domestic type and doesn't want a fixed and settled home life unless Uranus is in a Fixed sign. Restlessness in the roots of being can cause unstable conditions in life. There are likely to be many changes of position and location. Possibly an interest in astrology and metaphysics in later years. Unsettled conditions around the mother affect you emotionally.

Home and family life will be unusual, to say the least. Even the house itself may be of unusual or distinctive architecture and may contain any variety of electronic devices and gadgetry. Family members desire the freedom to come and go as they please, and there is the likelihood of one of the parents being exceptional or even strange in some regard. Close friends will be accepted as family members, as the home is a centre for group activities. You may have sudden changes of residence and many changes in family life.

5th House

Self-restraint and self-knowledge needed as you can be reckless and foolhardy. Too strong an assertion of individualism if Uranus is afflicted. Children are original, independent and unusual. Very creative and inventive person. Prefer to work for yourself rather than others.

There will be sudden and unusual romantic involvements that are prone to end as abruptly as they began. You want to feel free no matter what the cost. Romantic partners may be eccentric in some way. Excitement is sought through the pursuit of pleasure, and attitudes toward sexuality are sometimes unconventional. Your children may be gifted in some special way. Many rock stars, movie stars and television personalities have this placement of Uranus. In a woman's chart, there is a possibility of pregnancy out of wedlock.

6th House

Good worker, but needs a job that enables you to move around. Ingenious and original in nature. You either drive yourself mercilessly far beyond your physical strength or fight your job all the way. You have to learn the hard way to be obedient and do as you are told. Apt to be hasty and impatient with others.

This indicates innovative and advanced methods employed in work and service. This can take the form of alternative approaches to healing, medicine and diet, as well as working with advanced technology. Computer programmers and electronic engineers often have Uranus in the 6th house. Often friends are made through work, as relationships with coworkers, employers and employees are amicable and mentally stimulating. You are highly sensitive to your working conditions and relationships and will leave a job if these are unsatisfactory. You require freedom to do your work in your own way and will rebel against strict or rigid supervision.

7th House

There can be difficulties in marriage. Too independent. Apt to attract a partner who wants to feel free and be a law unto themselves. Partnerships in business as well as marriage or unions will demand a great deal of discipline.

There is a strong desire for freedom in marriage and other personal relationships. Marriage is often sudden and under unusual circumstances, and the spouse is often eccentric or brilliant in some way. Your married life will never be dull and there will be lots of surprises. Other relationships tend to be either very close or superficial, shallow and fleeting. You may have frequent changes of mood, attitudes and opinions that can leave others feeling confused.

8th House

Very strong psychic abilities. Must be very careful where business partnerships are concerned. You should not go into partnerships without a great deal of forethought.

This denotes a quest for freedom of expression through esoteric traditions and also possibly sexuality. As the 8th House involves other people's resources, you may receive an unexpected inheritance or benefit from your business or marriage partners. This can also indicate an intense and unusual dream life, and you are probably very intuitive. You may have sudden changes in your fortunes – from positive to negative. It will not be easy for you to settle down into a humdrum routine.

9th House

Success in publishing, teaching or foreign affairs. Often unusual journeys, either on the material plane or unusual experiences where the superconscious planes are concerned. May marry someone from another country.

This confers highly evolved, advanced, and innovative ideas in regard to philosophy, religion and higher education. Ideas about education will be especially progressive, with interest in new methods of teaching. Religious views are often unorthodox, with an interest in the occult and esoteric. You are likely to travel far and wide in search of new experiences and ideas. You have a keen interest in the remote past and the distant future. You will be able to hold onto your ideals and integrity against all the odds.

10th House

Not a conformer. You need to be your own boss due to your strong individualistic nature. You are altruistic and humanitarian in outlook with a strong imagination and originality. Generally there is an interest in astrology and the occult.

This often indicates an unusual profession and an outstanding or unique reputation within its ranks. You are apt to be leaders and innovators in your chosen field. You are generally politically liberal or radical, almost certainly never conservative. You have a driving ambition to achieve prominence and make unique contributions in your profession. However, changes in fortune can be sudden and drastic. You will not submit to any kind of routine in your work life.

11th House

Unpredictable changes where goals and objectives are concerned. Two types of friends: the conventional Saturnians and the bohemian Uranians and never the twain shall meet. Feelings of sympathy and antipathy very strong and changeable.

You are open-minded, impartial and humanitarian in your outlook. You have little to no regard for traditional opinions and mores in the face of objective truth, which you have an intuitive ability to perceive, along with universal laws and principles. You have many unusual friendships and group associations that are mentally and spiritually stimulating. You have an impersonal attitude to marriage and romantic partnerships, possessing a powerful desire for freedom. You have a strong sense of equality.

12th House

You have a tremendous desire to feel free but often feel confined. In dealing with people and situations you must use persuasion and not force. Good position for researchers or those who work behind the scenes. Apt to be a loner.

This indicates the mystical quest for spiritual identity and a deep probing into the hidden recesses of the unconscious. Interest in and understanding of esoteric teachings and practices such as yoga and meditation are likely. Intuitive and psychic abilities may be highly developed. You have a great desire to help your fellow man. You are very intuitive and likely to be clairvoyant. You may join secret organisations.

Neptune in Signs and Houses

As Neptune stays in a sign for between 13 – 16 years, it is interesting to look at the different periods in history that are associated with each sign.

Aries (1861/62 – 1874/75)
This indicates a strong concern with mystical and spiritual ideas. The initiative and drive for spiritual creativity and regeneration mean that pioneering advances are made in these fields. Spiritual pride and egotism, and the use of knowledge for personal power and self-aggrandisement, are the darker side of this expression.

Taurus (1874/75 – 1887/89)
Here, there is a strong idealism regarding the proper and ethical use of money and resources, with an active seeking of practical applications for idealistic visions and theories. On the negative, side, there can be a preoccupation with money and materialism.

Gemini (1887/89 – 1901/02)
This is the generation that produced Ernest Hemingway, William Faulkner, F. Scott Fitzgerald – those who have much to do with giving creative expression to the intuitive and image-making faculties of the mind through poetry and literature. These people are gifted with highly active and versatile imaginations and are able to channel and communicate ideas from the collective consciousness.

Cancer (1901/02 – 1914/16)
This is a generation with strong psychic ties to home, family, and the earth. You are emotionally sensitive and sympathetic and, if Neptune is strongly placed (on the cusp of the 4th House or in the 12th) and aspected, can have psychic and medium gifts.

Leo (1914/16 – 1928/29)
This is a generation with strong musical and artistic talents, with a special interest in the theatre and other performing arts. It is also strongly inclined to romantic idealism in love and courtship. Neptune is the planet of illusions. The movie industry is also included under its rulership. Time of the "Roaring Twenties."

Virgo (1928/29 – 1942/43)
Neptune is in its detriment in Virgo, the opposite sign of Pisces, of which Neptune is one of the rulers. This is a generation whose creative and imaginative faculties are blocked by adverse material circumstances. Neptune was in Virgo through the Great Depression, a time of mass unemployment and poverty. Chemical abuse of food began during this period. Also food was rationed.

Libra (1942/43 – 1955/57)
This has a natural instinct for emotional and social conformity. There is a strong intuitive awareness of social relationships and responsibilities. Mutual social responsibility is based more on the spirit than the letter of the law. Neptune in Libra can give rise to new forms of art. Emotional and social conformity manifested as drug abuse and the popularity of rock music grew.

Scorpio (1955/57 – 1970)
Scorpio is the sex sign, and Neptune rules drugs. Neptune in Scorpio is a period in which the natural desires are exploited. There is much emotional intensity and confusion, causing the turmoil within the unconscious to break out. This period was marked by the exploitation of sex for commercial purposes. Sexual permissiveness and promiscuity led to the widespread outbreak of venereal diseases, along with drug use as a means of psychological escape.

Sagittarius (1970 – 1984)
This signifies a period of higher spiritual and religious values and an intuitive exploration of the mysteries of the mind. There is much foreign travel and exchange of ideas, and artistic expression is also spiritually oriented. There is an increased practice of meditation and aimless wandering among the hippie generation. There were many false prophets and gurus at this time.

Capricorn (1984 – 2000)
This is a period in which world governments are in chaos, and economic and political structures are in upheaval. Spiritual responsibility for the world is expressed here in

practical ways. Out of the chaos will come true spiritual responsibility and discipline. Some astrologers believe that this period has already heralded the beginnings of world government.

Aquarius (2000 – 2013)

This marked the true beginning of the Age of Aquarius. It is supposed to see the birth of a new civilization based on humanitarianism, globalisation, science and technology. This is a period where human rights issues come to the forefront of legal systems and governments. There may be a tipping of the balance where victims have fewer rights than criminals. This is an age of attempts by governments to eradicate poverty in the world.

Pisces (2013 – 2026)

This will be a time of peace following the upheavals of the birth of the Aquarian Age. The heights of Aquarian culture will begin, making use of the greatest accomplishments of the Piscean Age, expressing itself in exalted forms of music and art. Great strides will be made in medicine and healing. During this period many great artists, mystics, teachers, and spiritual leaders will be born.

Neptune in Houses

1st House

Those with Neptune in the 1st House, have a strong, sensitive, and intuitive awareness of self and environment. A strongly aspected Neptune can confer clairvoyant abilities and a deep understanding of the motives underlying human actions and events. You may have an air of mystery about you. It is advisable for you to avoid alcohol and drugs. Emotional disturbances react on the physical body, producing strange physical disorders that are difficult to diagnose. Vague approach to reality. Like a sponge absorbing the vibration of those around you.

2nd House

Do not look to matter for support. Neptune dissolves matter and material things will dissolve. Assets completely washed out unless there is absolute honesty. Poor judgment often where finances are concerned. Use it for others and you will find it comes back.

You are idealistic about the use of money and material resources. You are prone to donate generously to humanitarian causes and be liberal with your material resources. You are likely to have an intuitive ability to make money. However, you need to be careful of extravagance and make sure that you do not spend everything you earn. You may need to develop practicality.

3rd House

Artistic and imaginative type of mind but it does fog the clarity of thinking and the ability to concentrate. Not a good student for this reason. Dream your way through school unless there is a powerful Mercury Uranus aspect.

You have a great capacity for mental visualisation, especially if Neptune aspects Mercury. Telepathic abilities are often an attribute of Neptune in the 3rd house, making you a channel of information that you are compelled to share impartially with others. You may be able to put your intuition to practical use. There could also be learning challenges and a tendency to become lost in fantasy and daydreaming.

4th House

Domestic life involves some kind of self sacrifice. Unsettled home conditions. Often a skeleton in the family closet. Latter part of life can bring withdrawal from activity and an aloneness, self chosen.

There will be strong unconscious emotional ties to home and family that are karmic in nature. You may like to live near water and will have strong feelings for land and nature. Family secrets and mysteries surrounding aspects of home life are common. You may have a deep desire to mother the world and may bring strays and strangers into your home.

5th House

Secret love affairs or lack of freedom of emotional expression. Often in love with someone who is not free. Great sacrifices made for children but receive little in return. Powerful imagination that can often run off with common sense.

You have a strong unconscious desire for love and appreciation through romance and creative self-expression. You are a naturally gifted performer with a general love of the theatre. Unusual circumstances often surround romantic and sexual involvements. Disappointments in love may happen quite often. There may be an intuitive insight into the workings of the stock market, although you need to be cautious about your investments and speculations.

6th House

Tendency to inertia caused by lack of vital force, especially if Mars is not strong. It is hard to diagnose illness when Neptune is in the 6th house. More open to psychic infections than you are aware. Supersensitive. Apt to feel too much is demanded of you. Natural methods of healing and positive thoughts will aid more than traditional medicine.

This puts spiritual emphasis on work and service. Neptune is in its detriment in the 6th House, meaning that many sacrifices will be demanded and the lessons of work and health will be a challenge. There could be an intuitive understanding of how to work effectively and efficiently. You may be interested in alternative medicine, diet and spiritual healing. There is a strong inclination to care for animals and even communicate with them telepathically.

7th House

Always brings dreams of finding a true soul mate. Gives a constant yearning for perfection. Often is in love with someone who is not free and makes great sacrifices where reputation or fulfilment is concerned. Out of the ordinary type of marriage; usually to someone on a different wavelength. Needs to give a great deal and expect nothing in return.

This placement indicates that there are strong karmic connects in marriage and partnerships. There may even be a tight psychic link with your partner and an intuitive understanding of people in general. You are highly sensitive to the moods and feelings of those around you. The achievement of an ideal spiritual marriage is a possibility. You may be called upon to make sacrifices for a business or marital partner.

8th House

Not much gain through partnership, whether business or marriage relationships. Dreams very important as you can bring back knowledge gained while your body sleeps. Must give yourself away in order to help others gain their resources.

This indicates powerful psychic tendencies, often with an interest in the occult and spiritualism or communication with the dead. Secretive or deceptive circumstances may surround a partner's money and financial assets. This can confer clairvoyant abilities. You will need to be extra careful when dealing with other peoples' resources.

9th House

The mind is impressionable and easily influenced. All planets in this house have a higher vibration than when placed in any other area.

This shows a keen interest in mysticism and religion. This is a highly impressionable mind, capable of intuitive insights and prophetic visions. You may have a great interest in mystical affairs, including yoga, meditation and oriental religions. Care must be taken to distinguish the real teachers from the fakes.

10th House

An unusual career. Must give more than will be received in the area of career. Will never receive the satisfaction of credit given for work done. This is a good position for those who serve others. Good for medical work or humanitarian work of any kind.

Here, intuition will play an important part in your career. It is considered an excellent position for psychiatrists, psychologists and ministers. One of the parents is likely to be unusual in some way, and your work will be unusual and surrounded by strange circumstances. Many actors, artists and musicians have Neptune in the 10th House. This can bring honour as a result of outstanding personal achievement or sacrifice.

11th House

Can be too gullible in friendships. Very necessary to use discrimination in the choice of your friends. Needs to have definite goals and aims in order to achieve success in life. Apt to be a dreamer instead of a doer.

There will be idealistic and unusual friendships and group associations, with whom you form close spiritual links.

You are generous with friends, from whom you in turn receive spiritual guidance and assistance in the realisation of your goals. You are sensitive to the needs of humanity and may join philanthropic or spiritual groups and organisations.

12th House

Feeling of being confined and restricted very strong. Extremely sensitive. Often confused about your purpose in life. Deep seated loneliness that is alleviated through service to others.

Here, Neptune confers a strong intuitive link to the deep unconscious, often resulting in mystical religious tendencies. You will tend to seek seclusion and privacy in order to expedite your inner spiritual search. You may have a sense of memories of previous incarnations and gain much spiritual wisdom from this intuitive link to the past. You must guard against mental confusion. Often confers healing abilities along with artistic, literary and musical talents. It is an excellent position for doctors, nurses or those who work in hospitals or institutions.

Pluto in Signs and Houses

Background on Pluto

When Pluto was discovered as a pinpoint of light on a photographic plate on February 18th, 1930, the world was in upheaval – financially because of the Wall Street crash, and politically because of the rise of fascism in Europe. Scientifically, early work in splitting the atom led to the development of the atom bomb, ultimately threatening the survival of humanity.

The principle of Pluto is that something infinitely small can have an effect out of all proportion to its size. In this sense Pluto is connected with miniaturisation. Computers that once filled whole buildings in the 1960s are handheld today.

As Pluto moves through the signs, it removes the comfort zone that humanity took for granted in connection with each sign, and when Pluto leaves that sign, something has been changed forever.

Aries (1823 – 1852)
Aries is the sign of the individual will and new experience, the beginning of a new cycle of action. Pluto in Aries saw the American expansion into the West and the golden age of the pioneer, a period of both dauntless courage in the name of freedom and settling a new frontier, and ruthless violence and bloodshed in the struggle for land and riches. In Europe and Asia, revolutionary movements heralded

the beginning of the overthrow of the ancient order in the name of the new.

Taurus (1852 – 1884)
Taurus is the sign of material resources and monetary concerns, and Pluto in Taurus marked a period of great economic expansion in which the Industrial Revolution reached its peak and corporations came into being.

Gemini (1884 – 1914)
Gemini rules ideas, communication, and inventiveness, and Pluto in Gemini was a period of great scientific discoveries and important inventions. The discovery and harnessing of electricity set the stage for the development of modern technology and communications. The telephone, automobile, and airplane are among the many significant inventions of this period.

Cancer (1914 – 1939)
Cancer is the sign of the Mother, the home, land, environment, food production and personal and instinctive expression. Pluto in Cancer was a time of economic struggle and the growth of strong nationalist sentiment that led finally to the outbreak of World War II. It also saw a revolution in agriculture, with the building of dams and the introduction of pesticides and chemical fertilisers. The threats to family and national security gave birth to new political philosophies – the New Deal in the USA, fascism in Europe and Japan, and communism in Russia and China.

Leo (1939 – 1957)

Leo is the sign of expressive will, power and leadership. Pluto in Leo saw the outbreak of World War II and a renewed thrust for world domination, the development of atomic energy (ruled by Pluto), and the unleashing of the atomic bomb. Humanity faced the possibility of the total destruction of civilisation alongside the heights of technological achievement and the harnessing of awesome power. The end of World War II gave birth to many new sovereign nations from the ashes of the old colonial empires and the global power struggle between capitalism and communism.

This period brought the rise of the superpower, based on the destructive power of the bomb. The generation of Pluto in Leo is obsessed with youth and self-indulgence. This first generation to grow up under the shadow of the bomb was the first to confront the fact that humanity really could be destroyed, that Armageddon could be a reality, and therefore they seized life with all their power.

Virgo (1957 – 1972)

Virgo is the sign of work, service, health, and the practical application of technology. Pluto in Virgo marked a period of revolutionary changes in industry, employment, and medicine. Computers revolutionised science, business, and industry; automation replaced many workers; and great strides and discoveries were made in medicine and science. America landed the first man on the Moon. The development of prepackaged food and the chemical adulteration and pollution of the food supply led to the widespread advocacy and promotion of organic food in the 1960s, while at the same time psychedelic drugs opened up formerly unknown realms of consciousness that brought about massive social upheavals.

The Pill enabled women to gain control over their biology – sex was on the rise, but, for the first time, birth rates started falling. Pluto has its own medical solution to the so-called population explosion.

Libra (1972 – 1984)

Libra is the sign of justice, human relations, social expression, and psychology. Pluto in Libra saw the awakening of a new consciousness of social responsibility and the development of new concepts of marriage, law and justice. Civil rights laws were strengthened, divorce was made easier, and America's involvement in Vietnam ended during this period, largely due to the growing antiwar movement both at home and abroad. During this period aesthetics and femininity were transformed as bras were burned, and equal rights insisted upon. Roles were reversed as men renounced masculinity, and women demonstrated that they could manage very well without the opposite sex. Men loved men, women loved women – leaving the Pluto in Libra children to ponder about love and relationships.

Scorpio (1984 – 2000)

Pluto has its fastest orbital motion while passing through Libra and Scorpio. Pluto rules Scorpio, the sign of death and rebirth. This is by far the most potent of all the planetary sign positions, marking the end of the Piscean Age and a period in which the consequences of human action or inaction will be felt profoundly on a grand scale. Regenerate or die was the order of the day. People began to want to know more about the deeper meaning of their lives.

After so much sexual experimentation, Pluto in Scorpio brought the spectre of AIDS. The most natural act in the world could result in death. Pluto focused paranoia on sex itself, and this led to a drastic change in sexual habits, not least in a new openness amongst governments regarding sexual health. Condoms were everywhere. Economically this was the time of the yuppie, of junk bonds and how to get rich by taking advantage of others.

Sagittarius (2000 – 2008)
This period has evoked the period of international terror and religious fundamentalism. As a Mutable sign Sagittarius creates polarity, and today we have the idea of a war of civilisations. Governments invest enormous resources into avoiding the consequences of terror. In Switzerland today, no new houses can be built without a nuclear fallout shelter. Likewise, a general political reaction to international terror today is control and surveillance.

Pluto in this sign has marked the beginning of new scientific discoveries and theories have resulted in a more comprehensive understanding of the underlying forces behind all existence. Both Pluto and Sagittarius can go to extremes. While we think of Sagittarius as good-hearted, it is capable of painting with a broad brush that refuses to see different points of view. Prejudice, therefore, has been a negative expression of this cycle.

Pluto in Sagittarius also brought the shadow side of religion. For example, the shadow side of the Church. In recent months the sexual habits of some Catholic priests have been unmasked all over the world. People have been blowing themselves up for their religious beliefs, dying for their beliefs and dropping bombs on foreigners all in the name of religion.

Sagittarius rules the media and entertainment, and the rise of a new compulsivity in celebrity journalism has grown up since Pluto entered Sagittarius, with the internet spawning a huge new gossip market. Sagittarius carries with it a nearly relentless optimism; ruled by Jupiter with its expansive need for growth, Pluto in Sagittarius has seen soaring home prices and a burgeoning stock market that seems to have no end. The "new economy" of the dot com era occurred under Pluto's Sagittarian influence, as did the explosion of the vacation home market.

Capricorn (1762 – 1777) (2008 – 2024)
This is a 16 year period where government consolidates autocratic power in the name of security.

Capricorn is the sign that deals with political and economic power structure, ambition, status, and leadership. Pluto in Capricorn saw the birth of new concepts of government, the most notable of which was the American Declaration of Independence in 1776. This period saw the birth of democratic governments and the displacement of aristocratic power structures. Pluto in Capricorn manifests itself as a dynamic and practical will in organisation, business, and government, based on the concept that all human beings are entitled to a fair chance to develop their own potential according to their abilities.

Capricorn is the sign of the builder, the achiever. Capricorn is rooted in the material world and understands that life on earth requires a practical approach to the matters of earning a living. There is also a drive for success; to climb the highest mountains like the goat which is its symbol. For Capricorn, the ends justify the means and achievement of one's goals is the important thing and it is able to maintain a powerful focus.

Its rulership by Saturn gives respect for discipline and authority and Capricorn has tremendous respect for governmental structures and the stability of a moral system. However, Saturn also bestows its tendency towards pessimism and lack of humour as all things personal are sacrificed for the goal. There is often a tendency to prize material things above those of the emotional or spiritual realms, and this lack of balance can create a dry and miserable experience.

When Pluto goes through Capricorn we can expect the transformation of all things ruled by that sign - such as our religious institutions, halls of government and political structures, the way we inter our dead and take care of our old people, construction techniques and buildings, and how we handle ownership of property.

Pluto will be in Capricorn until 2024, and this occurs at a time when our Capricorn structures are ripe for transformation. Industry in developed and developing countries has become a major source of carbon emissions which threaten the survival of life on earth. The very way we do business (Capricorn) is being forever changed by the globalisation of politics and the economy.

Pluto causes endings and new beginnings - it forces us to surrender as it rebuilds us from the inside out. I suspect that throughout next year the intense optimism of Pluto in Sagittarius will battle with the necessity for realism of Pluto in Capricorn, and it will be a while before the economic problems really hit home.

Once Pluto is firmly entrenched in Capricorn beginning in December 2008, we will begin to really see it at work. This of course will follow the US presidential election in November 2008. Pluto seeks to focus and intensify as well as break down and regenerate. The structures of our world keep societies in order and functioning: churches, governments, buildings – all of these are ruled by Capricorn. But so are bridges and tunnels, and the entire infrastructure upon which we live, particularly in urban areas, is likely to experience a severe breakdown while Pluto travels through Capricorn. Underground transportation, under the domain of the God of the Underworld, could become a battleground as Pluto often brings warfare or death in the areas of the sign through which it passes (such as September 11th during Pluto in Sagittarius, where air travel became a conveyance of death and total world transformation).

During the passage of Pluto, we see extremes and compulsions in the area of life associated with the sign through which Pluto travels, and with the Capricornian association with governments and government buildings I would expect a worldwide attempt to solidify a global government and minimise individual liberties. Pluto deals with issues of power – on a personal level such as personal empowerment as well as with the power structures that govern all of humanity that fall under the rubric of the Capricorn theme. When Uranus enters Aries in 2010-2011, there may be turmoil as the pendulum swings back towards individual liberties. By the time Uranus forms a square to Pluto in Capricorn in 2012-2013 there will be tremendous cultural, social and political upheaval which will further transform governments and political structures.

Pluto's reach will extend beyond governments, however. Capricorn also rules the elderly and end of life issues, and Pluto's passage through Capricorn could transform the way we view the entire process of death and dying, including the disposal of the body after death.

Often Pluto's passage through one sign is a reaction to Pluto's passage through the previous sign, and in Capricorn there may be a reaction of the practical and materialistic Capricorn against the ideological idealism of Pluto's travel through Sagittarius. An overdose of pragmatism could lead to the negativity and depression with which Capricorn is sometimes associated. Capricorn is associated with achievement and can be ruthless in its efforts to climb to the top, and we could see an increased obsession (Pluto) with climbing the ladder of success that leads to a breakdown in certain segments of society.

With Pluto in Capricorn we are likely to see an increase in stability and a more practical approach to economics and business than we saw under the Sagittarian influence. The inflated (Sagittarius) bonuses for CEOs that we saw in recent years are likely a sign of the past as businesses and corporations become more concerned with Capricornian fundamentals than with Sagittarian appearance and image.

Capricorn is essentially practical and prizes achievement above all else, which means achievement of real goals and objectives. Although Pluto in Capricorn will bring out secrets (Pluto) of governments and other political entities (Capricorn), there will be an increased focus on proficiency, skill, and a successful outcome rather than the spin and propaganda of the Sagittarian era.

The signature of Pluto in Capricorn has already been built, and it can be seen in the Shanghai World Financial Centre, which coincidentally is 492 metres in height. (A Neptune/Pluto conjunction takes place every 492 years.) This building may be a symbol of the shift of economic power from West to East – the destruction of the World Trade Centre clearing the path for one of the tallest buildings in the world, the Shanghai World Financial Centre. The exporting of jobs overseas in the Pluto in Sagittarius era has empowered Asia and there may be little the outdated institutions of Europe and the USA can do about this. Pluto in Capricorn will initiate a painful transformation of Western business structures. Business has already started to move east and this is set to continue.

When Pluto transits a sign it leaves a swathe of destruction, but what is destroyed has often outlived its relevance. Big business elites will not survive the Pluto transit, but will in turn be transformed. The invasive hand of government will not be able to stifle individuals, or reduce those who do not have the privilege of power to slaves in the hierarchy. By the time Pluto enters Aquarius in 2023 / 2024 – humanitarian concerns will sweep away autocracy.

Aquarius (2024 – 2044)
This places the planet of death and rebirth in the sign of sudden, radical changes. The last time this happened was during the French Revolution, a time period that shook Europe to its very foundations. Many people born during that time were obsessed, as a generation, with the new ideas of Liberty, Fraternity, and Equality, all of which have an Aquarian nature.

In my next book, I will look more deeply at the Aquarian Age cycles to come – especially Pluto's movement in this sign from 2024-2044. For the moment, realise that all our dreams, ideals and visions don't have to occur in the next couple of years. We are just beginning to taste the Aquarian Age potential. Think literally of a near future of mental telepathy, time travel (perhaps via the intuition and "higher planes"), contacts with extraterrestrials, clairvoyance, clairaudience, past-life and even future-life "recall," great advances in medicine, science, technology and environmental protection.

Pluto in Aquarius sets the pattern for future generations. The old and the new unite to form the ideal society as social problems are solved. The ashes of what remains from Pluto's stay in Capricorn are rekindled, and something pure and new emerges from the light.

Humanitarian interests are in focus. Care will have to be exercised lest release of the powerful new forces brings destruction rather than reconstruction. False hopes are exposed, and new, attainable aspirations are formed.

Pisces (2044 – 2068)

This placement of Pluto releases great psychic and spiritual power and the elevation of the conscious mind through magnetic healing and magic to a superconscious level. Places of incarceration such as prisons and hospitals, undergo a metamorphosis: more charitable and human methods of treatment and rehabilitation will unfold.

It is likely that reincarnation will be widely accepted at this time. It could be a time of great cultural change and innovation with the creation of many great works of art of lasting meaning and value.

Pluto in Houses

Pluto in the houses shows those areas in life in which we must exercise conscious, creative willpower over our self and environment. Pluto deals with issues of mass destiny, and its house position shows the individual effects and personal interpretations of these changes.

1st House

This position indicates a person with intense spiritual self-awareness and strong willpower. Your childhood may have been marked by extreme hardship, which may have made you a bit of a loner who hides his or her innermost feelings. You possess considerable initiative, but may find it difficult to cooperate with others or conform to traditional conduct and mores. Pluto is accidentally dignified in the 1st House, for it is one of the rulers of Aries, the natural resident of the 1st House. Thus, Pluto here confers a highly developed sense of personal power and will. The strong individualism and innate nonconformity of this position can make it challenging for you to get along at home and in your relationships. If Pluto is in conjunction with the Ascendant, you may possess clairvoyant abilities.

2nd House

This confers a driving ambition to obtain money and material resources. As Pluto rules Scorpio and the 8th House, which is opposite Taurus in the 2nd House, this can indicate that these ambitions are likely to be met through the use of other people's money. There can be great resourcefulness in money-making through the ability to perceive hidden financial opportunities. The great lesson of Pluto in the 2nd House is that material resources are fluid and must be used for the benefit of everyone.

3rd House

This bestows mental resourcefulness and scientific abilities, with an innate and penetrating comprehension of the causes underlying life's experiences and manifestations. Generally you will have strong opinions and will only compromise your beliefs in the face of factual evidence to the contrary. You may be privy to secret or exclusive information pertaining to matters of great importance and what you think and communicate can have serious consequences. You are a dynamic communicator.

4th House

You are inclined to be master of the home and family. You are probably very resourceful in providing for and improving the domestic situation, as well as possessing a powerful psychic connection to the earth that bestows an intuitive knowledge of its mysteries and hidden resources. There could be a power struggle with other members of the family. You may have a love of nature. In your later years, you are likely to have an interest in the occult.

5th House

This is an indicator of creative power that can find its expression in many forms: art, love, procreation, performing, nurturing. Many famous artists have this placement of Pluto. Spiritual regeneration is experienced through love and any children you have will be blessed with talent, genius and self-determination. You may dominate or be dominated by your romantic partner. You need to be careful about any speculation as serious losses can occur.

6th House

This confers an ability to improve existing work methods and employment and conscientious hard work toward this aim will bring financial gain and recognition. You will also apply your will to improve your health by adopting good dietary practices, exercise and mental discipline. People involved in the construction, salvage and atomic energy programmes often have Pluto in the 6th House. This placement of Pluto can often mean that serious attention must be paid to personal health. You must learn to cooperate with other workers.

7th House

You are likely to experience drastic alteration as a result of marriage and other partnerships, both personal and professional. You tend to attract a partner who is strong-willed and domineering. Pluto imbues a strong sense of justice that reacts intensely against the wrongdoings of others. You may have a profound intuitive insight into other people and their motives. It is important for you to strive for a balanced sharing of initiative and responsibility in your relationships and dealings with other people.

8th House

This confers a fierce and powerful will along with strong psychic and clairvoyant abilities. You will have an innate and deep understanding of karma, the soul and other issues of life after physical death. This intuitive awareness of the invisible behind the visible can give you a profound insight into subjects that deal with the nature of energy and matter, such a physics. You are often able to rejuvenate the discarded resources of others. Life is probably taken very seriously, with no time for trivialities and often a severe do-or-die attitude. You can show great resourcefulness and strength in times of crisis.

9th House

This indicates a strong interest in improving legal, educational, moral and philosophical systems. There is an intuitive ability to identify fundamental problems within the larger social order, bestowing a profound insight into the future of humanity. You may have a capacity for spiritual leadership. You can experience great achievements through higher education and you have little tolerance for hypocrisy or injustice. Yet, ambition to achieve distinction, when carried too far, can result in excessive pride and competitiveness. You need to watch out that you do not impose your beliefs upon others.

10th House

Pluto in the 10th House, ruled by Capricorn, indicates a strong will and a relentless drive to succeed. There is an equally compelling desire to reform and rehabilitate existing power structures, which can make for powerful friends as well as enemies. You can be misunderstood and may be a controversial figure. Crises in your career may force you to change your profession. You can be a leader in science as well as politics. Adept at handling positions of power, this is a favourable position for politicians. You may sometimes feel isolated by your responsibilities.

11th House

Reformist tendencies are expressed through friendships and group associations. You possess an immense capacity for dynamic group leadership through which scientific and humanitarian advances are achieved. Pluto is accidentally in its detriment in the 11th House, and you must be very careful about respecting the rights of others and to use your will cooperatively in order to work effectively within a group. You are likely to attract some powerful friends.

12th House

You have profound insight and clairvoyant abilities. The need here is to regenerate the unconscious mind by bringing its contents into consciousness. There is a deep sympathy and ability to assist and improve the conditions of the less fortunate, along with an intuitive understanding of life's so-called occult mysteries. You are telepathically sensitive to the thoughts, feelings, and motives of others. You may sometimes withdraw into privacy or seclusion. Meditation will be important to you.

Chapter 8

"There is no better boat than a horoscope to help a man cross over the sea of life."

Varaha Mihira – Astronomer, mathematician

Aspects

According to the ancient philosophers there are two lines of force in operation whereby nature is maintained in a state of equilibrium in order to produce life. These are the dual forces with which you have to reckon in every phase of living in a dual universe. Positive and negative, inbreath and outgoing breath, construction opposite to destruction, expansion and contraction. Since these forces are equal each complements the other.

An Aspect is the angle formed between two points in the chart. It may be formed by two planets to each other, or by a planet to some other point in the chart, for example, the Ascendant.

All organic structure is built on cells which in their simplest form are hexagons, similar to those of the honeycomb. Therefore the hexagon is the primary pattern of benefit and harmony. When light enters at the external angle of 60 degrees and the internal angle of 120 degrees, it necessarily illuminates all parts of the structure in equal lines of influence. The light that comes in at either of these angles imparts harmonious vibrations which stimulate growth.

Opposed to this process of construction is the process of crystallisation, recognised in magnetism and electricity, wherein two forces operate at right angles to one another – a geometrical relationship that is destructive to organic form. This is an angle of 90 degrees or 180 degrees. As a result, side by side through nature two mutually antagonistic forces exist, which despite their antipathy toward each other, work together toward the ordered disposition of the whole; one based on quadrature, the other upon the hexagon – the square and the trine.

Astrology shows that the square relationship between energy sources is destructive to form through releasing the energy that is locked up in the various structures Nature has built; the trine aspects constitute the constructive side of nature, whereby organic forms are created, nourished, and held to be released when subsequent destructive configurations are encountered.

To fully understand the laws of polarity inherent in the universe would be to comprehend the mystery of life itself. The laws of opposites apply in every phase of earth living and from the combination of the two opposites, a third force is born, higher than either force. This secret is hidden in the triangle.

Two of the most important aspects in a birth chart are the conjunction and the opposition. In a conjunction the two energies involved are as close together as they can be; in an opposition, the two forces are as far apart as they can get. When the Sun and Moon are together we have a new moon; when they are opposed to each other we have a full moon.

The major aspects the astrologer deals with are the following:

Aspect	Symbol	Degrees Apart	Keywords
Conjunction	☌	0	Power
Opposition	☍	180	Awareness
Square	□	90	Obstacles
Trine	△	120	Harmony, creation
Sextile	✶	60	Opportunity
Semisextile	⊻	30	Slightly beneficial
Inconjunct (Quincunx)	⋏	150	Discord

If you have learned the lessons on triplicities and quadruplicities you will have no trouble in recognising your trines and squares and oppositions in a chart.

Elements of the same nature – for example, two Fire signs, are of the same Element and trine each other. The same with two Water signs and so on. In the quadruplicities are shown the oppositions and the squares. Fire is not in harmony with Water; Aries planets square those in Cancer, and Scorpio (Water) is not in harmony with Aquarius (Air).

The orb of a planet is important. The closer the aspect, the stronger its effect.

Aspects to the Sun, Moon and Mercury operate from 8 degrees to 12 degrees apart. The others operate up to 8 degrees apart: the square, trine, sextile and opposition. It is important that you are not too rigid with the orbs, because there must be some degree of flexibility in your interpretation of a chart.

Aspects to the Ascendant and Midheaven are important only if you are sure of the birth time within five minutes.

Conjunction

0 degrees apart

Planets within 10 degrees of one another. These emphasise the bringing together of the two different energies. It is known as power operating. The conjunction can be harmonious or inharmonious, according to the planets involved. For example, Mars conjunct Saturn would be extremely challenging. As they are opposed in nature, they are likely to fight each other. Mars is dynamic, positive, active and quick; Saturn is slow, limiting and slows impulsive action. Venus and Jupiter together would be beneficial; both are harmonious and work well together. When one planet is positive (masculine) and the other is receptive (feminine) – for instance Mars conjunct Venus – there will be a complex in the nature that must be released or understood in order to use the energy wisely. Note the signs the planets are in. The planet most at home in the sign will be the stronger planet. Mars conjunct Venus in Scorpio will be very different to Mars conjunct Venus in

Libra. In the former, Mars will override Venus; in the latter Venus is in its own sign and will be able to overcome and subdue the energy of Mars. A conjunction is a concentrated mass of energy.

Opposition

180 degrees apart
Oppositions are opposing forces that need to be reconciled. They are easier to handle than squares, but call for cooperation. Opposing forces come from outside as well as inside and often involve other people. Often there is the need for compromise. Oppositions can cause you to be pulled apart by two contrary forces, like the two poles of a battery. Without opposing forces how could we have any choice? Without choice there would be no growth in discrimination and awareness. Oppositions do not give you difficulties if you learn how to handle people who disagree with you. It is necessary to learn diplomacy and tact. In the conjunction *you* do something; in an opposition, *the other person* does.

Sextile

60 degrees apart
Planets that are two signs apart. These energies work together harmoniously and in such a way that opportunities for success manifest through the energies involved. A chart with many sextiles indicates a life filled with opportunities. They must be activated or they will not function.

Trine

120 degrees apart

Like Jupiter, trines give a protective influence. Benefits come without any effort or any activity of the person concerned. Trine aspects are the good we have given out returning to us.

Semi-sextile

30 degrees apart

This aspect is one sign apart, and acts as a 2nd House aspect. Because the 2nd House is about values and resources, this aspect gives you a clue to finances.

Square

90 degrees apart

This aspect has more power than a trine if you learn how to deal with it. Trines are static; they ease. Squares are dynamic; they force you to face issues and in the process you grow and learn. Squares represent the lessons we have failed to learn and trines are the harmonies we have earned.

Inconjunct (Quincunx)

150 degrees apart

This aspect appears on one side or the other of an opposition. If it is in the sign before the opposition it is a 6th house relationship. If on the other side, it is an 8th House relationship. This makes a difference in how it operates. The 6th House inconjunct gives difficulties in either work or health. The 8th House inconjunct is concerned with the necessity of regeneration and transformation where character is concerned.

We may experience the energy of aspects in different ways at the physical, emotional and mental levels. Here is a guide to these levels:

Conjunction	Sense of energy, aliveness
	Individuality
	Magical power, source of inspiration
Opposition	Block, fixation
	Polarisation, vacillating
	Repression, antagonism
Sextile	Love of comforts, beauty, serenity
	Striving for harmony, peace-loving
	Aiming for perfection
Semisextile	Thinking, awareness
	Searching
	Sensitivity, flexibility
Trine	Lethargy, need for tranquillity
	Enjoying, sense of happiness, desire
	Fulfilment, superiority, serenity
Square	Energy, activity, achievement
	Soul energy, euphoria
	Confrontation, conflict
Inconjunct	Yearning, longing
	Searching, thinking
	Change, transformation

The energy shown through the aspects in the birth chart is neither constructive nor destructive. The energy is pure and for us to either use or abuse. It is how we use it that labels it good or bad.

There is only one planet whose power is completely out of our hands and that is Uranus. We can change the way in which we use any of the other energies, but Uranus is the planet of destiny and it operates suddenly, unpredictably and through other people. We have no control over other people's actions. The only decision we have is how we react to them.

Many oppositions and squares in a chart give a difficult life and obstacles to overcome, but there is the potential for strength and character. These are the people that attain success in many different fields. They are forced to go through painful events in order to learn and grow. Too easy a birth chart often gives an easy and pleasant life, but with little stamina or character. This person is apt to drive along and have an uneventful life. Welcome the challenges as they are opportunities to lead a rich and fulfilling life.

Chapter 9

"My evenings are taken up very largely with astrology. I make horoscopic calculations in order to find a clue to the core of psychological truth."

C. G. Jung in a letter to Sigmund Freud.

Astrological Humour

Light Bulb Joke:
How many members of your sign does it take to change a light bulb?

Aries:
Just one. You want to make something of it?

Taurus:
One, but just try to convince them that the burned-out bulb is useless and should be thrown away.

Gemini:
Two, but the job never gets done – they just keep discussing who is supposed to do it and how it's supposed to be done.

Cancer:
Just one. But it takes a therapist three years to help them through the grieving process.

Leo:
Leo's don't change light bulbs, although sometimes their agent will get a Virgo to do the job for them while they're out.

Virgo:
Approximately 1.00000000 with an error of + / - 1 millionth.

Libra:
Or, two. Or maybe one. No, on second thought, make that two. Is that OK with you?

Scorpio:
That information is strictly secret and shared only with the Enlightened Ones in the Star Chamber of the Ancient Hierarchical Order.

Sagittarius:
The sun is shining, the day is young, we've got our whole lives ahead of us, and you're inside worrying about a stupid burned-out light bulb?

Capricorn:
I don't waste my time with these childish jokes.

Aquarius:
Well, you have to remember that everything is energy, so....

Pisces:
Light bulb? What light bulb?

Here's another variation of the Light Bulb joke:

Aries:
Only one, but it takes a lot of light bulbs.

Taurus:
What, me move?

Gemini:
II

Cancer:
Only one, but he has to bring his mother.

Leo:
A dozen. One to change the bulb, and eleven to applaud.

Virgo:
Five. One to clean out the socket, one to dust the bulb, one to install, and two engineers to check the work.

Libra:
Librans can't decide if the bulb needs to be changed.

Scorpio:
None. They LIKE the dark.

Capricorn:
The light's fine as it is.

Aquarius:
Have you asked the bulb if it WANTS to be changed?

Pisces:
What light bulb?

Here's another version. You need twelve:

An Aries to get mad at the light bulb for burning out.

A Taurus to worry about how much a new one will cost.

A Gemini to tell the light bulb's life story and how it came to need changing.

A Cancer to reassure the bulb that it will be okay.

A Leo to sing the praises of illumination.

A Virgo to analyse the situation, figure out the best bulb to use as a replacement, and determine if the old one can be recycled.

A Libra to keep everyone else from fighting about it.

A Scorpio to insist that we should learn to face the darkness without a night light.

A Sagittarius to pontificate on the moral implications of trying to change someone.

A Capricorn to oversee the whole procedure and drive everyone crazy giving orders.

An Aquarian to break the light bulb and etch graffiti on the walls with the shards, writing that "every piece of the whole has meaning and value."

And a Pisces to…to… what was the question?

After Sex Comments by Sun Sign:

Aries: "Okay, let's do it again!"

Taurus: "I'm hungry – pass the pizza."

Gemini: "Have you seen the remote?"

Cancer: "When are we getting married?"

Leo: "Wasn't I fantastic?"

Virgo: "I need to wash the sheets."

Libra: "I liked it if you liked it."

Scorpio: "Perhaps I should untie you."

Sagittarius: "Don't call me – I'll call you."

Capricorn: "Do you have a business card?"

Aquarius: "Now let's try it with our clothes off!"

Pisces: "What did you say your name was again?"

Cleaning by the Signs

Aries: gets competitive over who's the speediest sweeper or whose rag is dustiest.

Taurus: goes over the same spot a million times with the vacuum, refusing to bend down to pick up the offending crumb.

Gemini: finishes their chores in half the time of everyone else.

Cancer: becomes preoccupied with your photo collection.

Leo: spends all day polishing the mirrors.

Virgo: SO doesn't need your help.

Libra: keeps saying: "Don't I look adorable in this apron?"

Scorpio: makes the bed, fluffs the pillows and asks for volunteers to test it out with them.

Sagittarius: doesn't like being stuck inside. Send them out for some fun on your riding lawnmower.

Capricorn: weighs the pros, cons and financial incentives and may decide to go with a better offer.

Aquarius: organises your piles of junk into charity, recycling and compost.

Pisces: asks to do the windows and then keeps staring out into your garden.

APPENDICES

Appendix I: Zodiac signs and body parts in more detail

Aries – the head, brain, eyes, skull, upper jaw, pineal gland, arteries to the head and brain

Taurus – the throat, neck, ears, lower jaw, larynx, vocal chords, jugular vein, tonsils, ears, chin

Gemini – shoulders, arms, wrists, hands and fingers, upper ribs, upper respiratory system

Cancer – breasts, lungs, rib cage, stomach and digestive organs, alimentary canal, sternum, womb, pancreas

Leo – the spine – especially the upper back – the spinal cord, the heart, the arteries – especially the aorta – the circulation, the spleen

Virgo – the lower digestive system, the bowels, the lower dorsal nerves, the skin, the nervous system and the mind

Libra – kidneys, bladder, lumbar region, haunches to buttocks, adrenal glands, lumbar nerves and blood vessels

Scorpio – sexual organs – especially the cervix – the lower stomach, the lower spine, the groin, anus, genito-urinary system, prostate gland, eyes

Sagittarius – hips and thighs, the pelvis, the sacrum, the liver, the sciatic nerve, the arterial system – especially the femoral artery

Capricorn – skin, ears, teeth, bones, skeletal system as a whole, knees

Aquarius – ankles, calves and shins, breathing, the circulatory system – especially the extremities

Pisces – feet, toes, lungs, lymphatic system, pituitary gland. Also the "ethereal body" – that is, the part that can be upset by psychic disturbances or imbalances in the aura or the psychic system

Appendix II: Natal Charts of Famous People

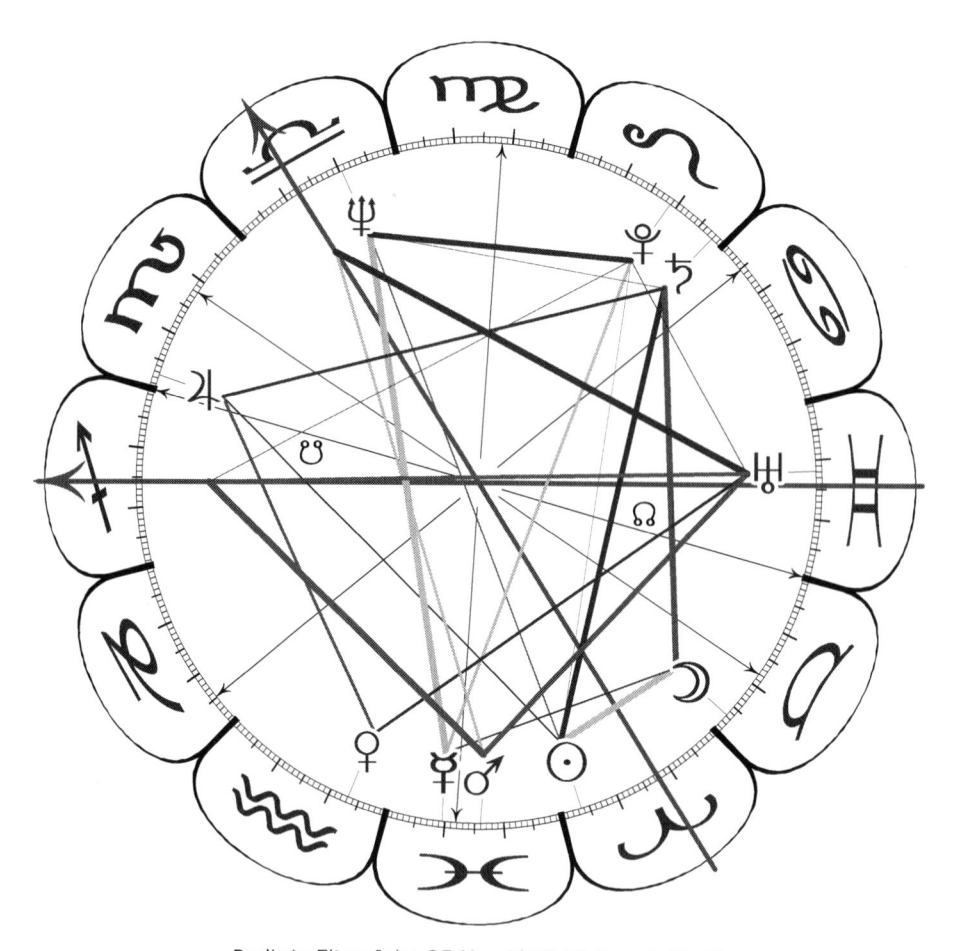

Radix1: Elton John 25 Mar 1947 AD Tue 2 00 00

Sun in Aries, Moon in Taurus, Ascendant Sagittarius

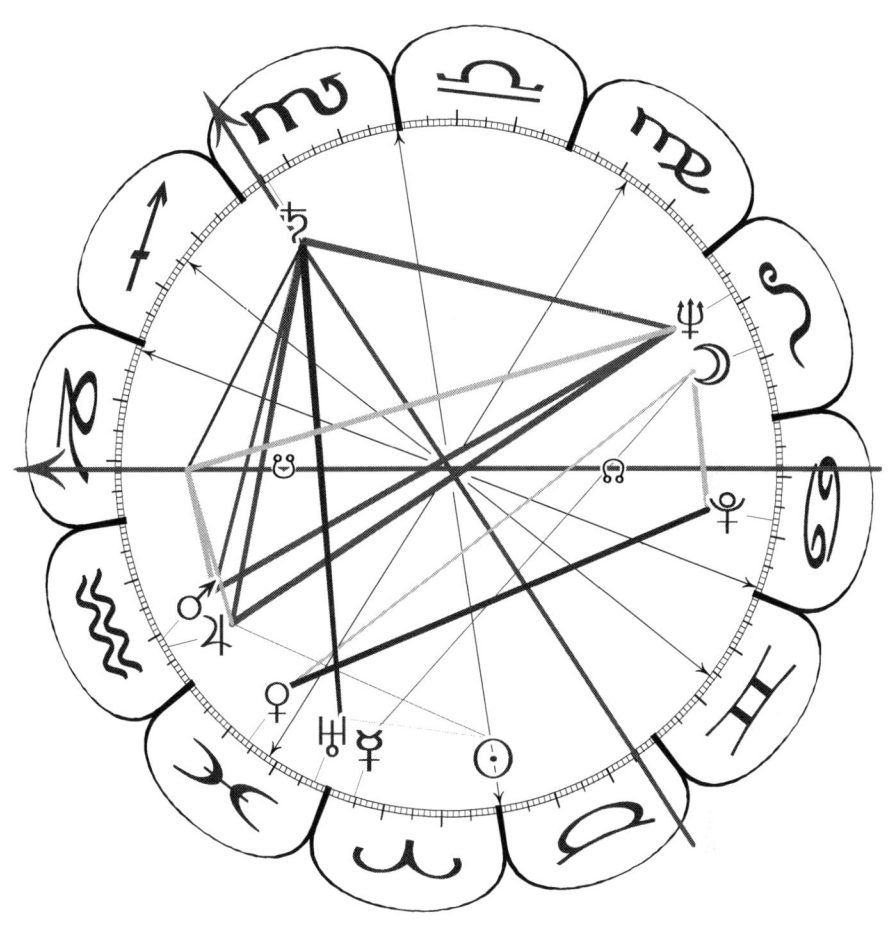

Radix1: Queen Elizabeth 21 Apr 1926 AD Wed 2 40 00

Sun in Taurus, Moon in Leo, Ascendant Capricorn

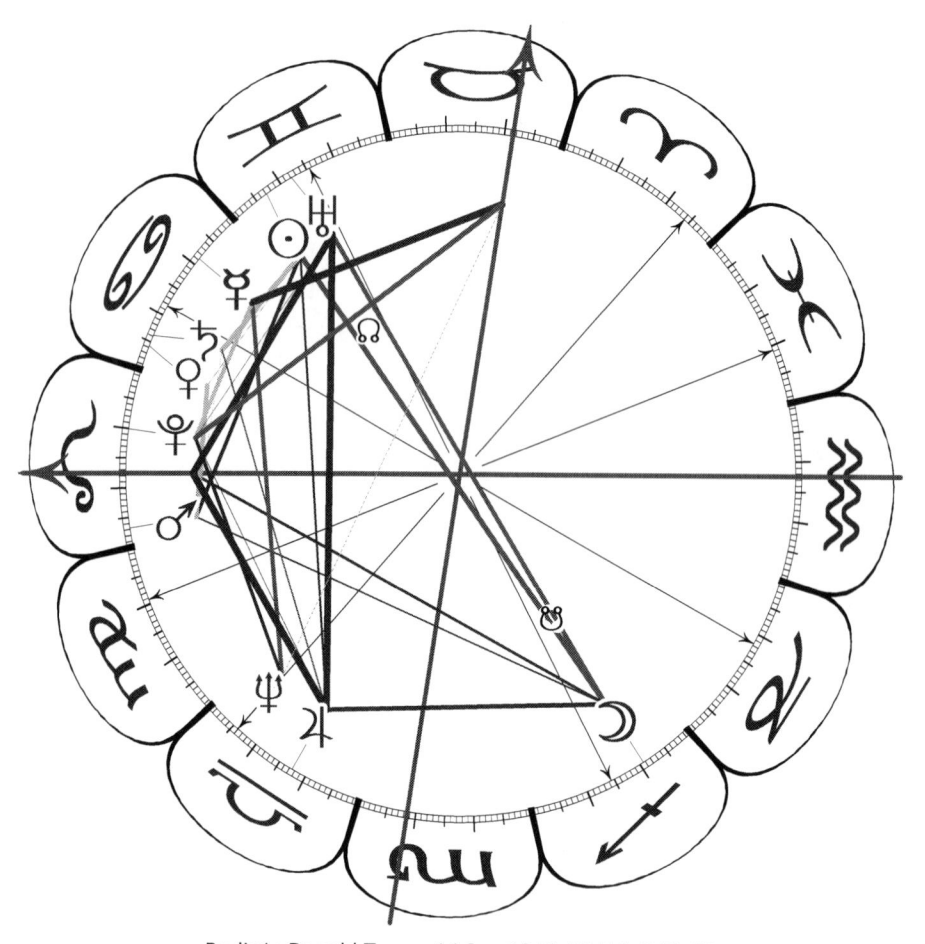

Radix1: Donald Trump 14 Jun 1946 AD Fri 9 51 00

Sun in Gemini, Moon in Sagittarius, Ascendant Leo

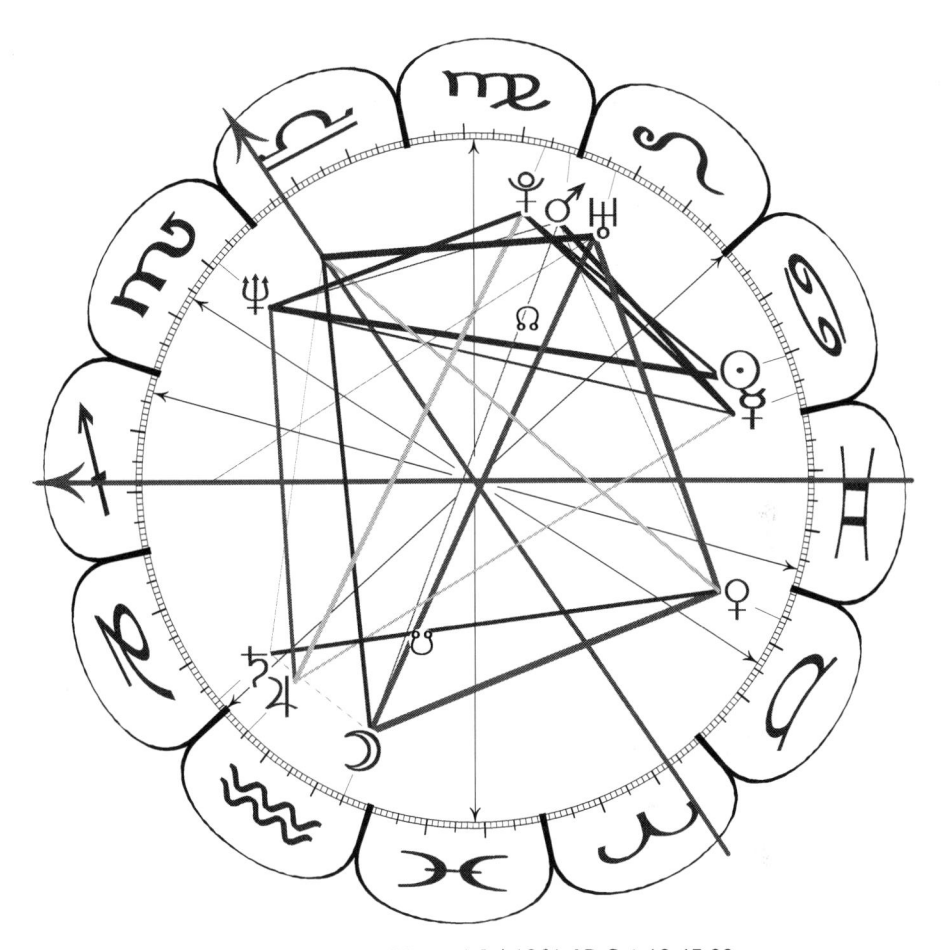

Radix1: Princess Diana 1 Jul 1961 AD Sat 19 45 00

Sun in Cancer, Moon in Aquarius, Ascendant Sagittarius

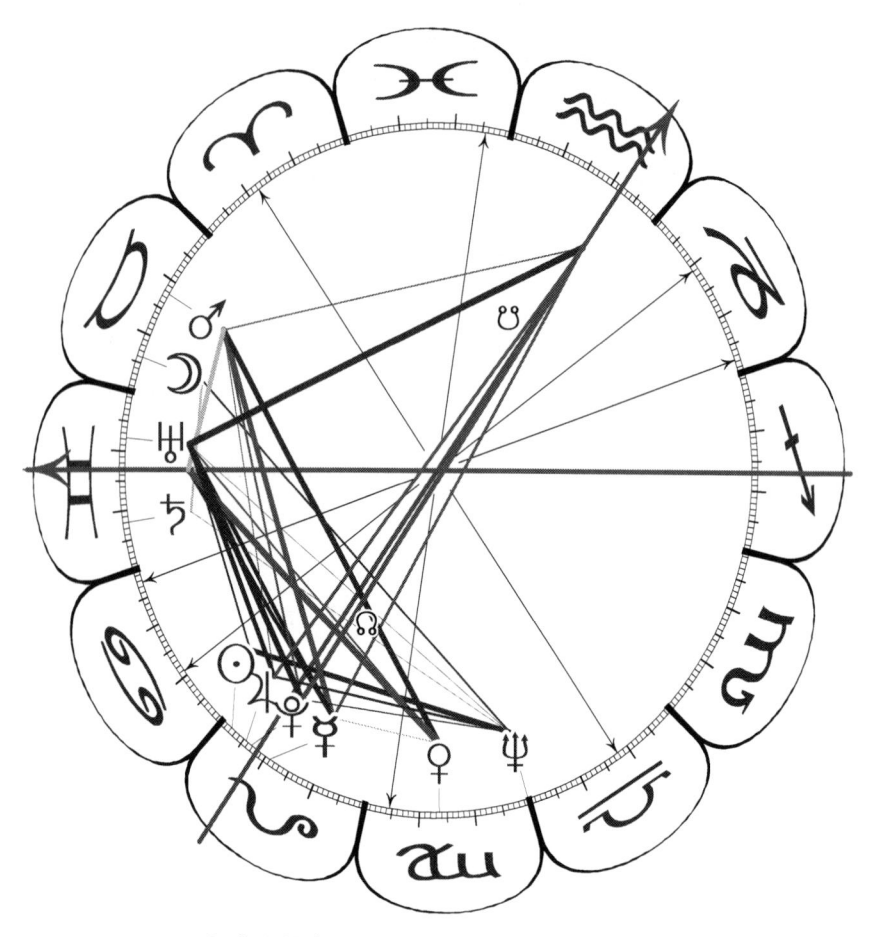

Radix1: Mick Jagger 26 Jul 1943 AD Mon 2 30 00

Sun in Leo, Moon in Taurus, Ascendant Gemini

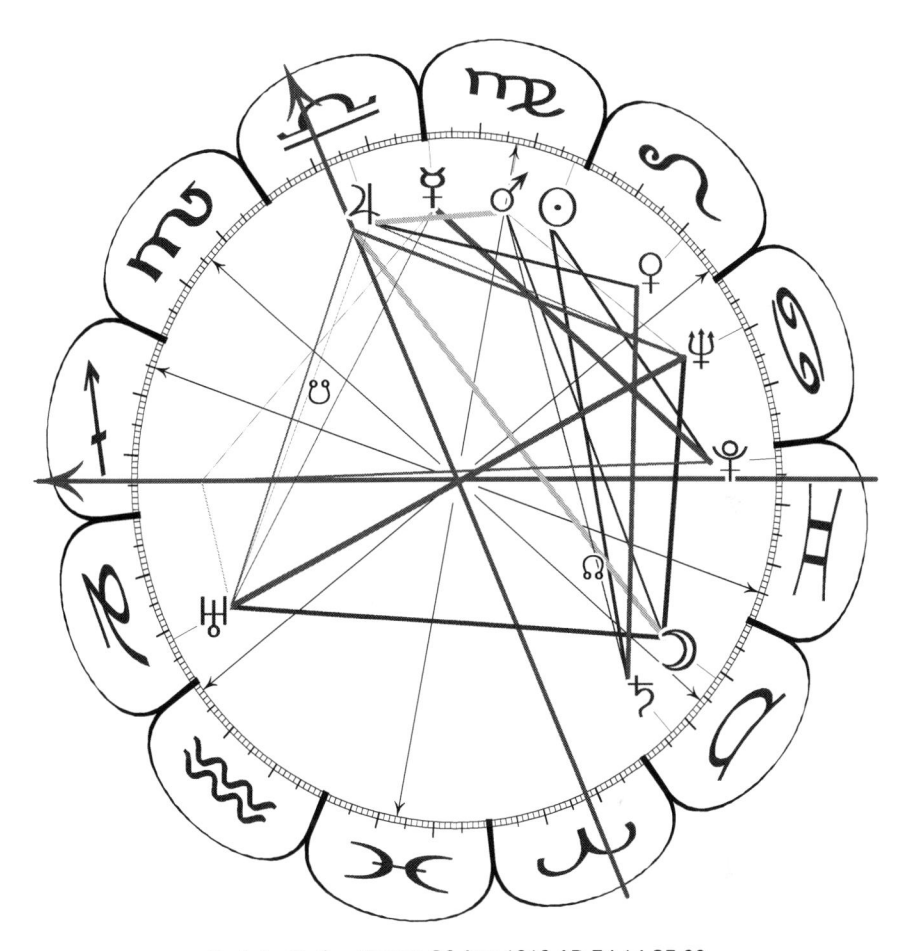

Radix1: Mother Teresa 26 Aug 1910 AD Fri 14 25 00

Sun in Virgo, Moon in Taurus, Ascendant Sagittarius

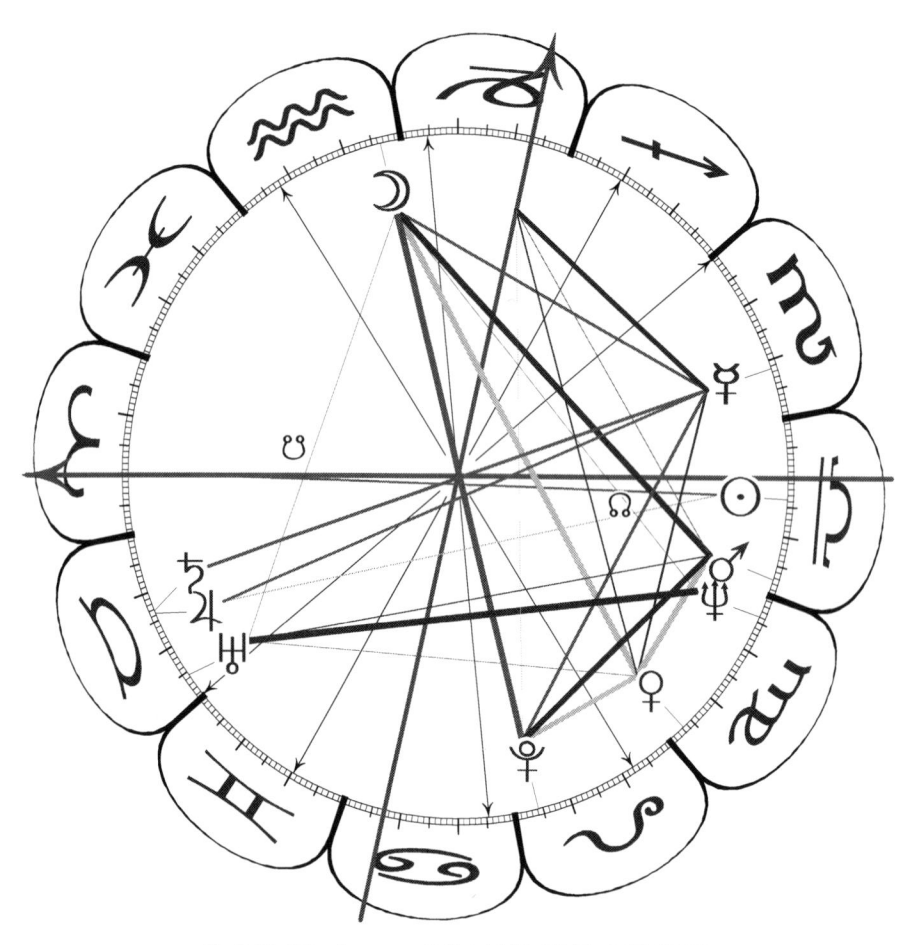

Radix1: John Lennon 9 Oct 1940 AD Wed 18 30 00

Sun in Libra, Moon in Aquarius, Ascendant Aries

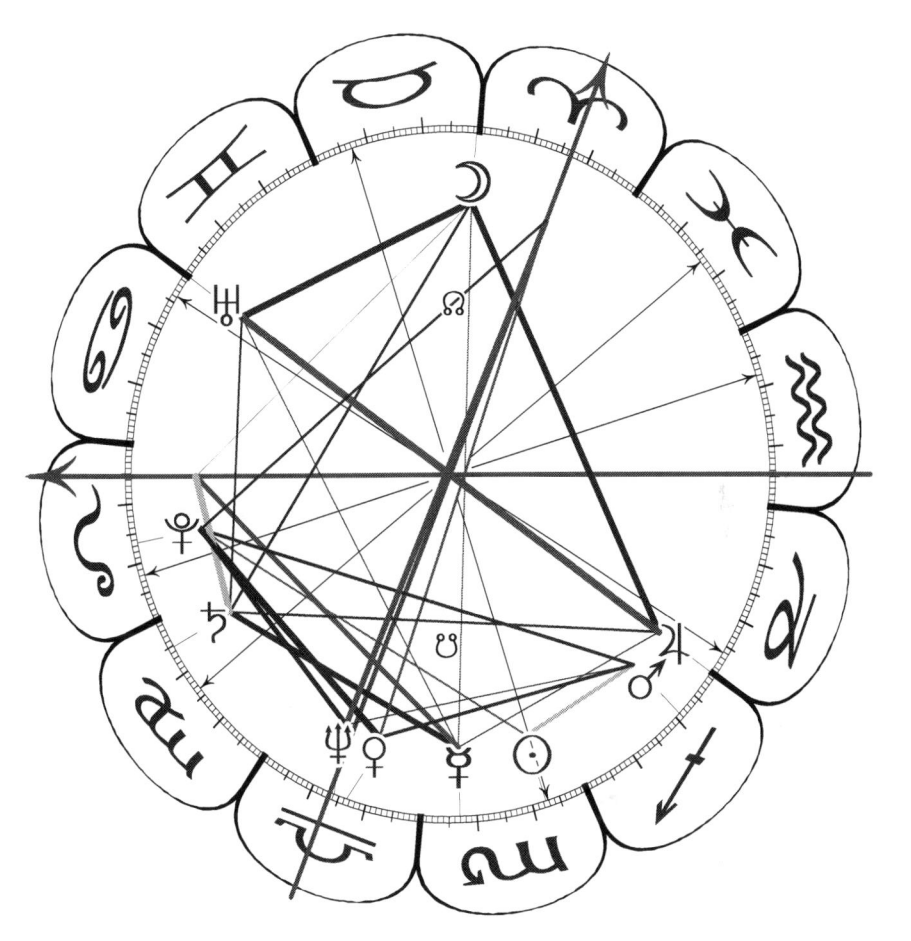

Radix1: Prince Charles 14 Nov 1948 AD Sun 21 14 00

Sun in Scorpio, Moon in Taurus, Ascendant Leo

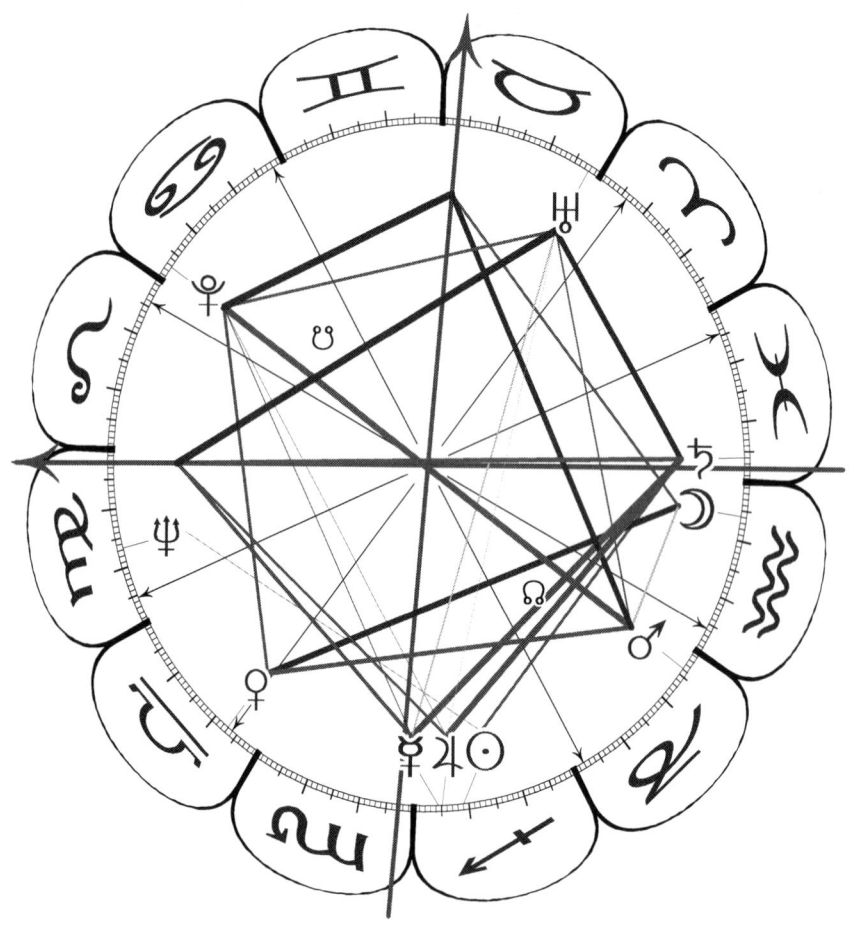

Radix1: Woody Allen 1 Dec 1935 AD Sun 22 55 00

Sun in Sagittarius, Moon in Aquarius, Ascendant Virgo

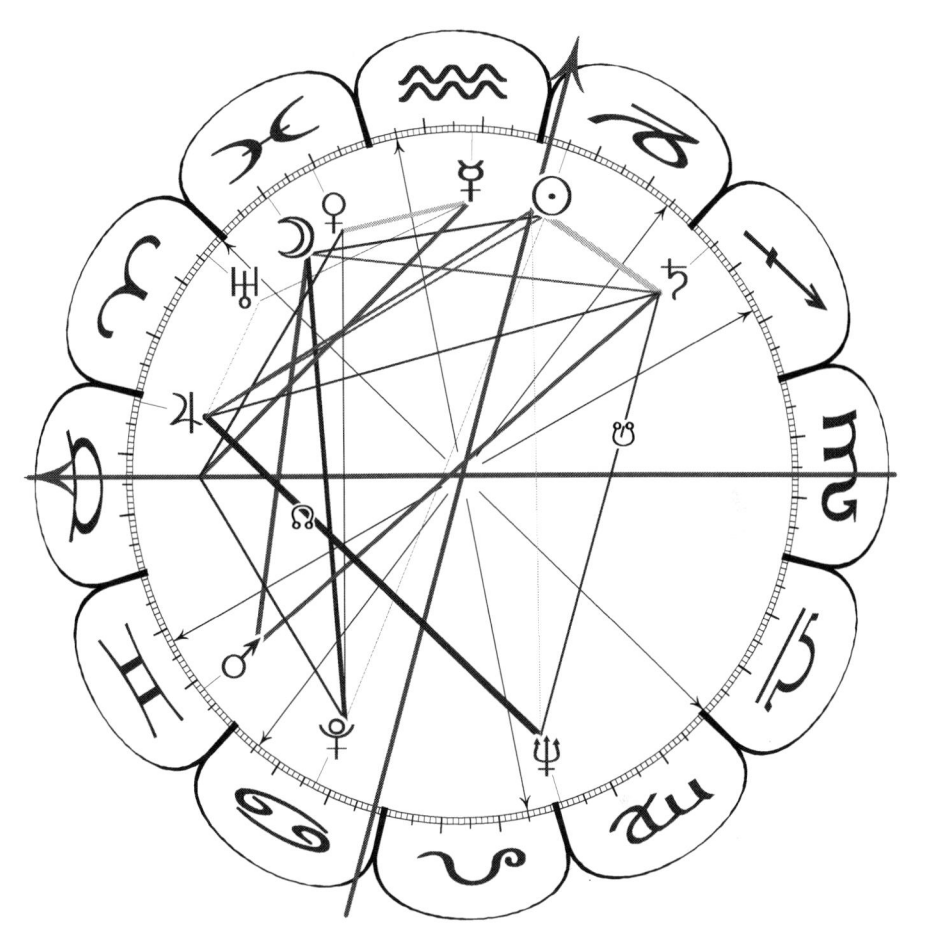

Radix1: Martin Luther King 15 Jan 1929 AD Tue 12 00 00

Sun in Capricorn, Moon in Pisces, Ascendant Taurus

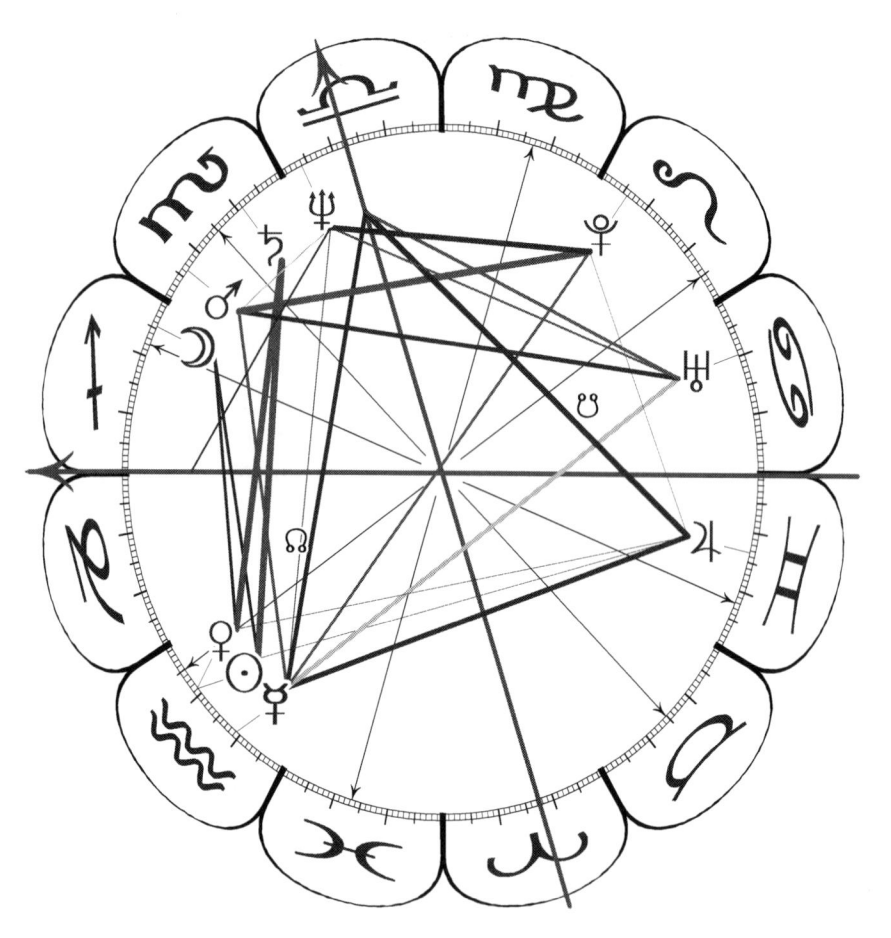

Radix1: Oprah Winfrey 29 Jan 1954 AD Fri 4 30 00

Sun in Aquarius, Moon in Sagittarius, Ascendant Sagittarius

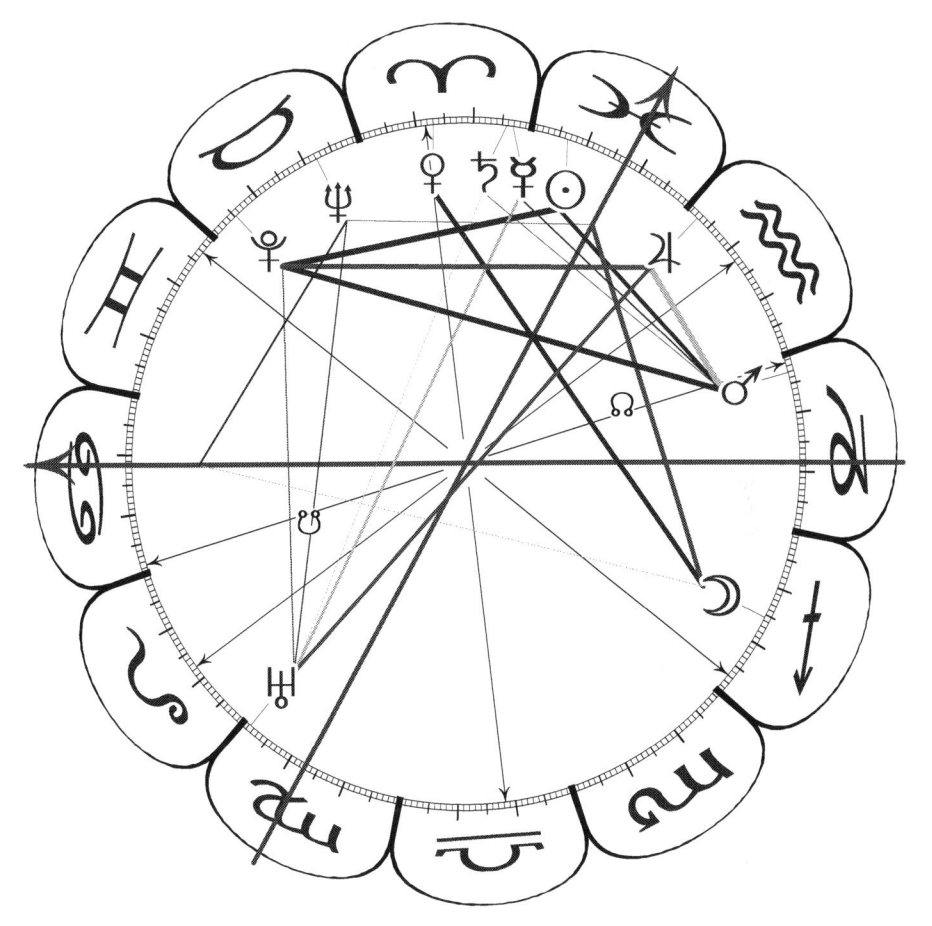

Radix1: Albert Einstein 14 Mar 1879 AD Fri 11 30 00

Sun in Pisces, Moon in Sagittarius, Ascendant Cancer

Appendix III: Glossary

Angle Any of the four Cardinal points are called Angles. The Cardinal points are the axis of the chart, that is, the horizontal and vertical lines. The Eastern angle is also known as the Ascendant; the Western angle as the Descendant; the Southern angle is the Medium Coeli (MC); and the Northern angle is the Imum Coeli (IC).

Angular The 1st, 4th, 7th and 10th Houses and corresponding to the Cardinal signs.

Ascendant The point at which the Eastern horizon intersects the ecliptic. The 1st house or Rising sign.

Aspect The angle formed between two imaginary lines connecting two planets or points with the Earth.

Birth Chart A map of where the planets, signs and houses are positioned at the time of birth.

Cadent The 3rd, 6th, 9th and 12th Houses. These are ruled by Mutable House signs.

Conjunction The occurrence of a direct or nearly direct line-up of two planets as seen from the Earth.

Cusp The line of division between two houses.

Descendant The point at which the Western horizon intersects the ecliptic. It is also the cusp between the 6th and 7th Houses.

Detriment When a planet is in the sign opposite the sign it rules, the planet is in detriment.

Ecliptic The apparent path of the Sun around the Earth. This path is at an angle of 23.45 degrees to the equator.

Exaltation Some signs match the energy of certain planets so well that, when the planets enter the sign, they are said to be in exaltation. These are: Sun in Aries, Moon in Taurus, Jupiter in Cancer, Neptune in Cancer, Mercury in Aquarius, Saturn in Libra, Uranus in Scorpio, Mars in Capricorn, Venus in Pisces.

Fall When a planet is in the sign opposite to the sign in which it finds its exaltation, the planet's energy is stifled: Saturn in Aries, Uranus in Taurus, Mars in Cancer, Mercury in Leo, Venus in Virgo, Jupiter in Capricorn, Sun in Libra, Moon in Scorpio, Jupiter in Capricorn, Neptune in Capricorn, Mercury in Pisces.

Horoscope A map or chart of the position of the planets in the heavens at the exact time and place of birth. The map covers the entire sky, a full circle of 360 degrees. This is also called the natal chart.

House One of the 12 divisions made in the cycle of the Earth's daily rotation. Each House represents an approximate 2 hour period during which one-twelfth of the zodiac appears to pass over the horizon. Each House presides over a different department of practical affairs.

House Systems The best-known systems are the Equal, Koch, Placidus, Campanus and Regiomontanus House Systems.

Intercepted A sign is intercepted when it lies wholly within a single House Sign and does not occupy the cusp at either end of the House. Being intercepted may restrict the freedom of a planet to act.

Meridian A great circle on the celestial sphere passing through the north and south points of the horizon and the zenith, which is directly above the observer.

Midheaven (Also written M.C. from the Latin Medium Coeli) The point at which the meridian intersects the ecliptic.

Nadir The point on the ecliptic directly opposite the Midheaven looking downward from the observer. Also called the 4th house cusp.

Node Each of the two points at which a planet's orbit intersects the ecliptic: once when the planet moves north across the ecliptic, and once again when it moves south. In astrology, the Nodes of the moon are especially significant.

Opposition An aspect representing an angular relationship of 180 degrees between two planets. Planets in opposition generally occupy approximately the same number of degrees in two signs directly across the zodiac from each other.

Planets The various energies or influences, along with the signs, operating in and through a birth chart. It usually includes: Sun, Moon, Mercury, Venus, Mars, Jupiter, Saturn, Uranus, Neptune, Pluto.

Progression A method of advancing the planets and points of a natal chart to a particular time after birth. Used to illustrate a person's evolution.

Quadruplicity One of the three fixed groups of signs, each containing four signs. The three quaduplicities relate to three characteristics – Cardinal, Fixed and Mutable – and are concerned with basic modes of activities.

Rectification The process of adjusting or determining a birth time. By referencing known events and dates and progressing planets, the birth chart most likely to match the person is identified.

Retrograde When a planet appears to be travelling backwards form the perspective of Earth. The energy of a retrograde planet is less assertive and more internalised.

Sextile The aspect representing an angular relationship of 60 degrees, or one sixth of a circle. Planets in sextile aspects are placed two signs apart and occupy approximately the same number of degrees in these signs, plus or minus 6 degrees.

Solar Chart A chart devoid of houses due to the subject of the chart not knowing their time of birth.

Solar Return A horoscope cast for the moment when the Sun returns to the exact place in the sky that it occupied at birth. Approximately one day after birth. Considered symbolic of the coming year.

Square The aspect representing an angular relationship of 90 degrees. Planets in square aspect generally occupy the same number of degrees in signs which are three signs apart.

Stellium Three or more planets linked together by conjunct aspects. The outer planets of the chain are not necessarily conjunct, but are joined by planets between them. A stronger configuration when the planets are grouped in one sign or house.

Succedent The houses that follow the angles, namely the 2nd, 5th, 8th and 11th Houses.

Sun signs The twelve traditional signs of the zodiac: Aries, Taurus, Gemini, Cancer, Leo, Virgo, Libra, Scorpio, Sagittarius, Capricorn, Aquarius, and Pisces.

Synastry A branch of astrology that studies relationship potential.

Transit The position and movement of a planet or point on any given day.

Trine The aspect representing an angular relationship of 120 degrees or one third of a circle between two planets. Planets in trine aspect generally occupy the same number of degrees in signs four signs apart.

Triplicity One of the four fixed groups of signs, each containing three planets. The four triplicities relate to the four elements: Fire, Earth, Air and Water. They are concerned with tendencies of the temperament.

Zenith The point in the celestial sphere directly above the observer.

Zodiac The band of sky 18 degrees wide having the ecliptic as its central line. It consists of twelve parts, each 30 degrees wide, which represent the twelve signs of the zodiac.

Printed in Great Britain
by Amazon